World Health Organization

Legislative Responses to Tobacco Use

MARTINUS NIJHOFF PUBLISHERS
DORDRECHT/BOSTON/LONDON

Library of Congress Cataloging-in-Publication Data

Legislative responses to tobacco use / World Health Organization.
p. cm.
ISBN 0-7923-1149-3 (alk. paper)
1. Tobacco--Law and legislation. 2. Smoking--Law and legislation.
I. World Health Organization.
K3593.A48 1991
344'.046342--dc20
[342.446342] 91-7274

ISBN 0-7923-1149-3

Published by Martinus Nijhoff Publishers,
P.O. Box 163, 3300 AD Dordrecht, The Netherlands.

Sold and distributed in the U.S.A. and Canada
by Kluwer Academic Publishers,
101 Philip Drive, Norwell, MA 02061, U.S.A.

In all other countries, sold and distributed
by Kluwer Academic Publishers Group,
P.O. Box 322, 3300 AH Dordrecht, The Netherlands.

Printed on acid-free paper

Printed in the Netherlands

“A decree against excesse in drinking, drunkennes and taking Tobacco”, issued by the Vice-Chancellor and Heads of Cambridge University, 23 February 1606.

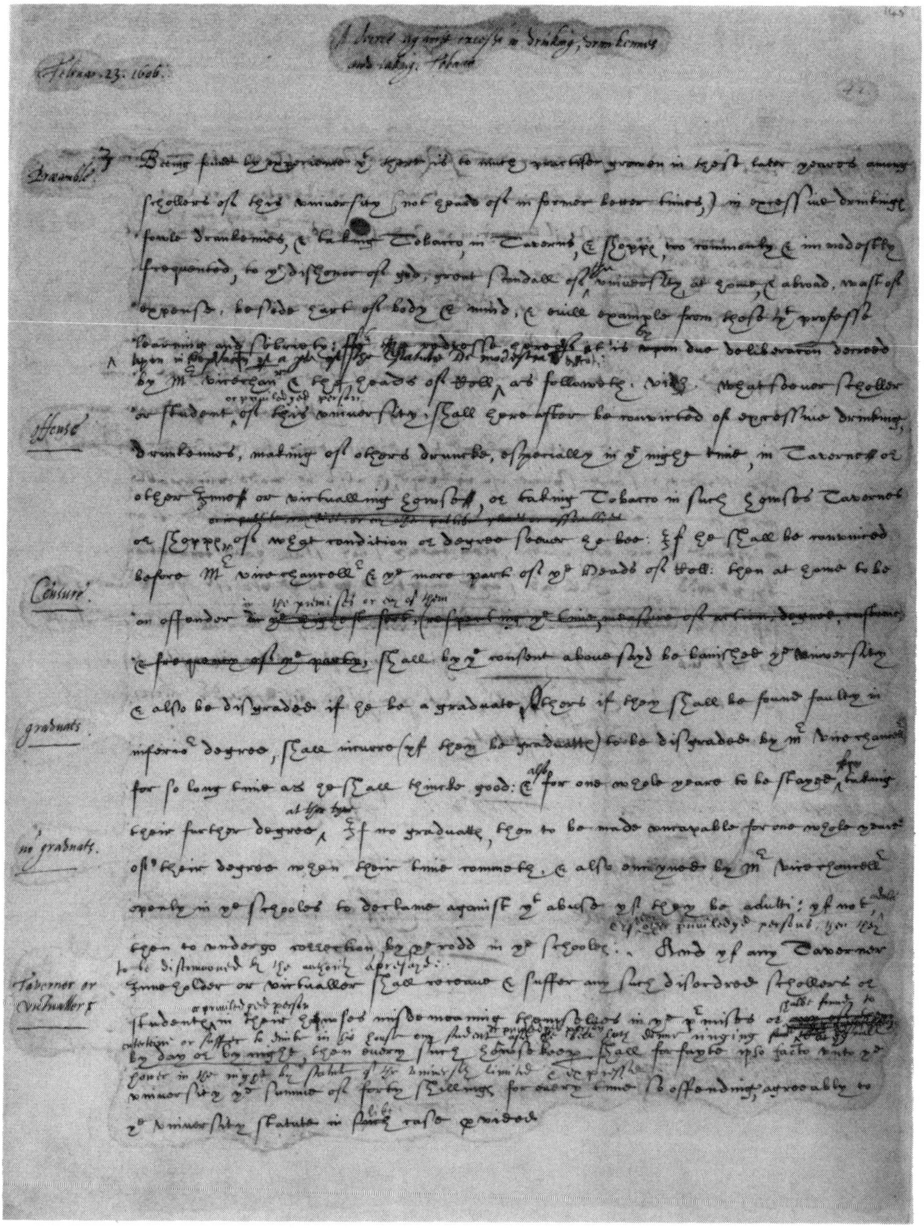

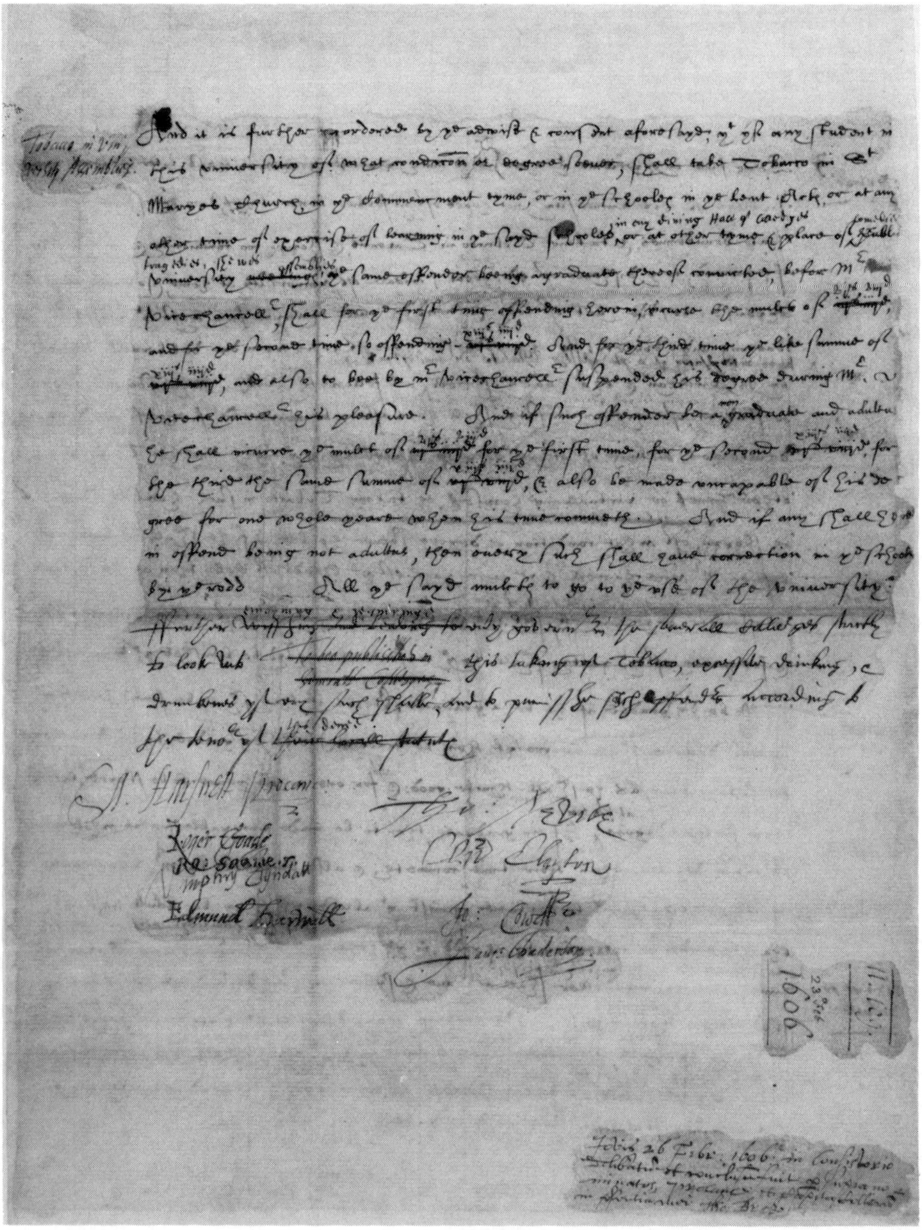

Tobacco in University Assemblies.

And it is further ordered by ye advise & consent aforesayd, yt if any student in this University of what condition or degree soever, shall take Tobacco in St Maryes church in ye commencement tyme, or in ye Scholes in ye Lent Acts, or at any other tyme of exercise of learning in ye sayd Scholes, in any dining Hall of Colledges or at other tyme & place of solemn University assemblies, the same offender being undergraduate thereof convicted before Mr Vicechancellor, shall for ye first time offending therein incurre the mulct of vjs viijd, and for ye second time so offending xiijs iiijd. And for ye third time ye like summe of xiijs iiijd, and also to bee by Mr Vicechancellor suspended his degree during Mr Vicechancellor his pleasure. And if such offender be a graduate and adultus he shall incurre ye mulct of vjs viijd for ye first time, for ye second xiijs iiijd, for the third the same summe of xiijs iiijd, & also be made uncapable of his degree for one whole yeare when his time commeth. And if any shall hereafter offend being not adultus, then every such shall have correction in ye Schools by ye rodd. All ye sayd mulcts to go to ye use of the University.

Further [illegible] to look into [illegible] this taking of Tobacco, excessive drinking, and drunkenness [illegible] and to punish such offenders according to their [illegible]

[illegible] Procan.

Roger Goade

Ro. Soame

Umphry Tyndall

Edmund Barwell

Tho. Nevile

Rich. Clayton

Jo. Cowell

Laur. Chaderton

1606

Lectis 26 Febr. 1606 in Consistorio [illegible]

A decree against excesse in drinking, drunkennes and taking Tobacco

Februar.23.1606

Preamble Beeing found by experience yt there is to much practise growen in these later yeares among schollers of this vniuersity (not heard of in former better times,) in excessiue drinkings, fowle drunkennes, & taking Tobacco in Taverns, & shoppes, too commonly & immodestly frequented, to ye dishonor of god, great scandall of the vniuersity at home & abroad, wast of expense, beside hurt of body & mind, & euill example from those yt professe learning and sobriety: redresse hereof it is by due deliberacion decreed by Mr Vicechancellor & the heads of Coll: vpon interpretacion of a parte of the Statute De modestia
Offense & caet: as followeth: viz: Whatsoeuer scholler or student or priuiledged person of vniuersity, shall hereafter be convicted or exessiue drinking, drunkennes, making of others druncke, especially in ye night time, in Taverne or other Inne or victualling howse, or taking Tobacco in such howses Tavernes or shoppes of what condition or degree soeuer he bee: If he shall be convinced before Mr vicechancellor & ye more part of ye
Censure Heads of Coll: then at home to be an offender in the premises or eny of them shall by ye consent abouesayd be banished ye
graduats University & also be disgraded if he be a graduate; others if they shall be found faulty in inferior degree, shall incurre (yf they be graduattes) to be disgraded by Mr Vicechancellor for so long time as he shall thincke good: & also for one whole yeare to be stayed from taking their further degree at ther tyme If no
non graduats graduattes, then to be made vncapable for one whole yeare of their degree when their time commeth, & also enioyned by Mr vicechancellor openly in ye schooles to declame against yt abuse yf they be adults: yf not adults, then to vndergo correction by ye rodd in ye schooles: & yf other priuiledged persons, then they
Taverner or victualler [are] to be discommoned by the authority aforesayde. And yf any Taverner Inneholder or victualler shall receaue & suffer any such disordered schollers or studentes or priuiledged person in their howses misdemeaning themselues in ye premises or shalbe found to enterteine or suffer to drinke in his house eny student or priuiledged person after the bell hath donne ringing at ye vsuall howre in the night by statute of the vniuersity limited &

Tobacco in Vniversity Assemblies

expressed such howsekeeper shall forfayte ipso facto vnto ye vniuersity ye summe of forty shillinges for euery time so offending, agreebly to ye vniuersity statute in like case provided. And it is further ordered by ye advise & consent aforesayd, y^{t} yf any student in this vniuersity of what condicion or degree soeuer, shall take Tobacco in St Maryes Church, in ye Commencement tyme, or in ye schooles in ye Lent Actes, or at any other time of exercise of learning in ye sayd schooles in eny dining Hall of Colledges or at other tyme & place of Comedies, tragedies, shewes of publike vniuersity assemblies, ye same offender beeing a graduate thereof convicted, before Mr Vicechancellor, shall for ye first time offending herein, incurre the mulct of vjs viijd, and for ye second time so offending – xiijs iiijd. And for ye third time ye like summe of xiijs iiijd, and also to bee by Mr Vicechancellor suspended his degree during Mr Vicechancellor his pleasure. And if such offender bee a non graduate and adultus he shall incurre ye mulct of vjs viijd for ye first time, for ye second yiijs iiijd, for the third the same summe of xiiijs iiijd & also be made vncapable of his degree for one whole yeare when his time commeth. And if any shall herein offend being not adultus, then euery such shall haue correction in ye schooles by ye rodd. All ye sayd mulcts to go to ye vse of the vniuersity.

Furter enioyning & requiringe euery governor in the seuerall Colledges strictly to look vnto this taking of Tobacco, excessive drinking, & drunkenes yf eny such shalbe, and to punisshe such offenders according to the tenour of this decree

Sa. Harsnett Procan*cellarius*
Roger Goade
Ro: Soame
Umphry Tyndall
Edmund Barwell

Tho: Nevile
Ric: Clayton
Jo: Cowell
Laur: Chaderton

These two decrees of the Vice-Chancellor and Heads were transcribed by Dr Elisabeth Leedham-Green, Assistant to the Keeper of the University Archives. Reproduced with the permission of the Editor of "Cambridge", the magazine of the Cambridge Society.

FOREWORD

Legislation is one of the strongest weapons to combat the world smoking epidemic. About 90 countries in the world and many sub-national jurisdictions have enacted laws in response to the largest single cause of preventable disease and premature death. Laws establish governmental policy on use of tobacco, enlist the resources of governmental departments, strengthen the activities of voluntary agencies, energize citizens' groups, and contribute to the development of a smoke-free environment.

The World Health Organization early recognized the crucial role of legislation in national strategies to control use of tobacco. Over the years, Mr. S.S. Fluss, Chief of WHO's Health Legislation unit in Geneva has made special efforts to obtain, translate, and make available important legislation on tobacco and health. These statutes and regulations are a gold mine of information on the legislative approaches of different countries to controlling use of tobacco, but until now they have been available only to those with access to a full set of the volumes of the WHO quarterly journal, the *International Digest of Health Legislation.*

With the publication of *Legislative Responses to Tobacco Use*, this legislation is now available in a convenient book that collects in a single volume all the statutes and other legislative instruments on tobacco and health published in the *International Digest of Health Legislation* from 1978 to late 1990.

This book is a most valuable tool for exchange of information on legislative strategies to control promotion and use of tobacco. Any country desiring to enact legislation in this field or to improve existing legislation can readily learn what other jurisdictions have done on the various aspects of tobacco control. The subjects covered deal with (1) measures to control the production, manufacture, promotion, and sale of tobacco and (2) measures designed to achieve changes in smoking behavior.

This volume is appearing at an opportune time – when national governments and local communities all over the world are taking action to ban tobacco advertising, to strengthen health warnings, to control the levels of harmful substances in tobacco, and to make public places and workplaces smokefree. This volume will be an important aid to these dynamic developments.

A leading advocate of global efforts to combat tobacco use, Dr. Keith Ball, Senior Lecturer in Preventive Medicine and Cardiology at the Middlesex Hospital Medical School, London has called tobacco the greatest single threat to the health of the world's people, short of nuclear war, famine, and pestilence. While legislation cannot by itself overcome this threat, it can lay the basis for other actions that can encourage smokers to quit, protect the health of nonsmokers, dissuade young people from starting to smoke, and achieve a smoke-free society. *Legislative Responses to Tobacco Use* is a user-friendly resource that will be helpful to all countries concerned about the needless suffering caused by tobacco.

Ruth Roemer, J.D.
Adjunct Professor of Health Law
School of Public Health
University of California, Los Angeles (USA)
Past President (1987)
American Public Health Association

TABLE OF CONTENTS

Tasmania

Victoria

Western Australia

BELGIUM

CANADA

Ontario

Quebec

CAYMAN ISLANDS

CHILE

EGYPT

EL SALVADOR

FEDERAL REPUBLIC OF GERMANY

FINLAND

FRANCE

FRENCH POLYNESIA

GAMBIA

GREECE

HONG KONG

ICELAND

INDIA

IRELAND

ISRAEL

IVORY COAST

JORDAN

KENYA

KUWAIT

LEBANON

LUXEMBOURG

MALTA

MEXICO

NETHERLANDS

NEW ZEALAND

NIGERIA

NORWAY

PAKISTAN

PAPUA NEW GUINEA

PARAGUAY

PERU

PORTUGAL

Macao

SAUDI ARABIA

SENEGAL

SINGAPORE

SPAIN

Catalonia

Valencia

SUDAN

SWEDEN

UNION OF SOVIET SOCIALIST REPUBLICS

UNITED KINGDOM

UNITED STATES OF AMERICA

New York

URUGUAY

VENEZUELA

COUNCIL OF EUROPE

EUROPEAN COMMUNITIES

ARGENTINA

ARGENTINA. Law No. 23344 of 31 July 1986 on restrictions on the advertising of tobacco, cigars, cigarettes, and other products intended for smoking, and their packaging. (*Boletín Oficial de la República Argentina*, 29 August 1986, No. 25982, p. 1) **Arg. 86.1**

Secs. 1-3 of this Law read as follows:

"**1.** Packages in which the different types of tobacco, cigars, cigarettes, and other products intended for smoking are marketed shall carry the following legend in a legible and conspicuous manner: 'Smoking is harmful to health'.

2. Advertising for the different types of tobacco, cigars, cigarettes and other products intended for smoking shall be subject to the following restrictions:

(*a*) advertising is prohibited on radio and television between 8 a.m. and 10 p.m. every day, with the exception of advertising limited to the identification of the brand and not forming the subject of a specific broadcast;

(*b*) advertising is prohibited in publications intended for young persons and in theatres, cinemas, and the like to which persons under 18 years of age are admitted;

(*c*) promoting or distributing samples of such products is prohibited in schools, colleges, universities, and teaching establishments or during entertainments or activities where the public is composed essentially of young persons;

(*d*) featuring in advertising of personalities from artistic and cultural circles whose public essentially consists of young persons is prohibited;

(*e*) young models or persons dressed or made up in such a way as to represent young persons are prohibited in advertisements;

(*f*) the representation of persons smoking excessively is prohibited;

(*g*) the use of expressions or terms characteristic of young persons is prohibited;

(*h*) treatment or production processes intended to reduce the level of nicotine or tar may not be represented as beneficial or appropriate to health.

3. The Secretariat for Internal Trade shall be the authority responsible for the implementation of this Law."

AUSTRALIA

AUSTRALIA. Trade Practices Act 1974. Notice under subsection 65C(5) and Section 65P: notice of declaration of unsafe goods and of reasons for decision. Dated 11 October 1989. (*Commonwealth of Australia Gazette*, 12 October 1989, No. S 324, pp. 1-4) **Aust. 91.3**

NOTICE OF DECLARATION OF UNSAFE GOODS AND OF REASONS

FOR DECISION

WHEREAS:

A. On 4 January 1988 the Honourable Peter Richard Staples as Minister of State for Consumer Affairs prepared pursuant to sub-section 65J(1) of the *Trade Practices Act* 1974 ("the Act") a draft of a proposed notice under sub-section 65C(5) of the Act in respect of goods particularized as "Smokeless tobacco products intended for oral use and snuffs intended for oral use manufactured in, or imported into, Australia after 30 April 1988." ("the proposed notice") which was published in the Commonwealth Gazette (No GN1) dated 13 January 1988;

B. On 8 February 1988 the United States Tobacco Company requested the Trade Practices Commission ("the Commission") to hold a conference in relation to the proposed notice which conference commenced on 18 February 1988 and was conducted over a number of sitting days in February, March, June and November 1988 ("the conference");

C. On 25 September 1989 the Commission recommended pursuant to sub-paragraph 65K(a)(ii) of the Act by notice in writing given to the Minister that the Minister publish the proposed notice with modifications in terms that the relevant goods be particularized as "Snuffs intended for oral use manufactured in, or imported into, Australia after 30 September 1989." ("the recommendation");

D. The recommendation was presented by the Commission within a report it had prepared which also contained the reasons for making the recommendation and summarised the material on which its evaluation was based ("the report"); and

E. Oral smokeless tobacco products are produced in two general forms, namely, chewing tobacco and snuffs intended for oral use:

NOW THEREFORE, in pursuance of sub-section 65C(5) of the Act, I, NICK BOLKUS, Minister of State for Consumer Affairs, having had regard to the recommendation and the report, HEREBY DECLARE the goods specified below in the First Schedule to be unsafe goods in that it appears to me that the goods may cause injury to a person who uses the goods, AND IN SO FAR as I have decided to act otherwise than in accordance with the recommendation, in pursuance of section 65P of the Act, I SET OUT below in the Second Schedule the reasons for my decision.

FIRST SCHEDULE

Particulars of Goods:

Chewing tobacco and snuffs intended for oral use.

SECOND SCHEDULE

Reasons for Deciding to Act Otherwise than in Accordance with the Recommendation:

I have decided to act otherwise than in accordance with the recommendation in two respects: I have decided to expand the class of goods which I am declaring unsafe to cover chewing tobacco, and I have decided not to limit the class of goods which I am declaring to be unsafe by reference to a date of manufacture or import. The reasons for my decision are:

(1) Expansion to Cover all Oral Smokeless Tobacco Products

- I accept, for the reasons given in the report, that snuffs intended for oral use ought to be declared to be unsafe pursuant to sub-section 65C(5) of the Act.
- Having had regard to the information presented to the Commission during the course of the conference, which is specified below, and to the findings of the Commission contained in the report, which are specified below, it appears to me that:

  - chewing tobacco may cause injury to a person who uses chewing tobacco; and
  - I ought to declare both forms of oral smokeless tobacco products (i.e. chewing tobacco and oral snuffs) to be unsafe goods pursuant to sub-section 65C(5) of the Act.

Information Presented to the Commission

– The International Agency for Research on Cancer concluded, in its 1985 Monograph (Volume 37, September 1985) on the Evaluation of the Carcinogenic Risk of Chemicals to Humans, that:

- there was limited evidence that chewing tobacco of the types commonly used in North America and western Europe is carcinogenic;
- epidemiological studies that did not distinguish between chewing tobacco and snuff provide sufficient evidence for the carcinogenicity of oral use of smokeless tobacco products; and
- in aggregate, there is sufficient evidence that oral use of smokeless tobacco products is carcinogenic to humans.
- The 1986 Report of the United States Surgeon-General, while noting that the number of epidemiological investigations evaluating the relation between smokeless tobacco and oral cancer was not large, and that several studies have methodologic limitations, nonetheless concluded that users of smokeless tobacco face a strongly increased risk of oral cancer, particularly for the tissues that come into contact with the tobacco.
- The 101st Session of the National Health and Medical Research Council held in June 1986 noted that use of chewing tobacco was being promoted in some Australian States "despite medical and toxicological data clearly linking the practice of chewing tobacco with the development of tumours of the jaw and mouth".

Findings of the Commission

- Although the role played by nitrosamines in the mechanism of cancer causation is unclear, the general thrust of the evidence is that:
  - nitrosamines are powerful animal carcinogens;
  - they are present to a significant degree in smokeless tobacco products; and
  - they have the capacity to cause cancer in humans.

- In certain circumstances, the results of epidemiological studies alone could provide a sufficient basis for decisions on public health policy, even when there remain questions of concern to scientists about the nature and mechanisms of any causal relationship; and
- That long-term consumption of chewing tobacco will increase the health risks to users, although the Commission is not as confident in this conclusion as it is in relation to oral snuffs.

(2) Date of Manufacture or Import

– Were I to act in accordance with the recommendation in so far as it limits the relevant goods to those manufactured in or imported into Australia after 30 September 1989, it would have to be shown, for the purposes of determining in a particular case whether the goods in question were unsafe goods, that those goods were manufactured in or imported into Australia on or after 1 October 1989. When the goods in question were manufactured or imported may not be readily ascertainable and may, depending upon the relevant circumstances, be difficult to ascertain with any precision at all.

– Having regard to the objects of Division 1A of Part V of the Act, it would seem incongruous to permit the continued supply of goods of a kind which I am declaring to be unsafe merely because they were manufactured or imported on or before a particular date.

Dated this Eleventh day of October 1989

NICK BOLKUS
Minister of State for Consumer Affairs

AUSTRALIA (CAPITAL TERRITORY). An Ordinance (No. 49 of 1986) to provide for the printing of health warnings on containers in which certain tobacco products are packaged. Dated 20 August 1986. (The Tobacco Products (Health Warnings) Ordinance 1986). (4 pp.) **Ausl. (CT) 87.5**

The following is an outline of the principal provisions of this Ordinance, which is to come into operation on a date to be fixed by the Minister of State for Territories by notice in the *Gazette*. Sec. 3 defines various terms, including "tobacco product" ("pipe tobacco, roll-your-own tobacco, or cigarettes or cigars containing tobacco"). Subsection 1 of Sec. 4 (Tobacco product containers) reads as follows:

"**4.** (1) The phrase 'Health Authority warning', and one of the following warnings, shall appear on every container or wrapping in which a tobacco product is packaged:

'SMOKING CAUSES LUNG CANCER'

'SMOKING CAUSE HEART DISEASE'

'SMOKING DAMAGES YOUR LUNGS'

'SMOKING IS ADDICTIVE'."

The substantive provisions of Sec. 6 (Rotation of warnings) prescribe that "A person who imports tobacco products into the Territory, or who packs tobacco products, for sale or for advertising purposes, shall ensure that, within each calendar year, each warning specified in sub-section 4(1) appears on 25 per cent of the containers and of any cartons in which each brand of each type of tobacco product is packaged". Subsection 2 of Sec. 7 (Offences) reads as follows:

"(2) A person shall not—

(*a*) sell a tobacco product, or expose a tobacco product for sale; or (*b*) for advertising purposes, give a tobacco product, or cause a tobacco product to be given, to another person,

if the tobacco product is in a container on which the words 'non-injurious', 'non-hazardous', or any other words that convey, or tend to convey, an indication that smoking is not a hazard to health, or on which any words which expressly or by implication contradict, qualify or modify a warning appearing on the container, appear.

Penalty:...".

AUSTRALIA (CAPITAL TERRITORITY). Tobacco Products (Health Warnings) (Amendment) Ordinance 1987. No. 22 of 1987.

I, THE GOVERNOR-GENERAL of the Commonwealth of Australia, acting with the advice of the Federal Executive Council, hereby make the following Ordinance under the *Seat of Government (Administration) Act 1910*.

Dated 5 June 1987.

N. M. STEPHEN
Governor-General

By His Excellency's Command,

G. SCHOLES
Minister of State for Territories

An Ordinance to amend the *Tobacco Products (Health Warnings) Ordinance 1986*

Short Title

1. This Ordinance may be cited as the *Tobacco Products (Health Warnings) (Amendment) Ordinance 1987.*[1]

Principal Ordinance

2. In this Ordinance, "Principal Ordinance" means the *Tobacco Products (Health Warnings) Ordinance 1986.*[2]

3. Section 2 of the Principal Ordinance is repealed and the following section substituted:

Commencement

"2. (1) Section 1, this section and subsection 7 (2) shall come into operation on 1 July 1987.

"(2) The remaining provisions of this Ordinance shall come into operation on 1 September 1987."

Interpretation

4. Section 3 of the Principal Ordinance is amended:

(a) by omitting "or a carton, or a label on a carton" from the definition of "brand name" in subsection (1) and substituting ", carton or wrapping, or a label on a carton or wrapping";

(b) by omitting "or carton" from the definition of "brand name" in subsection (1) and substituting "carton or wrapping";

(c) by omitting from subsection (1) the definitions of "carton" and "container";

(d) by omitting from subsection (1) the definition of "tobacco product" and substituting the following definition:

"tobacco product" means:

(a) cigarettes containing tobacco;

(b) roll-your-own tobacco; or

(c) pipe tobacco;";

(e) by omitting from paragraph (2) (a) "or a carton" and substituting ", carton or wrapping";

(f) by omitting from subparagraph (2) (a) (i) "outer";

(g) by omitting from subparagraph (2) (a) (ii) "outer"; and

(h) by omitting from paragraph (2) (b) "to a cigar sold individually or".

Tobacco product containers

5. Section 4 of the Principal Ordinance is amended:

(a) by omitting from subsection (1) "IS ADDICTIVE" and substituting "REDUCES YOUR FITNESS"; and

(b) by omitting subsections (2) to (6) (inclusive) and substituting the following subsections:

"(2) A warning shall be printed in Universe 57 Medium Condensed Roman typeface in one horizontal line of upper case letters of not less than:

(a) 14 point size; or

(b) if the container or wrapping is so small that 14 point size would be impracticable – the largest practicable point size.

"(3) The prescribed phrase shall be printed in Universe 55 Medium Roman typeface in one horizontal line of letters with the initial letter of each word in upper case and the remaining letters in lower case, being letters of one-half the point size of the letters in which the warning is printed.

"(4) A warning and the prescribed phrase shall be printed in a colour that makes a distinct contrast with the colour of the background on which they appear, but may be printed in a colour that appears elsewhere on the container or wrapping.

"(5) A warning and the prescribed phrase shall be printed:

(a) if the container or wrapping has only 2 faces on which the brand name appears – on each of those faces;

(b) if the container or wrapping has more than 2 faces on which the brand name appears – on any 2 of those faces or, if those faces differ in area, on any 2 of those faces which are greater or greatest in area; and

(c) in any other case – in such a position or positions on the container or wrapping that they are clearly visible together with the brand name.".

Cartons

6. Section 5 of the Principal Ordinance is amended:

(a) by omitting from subsection (1), ", (3)";

(b) by omitting from subsection (1) ", or outer wrapping," and substituting "or wrapping";

(c) by omitting from subsection (1) "outer" (second occurring);

(d) by inserting in subsection (2) "or wrapping" after "carton" (wherever occurring);

(e) by omitting from subsection (2) "with sub-section 4 (6)" and substituting "with subsection 4 (5)";

(f) by omitting subsection (3);

(g) by inserting in subsection (4) "or wrapping" after "carton"; and

(h) by omitting from subsection (4) "sub-sections 4 (2) and (3) respectively" and substituting "subsection 4 (2)".

7. Section 6 of the Principal Ordinance is repealed and the following section substituted:

Rotation of warnings

"6. A person who imports tobacco products into the Territory, or who packs tobacco products, for sale or for advertising purposes, shall, as far as practicable, ensure that, within the period of 12 months commencing on 1 September in any year, each warning specified in subsection 4 (1) appears with equal frequency on the containers, cartons and wrappings in which each brand of each type of those products is packaged.

Penalty: (a) in the case of a body corporate–$2,500; and

(b) in the case of a natural person–$500.".

Containers without warnings–offence

8. Section 7 of the Principal Ordinance is amended:

(a) by inserting in paragraph (1) (c) "or wrapping" after "container";

(b) by inserting in paragraph (1) (d) "or wrapping" after "container";

(c) by inserting in paragraph (1) (e) "or wrapping" after "carton";

(d) by omitting the penalty set out at the foot of subsection (1); and

(e) by omitting subsection (2) and substituting the following subsection:

"(2) A person shall not:

(a) import a tobacco product into the Territory for sale or advertising purposes; or

(b) pack a tobacco product for sale or advertising purposes; unless:
(c) the tobacco product is in a container or wrapping;
(d) the container or wrapping complies with section 4; and
(e) any carton or wrapping in which the container is packed complies with sections 4 and 5.

Penalty: (a) in the case of a body corporate – $2,500; and
(b) in the case of a natural person – $500.".

9. After section 7 of the Principal Ordinance the following section is inserted:

Contradiction of warning – offence

"7 A. A person shall not:
(a) sell a tobacco product, or expose a tobacco product for sale;
(b) for advertising purposes, give a tobacco product, or cause a tobacco product to be given, to another person;
(c) import a tobacco product into the Territory for sale or advertising purposes; or
(d) pack a tobacco product for sale or advertising purposes;

in a container or wrapping on which the words "non-injurious", "non-hazardous", or any other words that convey, or tend to convey, an indication that smoking is not a hazard to health, or on which any words which expressly or by implication contradict, qualify or modify a warning appearing on the container or wrapping, appear.

Penalty: (a) in the case of a body corporate – $5,000; and
(b) in the case of a natural person – $1,000.".

Repeal of section 9

10. Section 9 of the Principal Ordinance is repealed.

Transitional

11. (1) During the period of 2 months commencing on 1 July 1987 a person who complies with the provisions of the Principal Ordinance in relation to cigarettes sold or exposed for sale or given or caused to be given for advertising purposes by that person shall be taken to have complied with the requirements of the *Cigarette Containers (Labelling) Ordinance 1972* in the relevant respect.

(2) Subsection 7 (2) of the Principal Ordinance as amended by this Ordinance does not apply before 1 September 1987 in relation to a tobacco product manufactured outside Australia.

NOTES

1. Notified in the *Commonwealth of Australia Gazette* on 15 June 1987.
2. No. 49, 1986.

AUSTRALIA (CAPITAL TERRITORY). Smoking and Tobacco Products Advertisements (Prohibition) Act 1989. No. 181 of 1989.

An Act to prohibit certain advertisements relating to smoking and tobacco products, and for related purposes

[*Assented to 28 December 1989*]

BE IT ENACTED by the Queen, and the Senate and the House of Representatives of the Commonwealth of Australia, as follows:

Short title

1. This Act may be cited as the *Smoking and Tobacco Products Advertisements (Prohibition) Act 1989*.

Commencement

2. This Act commences on the first day after the end of the period of 12 months beginning on the day on which it receives the Royal Assent.

Interpretation

3. **(1)** In this Act, unless the contrary intention appears:

"Australia" includes the external Territories;

"corporation" means:

(a) a body corporate that is a foreign corporation within the meaning of paragraph 51 (xx) of the Constitution; or

(b) a body corporate that is a trading corporation, within the meaning of paragraph 51 (xx) of the Constitution formed within the limits of the Commonwealth; or

(c) a body corporate that is a holding company of a body corporate of a kind referred to in paragraph (a) or (b); or

(d) a body corporate that is controlled by a corporation described in paragraph (a), (b) or (c); or

(e) a partnership at least one of the partners in which is a corporation described in paragraph (a), (b), (c) or (d);

"newspaper" includes a magazine, journal or periodical or any other publication copies of which contain:

(a) news, intelligence, information or reports of occurrences; or

(b) remarks, observations or comments in relation to any news, intelligence, information or occurrences or in relation to any other matter of interest to the public or any section of the public;

whatever language it is printed in and whether it is published at regular or irregular intervals;

"printed" includes made by any method of producing text or pictures in a material form;

"print medium" means a newspaper, handbill, program, ticket or other printed document, but does not include a document displayed as a poster;

"publish" does not include communicate to a person in the tobacco trade or in a tobacco product trade;

"smoking" means inhaling or puffing the smoke of cigarettes or cigars of any composition or tobacco in any form;

"tobacco product" means cigarettes or cigars of any tobacco composition or tobacco in any form, and includes snuff, cigarette paper, cigarette rollers and pipes;

(**2**)For the purpose of this Act, the question whether a body corporate is the holding company of another body corporate shall be determined in the same manner as that question is required to be determined by section 7 of the *Companies Act 1981*.

Extension to Territories

4. This Act extends to every external Territory.

Prohibition of advertising of smoking and tobacco products

5. (**1**) Subject to section 6, a corporation must not publish, or cause to be published, in a print medium an advertisement:

(a) for smoking; or

(b) for, or for the use of:

(i) cigarettes; or

(ii) cigarette tobacco; or

(iii) other tobacco products.

Penalty: $60,000.

(**2**) A reference in subsection (1) to the publication of an advertisement shall be read as not including a reference to the publication by a corporation of matter of an advertising character as an accidental or incidental accompaniment of the publication of other matter in circumstances in which the corporation does not receive payment or other valuable consideration for publishing the advertising matter.

Print media printed outside Australia

6. Subsection 5 (1) does not apply to a print medium:

(a) printed outside Australia; and

(b) not principally intended for distribution or use in Australia.

Certain actions do not lie

7. Where a contract entered into before or after the commencement of this Act relates to the advertising of tobacco products or smoking, an action does not lie in any court against a party to the contract for failing, neglecting or refusing, after the commencement of this Act, to publish an advertisement relating to tobacco products or smoking as required by the contract if the failure, neglect or refusal is attributable to, or occasioned by, the operation of this Act.

Conduct by directors, servants or agents

8. (1) Where, in proceedings for an offence against this Act, it is necessary to establish the state of mind of a body corporate in relation to particular conduct, it is sufficient to show:

(a) that the conduct was engaged in by a director, servant or agent of the body corporate within the scope of his or her actual or apparent authority; and

(b) that the director, servant or agent had the state of mind.

(2) Any conduct engaged in on behalf of a body corporate by a director, servant or agent of the body corporate within the scope of his or her actual or apparent authority is to be taken, for the purposes of a prosecution for an offence against this Act, to have been engaged in also by the body corporate unless the body corporate establishes that it took reasonable precautions to avoid the conduct.

(3) A reference in subsection (1) to the state of mind of a person includes a reference to:

(a) the knowledge, intention, opinion, belief or purpose of the person; and

(b) the person's reasons for the intention, opinion, belief or purpose.

(4) A reference in this section to engaging in conduct includes a reference to failing or refusing to engage in conduct.

(5) A reference in this section to an offence against this Act includes a reference to an offence created by section 6, 7 or 7A, or subsection 86 (1), of the *Crimes Act 1914*, being an offence that relates to this Act.

Additional operation of this Act

9 (1) Without prejudice to its effect apart from this section, this Act has effect as provided by this section.

(2) This Act has, by force of this subsection, the effect it would have if:

(a) in subsection 5 (1) "a corporation must not" were omitted and "a person must not, in the course of, or for the purposes of, trade or commerce to which this Act applies by virtue of subsection 9 (3)" were substituted; and

(b) in subsection 5 (1) "$60,000" were omitted and "$12,000" substituted; and

(c) in subsection 5 (2) "corporation" (wherever occurring) were omitted and "person" substituted.

(3) For the purpose of this Act having effect by virtue of subsection (2), this Act applies to trade and commerce:

(a) between Australia and places outside Australia; or

(b) among the States; or

(c) between a State and a Territory or between 2 Territories; or

(d) by way of the supply of goods or services to the Commonwealth or an authority or instrumentality of the Commonwealth.

(4) This Act has, by force of this subsection, the effect it would have if:

(a) in subsection 5 (1) "a corporation must not" were omitted and "a person must not in a Territory (not being the Australian Capital Territory, the Northern Territory or Norfolk Island)" were substituted; and

(b) in subsection 5 (1) "$60,000" were omitted and "$12,000" substituted.

[*Second reading speech made in –*
Senate on 31 August 1989
House of Representatives on 22 December 1989]

AUSTRALIA (CAPITAL TERRITORY). Tobacco (Amendment) Act 1990. No. 39 of 1990

An Act to amend the *Tobacco Act 1927*

[*Notified in ACT Gazette S76: 7 November 1990*]

The Legislative Assembly for the Australian Capital Territory enacts as follows:

Short title

1. This Act may be cited as the *Tobacco (Amendment) Act 1990.*

Commencement

2. **(1)** Section 1 and this section commence on the day on which this Act is notified in the *Gazette.*

(2) The remaining provisions commence on a day, or on respective days, fixed by the Minister by notice in the *Gazette.*

(3) If a provision referred to in subsection (2) has not commenced before the end of the period of 6 months commencing on the day on which this Act is notified in the *Gazette*, that provision, by force of this subsection, commences on the first day after the end of that period.

Principal Act

3. In this Act, "Principal Act" means the *Tobacco Act 1927.*[1]

Insertion of heading

4. Before section 1 of the Principal Act, the following heading is inserted:

"PART I – PRELIMINARY"

Substitution

5. Section 10 of the Principal Act is repealed and the following sections and Parts substituted:

Crown

"2. (1) This Act binds the Crown.

"(2) Nothing in this Act renders the Crown liable to be prosecuted for an offence.

Interpretation

"3. In this Act, unless the contrary intention appears–

'newspaper' has the same meaning as in the *Printing and Newspapers Act 1961*;

'public place' means a place to which the public ordinarily has access, whether by payment or not, but does not include a part of a place to which the public has access by reason only of the carrying on of a trade, business or profession on or in that place;

'sell' includes–

(a) barter or exchange;
(b) offer or expose for sale, barter or exchange;
(c) supply, or offer to supply, in circumstances in which the supplier derives, or would derive, a direct or indirect pecuniary benefit; and
(d) supply, or offer to supply, gratuitously but with a view to gaining or maintaining custom, or otherwise with a view to commercial gain;

'smoking' means inhaling or puffing the smoke of a cigarette or cigar of any composition, or tobacco in any form;

'theatre' means a place where any live entertainment or film is presented, performed or exhibited to which admission is or may be procured by payment or by ticket or by any other means, token or consideration;

'tobacco advertisement' means writing or a picture, symbol, light or other visible device, object or sign, or a combination of 2 or more of the foregoing, that gives publicity to or otherwise promotes–

(a) the purchase or use of a tobacco product; or
(b) a trademark or brand name, or part of a trade mark or brand name, of a tobacco product;

'tobacco product' means tobacco, a cigarette or cigar or any other product the main ingredient of which is tobacco and which is designed for human consumption;

'vending machine' means a machine, device or contrivance that is constructed to contain tobacco products that may be obtained from it by an operation that involves the insertion of money or a token or similar object.

"PART II – SUPPLY OF TOBACCO PRODUCTS

Supply of tobacco products to persons under 18 years

"4. (1) A person shall not sell, or cause or permit to be sold, a tobacco product to a person under the age of 18 years.

Penalty: $1,000.

"(2) The occupier of premises on which a vending machine is situated shall not permit a person under the age of 18 years to obtain a tobacco product from that machine.

Penalty: $1,000.

"(3) It is a defence to a prosecution under this section if it is established that the defendant–

(a) had reasonable cause to believe that the person purchasing or obtaining the tobacco product had attained the age of 18 years; or

(b) had taken all reasonable precautions to ensure that the tobacco product was not sold or supplied to a person under the age of 18 years.

Purchase of tobacco products for persons under 18 years

"5. A person shall not purchase a tobacco product for use by a person under the age of 18 years.

Penalty: $1,000.

Vending machines

"6. (1) A person shall not, without reasonable excuse, place, or cause, permit or authorise to be placed, a vending machine for operation by members of the public on any premises except licensed premises within the meaning of the *Liquor Act 1975*.

Penalty: $1,000.

"(2) A person who owns or possesses a vending machine shall take reasonable precautions to ensure that there is kept conspicuously displayed on the front of that machine a statement in the prescribed form.

Penalty: $500.

Smokeless tobacco

"7. A person shall not manufacture or sell a tobacco product other than a product prepared for smoking.

Penalty: $1,000.

Confectionery or toys resembling tobacco products

"8. (1) A person shall not sell, or import into the Territory for sale, confectionery, or a toy, that is designed to resemble a tobacco product.

"(2) A person shall not sell, or import into the Territory for sale, confectionery, or a toy, contained in packaging that is designed to resemble a tobacco product or the packaging of a tobacco product.

Penalty: $1,000.

Sale of cigarettes

"9. A person shall not sell cigarettes in a quantity of fewer than 20.

Penalty: $1,000.

"PART III – ADVERTISING AND SPONSORSHIP

Certain advertising prohibited

"10. (1) A person shall not for any direct or indirect pecuniary benefit–

(a) display, or cause, permit or authorise to be displayed, a tobacco advertisement in a theatre;

(b) sell, or cause, permit or authorise to be sold, a film or video tape that contains a tobacco advertisement;

(c) distribute, or cause, permit or authorise to be distributed, to the public any unsolicited leaflet, handbill or other document that is or that contains a tobacco advertisement;

(d) place or display, or cause, permit or authorise to be placed or displayed, a tobacco advertisement so that it is visible in or from a public place; or

(e) sell, or cause or permit or authorise to be sold, an object that is or that contains a tobacco advertisement.

Penalty: $5,000.

"(2) This section does not apply in relation to–

(a) a tobacco advertisement in or on–

(i) a newspaper or magazine;

(ii) a book; or

(iii) a package containing a tobacco product;

(b) a tobacco advertisement that is an accidental or incidental accompaniment to a film or video tape;

(c) a tobacco advertisement which is displayed inside a shop or warehouse adjacent to a place where tobacco products are offered for sale;

(d) a tobacco advertisement which is–

(i) displayed outside the entrance to a place where tobacco products are offered for sale; and

(ii) to the effect that tobacco products are offered for sale in that place;

where the advertisement–

(iii) does not contain a trademark or brand name, nor part of a trademark or brand name, of a tobacco product; and

(iv) does not contain the name of a manufacturer or distributor of a tobacco product;

(e) a document ordinarily used in the course of business; or

(f) tobacco advertising specified in a notice under subsection (3).

"(3) The Minister may, by notice published in the *Gazette*, exempt specified tobacco advertising from the operation of subsection (1).

"(4) A notice under subsection (3) is a disallowable instrument for the purposes of section 10 of the *Subordinate Laws Act 1989*.

Removal of tobacco advertisements

"11. (1) If an authorised officer believes on reasonable grounds that a person has contravened paragraph 10 (1) (d), the officer shall give the person a written notice stating that unless the relevant tobacco advertisement is removed, or obscured, in the specified manner within the period of 30 days after the notice is given, proceedings may be commenced against the person for an offence against that paragraph.

"(2) Proceedings against a person for an offence against paragraph 10 (1) (d)–

(a) shall not be commenced unless a notice is given to the person under subsection (1);

(b) shall not be commenced until after the period of 30 days after that notice is given; and

(c) shall not be commenced if the relevant tobacco advertisement is removed or obscured in accordance with that notice.

"(3) If a person is convicted of an offence against paragraph 10 (1) (d), the Court, in addition to imposing any other penalty, may order that the relevant tobacco advertisement be removed, or obscured, by the Territory.

"(4) If a tobacco advertisement is removed, or obscured, in accordance with an order under subsection (3), the person convicted of the relevant offence shall pay the Territory the reasonable costs incurred in removing or obscuring the advertisement.

"(5) In this section–

'authorised officer' means a person who is–

(a) an Inspector; or

(b) authorised;

for the purposes of the *Public Health Act 1928.*

Prohibition of sponsorships

"12. (1) A person shall not, under a contract, agreement, undertaking or understanding, whether or not legally binding, promote or agreed to promote–

(a) a tobacco product;

(b) a trademark or brand name, or part of a trademark or brand name, of a tobacco product; or

(c) the name or interests of a manufacturer or distributor of a tobacco product in association, whether directly or indirectly, with that tobacco product;

in exchange for a sponsorship, gift, prize, scholarship or like benefit given or agreed to be given by another person.

Penalty: $5,000.

"(2) A person shall not, under a contract, agreement, undertaking or understanding, whether or not legally binding, give or agree to give any sponsorship, gift, prize, scholarship or like benefit in exchange for a promotion, or an agreement to promote, referred to in paragraph (1) (a), (b) or (c).

Penalty: $5,000.

"(3) This section does not apply in relation to–

(a) a scholarship given, or agreed to be given, by a manufacturer or distributor of a tobacco product to an employee, or a member of the family of an employee, of the manufacturer or distributor; or

(b) a contract, agreement, undertaking or understanding specified in a notice under subsection (4).

"(4) The Minister may, by notice published in the *Gazette*, exempt a specified contract, agreement, undertaking or understanding from the operation of subsection (1) or (2).

"(5) A notice under subsection (4) is a disallowable instrument for the purposes of section 10 of the *Subordinate Laws Act 1989*.

"PART IV – MISCELLANEOUS

Conduct of directors, servants and agents

"13. (1) Where, for the purposes of this Act, it is necessary to establish the state of mind of a body corporate or a natural person in relation to particular conduct, it is sufficient to show–

(a) that a director, servant or agent of the body, or a servant or agent of the person, had that state of mind; and

(b) that the conduct was engaged in by that director, servant or agent within the scope of his or her actual or apparent authority.

"(2) A reference in subsection (1) to the state of mind of a body or person is to be read as including a reference to–

(a) the knowledge, intention, opinion, belief or purpose of the body or person; and

(b) the body's or person's reasons for the intention, opinion, belief or purpose.

"(3) Any conduct engaged in on behalf of a body corporate or a natural person by a director, servant or agent of the body, or a servant or agent of the person, within the scope of his or her actual or apparent authority is to be taken, for the purposes of this Act, to have been engaged in also by the body or person unless the body or person establishes that reasonable precautions were taken and due diligence was exercised to avoid the conduct.

"(4) A reference in this section to a director of a body corporate is to be read as including a reference to a member of a body corporate incorporated for a public purpose by a law of the Territory, the Commonwealth, a State or another Territory.

"(5) A reference in this section to engaging in conduct is to be read as including a reference to failing or refusing to engage in conduct.

Corporations – penalties

"14. Where a body corporate is convicted of an offence against this Act, the penalty that the Court may impose is a fine not exceeding 5 times the maximum amount that, but for this section, the Court could impose as a pecuniary penalty for that offence.

Regulations

"15. The Executive may make regulations, not inconsistent with this Act, prescribing matters–

(a) required or permitted by this Act to be prescribed; or

(b) necessary or convenient to be prescribed for carrying out or giving effect to this Act.".

NOTE

1. Ordinance No. 14, 1927 as amended by No. 5, 1930; No. 10, 1936; Nos. 19 and 27, 1937; No. 10, 1957; No. 14, 1966; No. 21, 1989.

[Presentation speech made in Assembly on 6 June 1990.]

AUSTRALIA (SOUTH AUSTRALIA). An Act (No. 79 of 1984) to prohibit the sale or supply of certain tobacco products to children; and to amend the Community Welfare Act, 1972. Dated 15 November 1984. (The Tobacco Sales to Children (Prohibition) Act, 1984). (2 pp.) **Ausl. (SA) 86.3**

Sec. 2 of this Act defines "supply" to mean "to give, lend or supply in any manner whatsoever", and "tobacco product" as "tobacco, a cigarette or cigar, or any other manufactured product, intended for smoking, of which tobacco is a constituent part". Secs. 3 (Prohibition of sale of tobacco products to person under sixteen years) and 4 (Vendor of tobacco products must display warnings) are substantially reproduced below:

"**3.** (1) A person who sells (whether directly or by way of a vending machine) or supplies, or offers to sell or supply, a tobacco product—

(*a*) to a person under the age of sixteen years; or

(*b*) to a person where the vendor knows, or has reasonable cause to believe, that the tobacco product is for the use of a person under the age of sixteen years,

shall be guilty of an offence and liable to a penalty not exceeding five hundred dollars.

(2) [*Penal provisions*]

4. The occupier of premises at which tobacco products are sold by retail shall ensure that a statement to the general effect of section 3, including the penalty provided in that section, is displayed at each place where the tobacco products are offered for sale on the premises, in such manner and position as to be readily noticed and understood by persons intending to purchase a tobacco product.
Penalty: Two hundred dollars."

AUSTRALIA (SOUTH AUSTRALIA). An Act (No. 74 of 1986) to regulate the sale, packing, importing, advertising and use of tobacco products; to repeal the Cigarettes (Labelling) Act, 1971, and the Tobacco Sales to Children (Prohibition) Act, 1984; and for other purposes. Dated 27 November 1986. (The Tobacco Products Control Act, 1986). (6 pp.) **Ausl. (SA) 88.6**

Sec. 2 (Commencement) reads as follows:

"**2.** (1) This Act shall come into operation on a day to be fixed by proclamation.

(2) The Governor may, in a proclamation fixing a day for this Act to come into operation, suspend the operation of specified provisions of this Act until a subsequent day fixed in the proclamation, or a day to be fixed by subsequent proclamation.

(3) The Governor shall not fix a day for section 7 to come into operation unless the Governor is satisfied that legislation similar in effect to section 7 has come into operation, or is likely to come into operation, in the Australia Capital Territory and at least 3 States of the Commonwealth apart from this State."

Sec. 3 defines various terms, including "sucking tobacco" ("tobacco that has been prepared for sucking but not chewing") and "tobacco products" ("tobacco, cigarettes, cigars and all other products the main ingredient of which is tobacco and which are designed for human consumption"). Secs. 4 (Sale of tobacco products by retail), 5 (Importing and packing of tobacco products), 6 (Tobacco products in relation to which no health warning has been prescribed), 7 (Advertisements of tobacco products), 8 (Notice of tar, nicotine, etc., content of cigarettes), 9 (Sale of sucking tobacco), 10 (Sale of confectionery), and 11 (Sale of tobacco products to children) read substantially as follows:

"**4.** (1) A person shall not sell a tobacco product by retail unless it is enclosed in a package that displays a health warning in the prescribed manner and form.

(2) A person shall not sell by retail a tobacco product that is enclosed in two or more packages unless each package displays a health warning in the prescribed manner and form.

(3) A person shall not sell cigarettes by retail in a package containing less than 20.

(4) The Governor may, by regulation, exempt a person from the operation of subsection (3) in relation to cigarettes of a prescribed class.

5. (1) A person shall not import tobacco products that have been packed for sale by retail unless—

(*a*) each package displays a health warning in the prescribed manner and form;

and

(*b*) where two or more health warnings have been prescribed—the various warnings are distributed in approximately equal numbers between the packages imported by that person in each financial year.

(2) A person who packs tobacco products for sale by retail shall ensure—

(*a*) that each package displays a health warning in the prescribed manner and form;

and

(*b*) where two or more health warnings have been prescribed—the various warnings are distributed in approximately equal numbers between the packages packed by that person in each financial year.

(3) Where tobacco products have been packed for sale by retail in two or more packages only the smallest of those packages and the warning it displays shall be taken into account when determining the number of packages on which each health warning is displayed.

6. Notwithstanding any other provision of this Act, where no health warning is prescribed in relation to a tobacco product of a particular class—

(*a*) a tobacco product of that class need not be enclosed in a package;

and

(*b*) a package that contains a tobacco product of that class need not (provided it does not also contain a tobacco product of a class in relation to which a health warning is prescribed) display a health warning.

7. (1) Subject to subsection (3), a person shall not publish, or cause to be published, an advertisement for a tobacco product unless the advertisement incorporates, or appears in conjunction with, a health warning.

(2) The warning must be published in the prescribed manner and form.

(3) The Governor may, by regulation, exclude a class of advertisements from the operation of this section.

8. (1) A person who sells cigarettes by retail shall display a notice setting out the quantity of tar and carbon monoxide that will be produced, and the quantity of nicotine that will be released, in the normal course of smoking each cigarette.

Penalty: $500.

(2) The notice must be in a form approved by the South Australian Health Commission and must be displayed in a manner and position that is likely to attract the attention of persons who purchase those cigarettes.

Penalty: $500.

9. (1) A person shall not sell sucking tobacco by retail.

(2) The Governor may, by regulation, exempt a person from the operation of subsection (1) subject to such conditions as are set out in the regulation.

10. A person shall not sell by retail confectionery that is designed to resemble a tobacco product.

11. (1) A person shall not supply, or offer to supply (whether by sale, gift or any other means) a tobacco product to a child or a person who the supplier knows or has reason to believe will supply the product to a child.

Penalty: $1000.

(2) A person shall not permit a child to obtain a tobacco product from a vending machine situated on premises that he or she occupies.

Penalty: $1000.

(3) [*Miscellaneous provisions*]."

Under Sec. 12, it is an offence, except as indicated, for a person to smoke a tobacco product in a bus that is carrying members of the public. Sec. 13 prohibits the smoking of tobacco products in a lift. Sec. 14 defines the powers of "authorized officers". Sec. 16 (Regulations) reads as follows:

"**16.** (1) The Governor may make such regulations as are contemplated by this Act or as are necessary or expedient for the purposes of this Act.

(2) In particular the regulations may—

(*a*) prescribe warnings that must be displayed on packages containing tobacco products and in, or in conjunction with, advertisements of tobacco products;

(*b*) prescribe the manner and form in which those warnings must be displayed or published.

(3) A regulation may prescribe a warning in relation to tobacco products generally or in relation to tobacco products of a particular class."

AUSTRALIA (SOUTH AUSTRALIA). An Act (No. 123 of 1986) to recover from consumers of tobacco products an appropriate contribution towards the State's revenues; to repeal the Business Franchise (Tobacco) Act, 1974; and for other purposes. Dated 18 December 1986. (The Tobacco Products (Licensing) Act, 1986). (19 pp.)

Ausl. (SA) 88.7

The Preamble to this Act is reproduced below:

"Preamble:

1. The consumption of tobacco products impairs the health of the citizens of the State and places a substantial burden on the State's financial resources.

2. In view of this financial burden, the Parliament considers it fair that consumers of tobacco products should make an appropriate contribution to State revenues irrespective of the source of the tobacco products.

3. The purpose of this Act is to establish a legislative scheme under which—

(*a*) a direct contribution to State revenues, in the form of a licence fee, will be made by a consumer who takes out a consumption licence;

but

(*b*) a tobacco merchant who chooses to be licensed and thus by payment of licence fee to make a contribution to State revenues on behalf of consumers will relieve a consumer from the obligation to hold a consumption licence for the consumption of tobacco products obtained through the merchant."

AUSTRALIA (TASMANIA). An Act (No. 49 of 1987) to prohibit the sale of tobacco products except in packages marked with health warnings and to provide for related matters. Date of assent: 18 August 1987. (The Tobacco Products (Labelling) Act 1987). (4 pp.)

Ausl. (Tas) 88.1

This Act, which repeals the Cigarettes (Labelling) Act, 1972 (see *IDHL*, 1974, **25**, 721). Sec. 3 defines various terms, including "tobacco product" ("a tobacco product prepared for smoking and includes cigarettes and any mixture that contains tobacco and is intended to be smoked, but does not include snuff, plug tobacco, or cigars that are sold individually"). The substantive provisions are contained in the following Sections: 5. Sale of unpackaged tobacco products prohibited; 6. Packing of tobacco products without health warning prohibited; 7. Sale of tobacco products without health warning prohibited; and 8. Prohibited words on packaged tobacco products.

Sec. 9 indicates the matters in respect to which the Governor may make regulations for the implementation of this Act.

AUSTRALIA (VICTORIA). The Tobacco Act 1987. Act No. 81 of 1987. Date of assent: 24 November 1987. (23 pp.) **Ausl. (Vic) 88.3**

Sec. 3 (Definitions) of Part I (Preliminary) (Secs. 1-5) defines various terms, including "tobacco advertisement" and "tobacco product", ("tobacco, cigarette or cigar or any other product, the main ingredient of which is designed for human consumption"). Sec. 4 (Application of Act) states that nothing in this Act applies to anything done by radio or television broadcast; furthermore, nothing in the Act or the regulations for its implementation applies to: (*a*) the labelling of packages of tobacco if the tobacco is packed for sale outside Victoria and is not sold in Victoria; or (*b*) anything which causes, permits, authorizes, or assists in the sale or promotion of the sale, purchase, use, or consumption of a tobacco product if the sale, purchase, use, or consumption occurs solely outside Victoria. Sec. 5 (Objects of Act) is reproduced below:

"**5.** (1) The objects of this Act are—

(*a*) the active discouragement of the smoking of tobacco—

(i) by encouraging non-smokers, particularly young people, not to start smoking; and

(ii) by limiting exposure of children and young people to persuasion to smoke; and

(iii) by encouraging and assisting smokers to give up smoking; and

(*b*) the promotion of health and illness prevention.

(2) In giving effect to the objects of this Act, the Minister shall cause steps to be taken to—

(*a*) plan and co-ordinate an integrated State-wide program to reduce the prevalence of smoking in Victoria; and

(*b*) encourage agreements to prohibit or limit the places and times at which people may smoke in enclosed public places or in the work environment; and

(*c*) ensure that tobacco usage by all age and sex groups in the population is monitored and reported upon regularly; and

(*d*) evaluate the effectiveness of anti-smoking programs and plan future activities and policies on tobacco usage."

Part 2 (Prohibition of advertising, etc.) (Secs. 6-15) includes substantive Sections imposing restrictions on various forms of advertising. Certain exemptions are laid down in Sec. 10. Under Sec. 11 (Packing), a person must not sell any tobacco prepared for smoking that is in a package: (*a*) that is not labelled in accordance with the regulations with a prescribed statement and warning (if any) applicable to packages of that class; or (*b*) that is not labelled with the prescribed statement (if any) applicable to packages of that class giving the tar content of the tobacco; or (*c*) that is not labelled with any other prescribed information applicable to packages of that class.

Provisions prohibiting the supply of tobacco to persons under 16 years of age are laid down in Sec. 12, while Sec. 13 lays down restrictions on the siting of vending machines. Under Sec. 14, a person may not sell cigarettes in a package containing less than 20 cigarettes. Sec. 15 prohibits any person from manufacturing or selling a tobacco product other than a product prepared for smoking (this provision does not apply to the manufacture or sale of prescribed tobacco products).

Part 3 (Victorian Health Promotion Foundation) (Secs. 16-36) provides for the establishment of the Foundation. Its objectives, as laid down in Sec. 17, are as follows: (*a*) to fund activities related to the promotion of good health, safety, or the prevention and early detection of disease; (*b*) to increase awareness of programmes for promoting good health in the community through the sponsorship of sports, the arts, and popular culture; (*c*) to encourage healthy lifestyles in the community and support activities involving participation in healthy pursuits; and (*d*) to fund research and development activities in support of these objects.

Details are given in Sec. 21 of the membership of the Foundation. Sec. 32 provides for the establishment of a Trust Fund known as the Victorian Health Promotion Fund. The monies paid into the Fund include the Victorian Health Promotion Levy referred to in Sec. 10 (8) of the Business Franchise (Tobacco) Act 1974.

The remaining Parts of the Act are as follows: 4. Miscellaneous (Secs. 37-43) (Sec. 43 empowers the Governor in Council to make regulations for the implementation of this Act); and 5. Amendment of other Acts.

AUSTRALIA (WESTERN AUSTRALIA). The Tobacco (Warning Labels) Regulations 1987. (*Government Gazette, Western Australia*, 23 January 1987, pp. 188-189) **Ausl. (WA) 88.1**

These Regulations have been made by the Governor in Executive Council, on the advice of the Drug Advisory Committee, in pursuance of the Health Act 1911; they repeal the Cigarettes (Labelling) Regulations (originally published on 21 June 1972 and amended by Regulations published on 21 June 1974). It is laid down that, as from 1 September 1987, a person may not sell a package containing tobacco (the term is defined to exclude cigars and plug tobacco) unless the package is labelled in accordance with these Regulations.

The warnings to appear in the warning labels are as follows:

"SMOKING CAUSES LUNG CANCER

Health Authority Warning";

"SMOKING CAUSES HEART DISEASE

Health Authority Warning";

"SMOKING DAMAGES YOUR LUNGS

Health Authority Warning";

"SMOKING REDUCES YOUR FITNESS

Health Authority Warning".

Packers are required to ensure, insofar as is reasonably practical, that each statement and warning is inscribed with equal frequency on labels attached to or printed on packages of tobacco packed during each 12-month period, commencing on 1 July 1987. Details are given of the conditions under which warnings are to appear.

It is also laid down that a package of tobacco must not be labelled with or bear: (*a*) any statement or words such as "non-injurious", "non-hazardous", "harmless to man", or any statement or words of similar import; or (*b*) any comment on, reference to, or explanation of any statement or warning which must be inscribed on a label under these Regulations.

AUSTRALIA (WESTERN AUSTRALIA). Tobacco Control Act. No. 104 of 1990.

AN ACT to regulate the sale and promotion of tobacco products, to establish the Western Australian Health Promotion Foundation, to amend the *Constitution Acts Amendment Act 1899*, the *Financial Administration and Audit Act 1985*, the *Government Employees Superannuation Act 1987*, the *Health Act 1911*, and the *Parliamentary Commissioner Act 1971* and to repeal the *Sale of Tobacco Act 1916* and to provide for matters incidental to or connected with the foregoing.

[*Assented to 2 January 1991.*]

The Parliament of Western Australia enacts as follows:

PART 1—PRELIMINARY

Short title

1. This Act may be cited as the *Tobacco Control Act 1990*.

Commencement

2. (1) Subject to this section, this Act shall come into operation on such day as is fixed by proclamation.

(2) Sections 5 (2), 6 (1), 11 (1) and (2), and 12 shall come into operation 6 months after the appointed day.

(3) Section 5 (1) shall come into operation 12 months after the appointed day.

Purposes of Act

3. The purposes of this Act are—

(a) the active discouragement of the smoking of tobacco by—

(i) encouraging non-smokers, particularly young people, not to start smoking;

(ii) limiting exposure of children and young people to persuasion to smoke; and

(iii) encouraging and assisting smokers to give up smoking;

and

(b) the promotion of good health and the prevention of illness.

Interpretation

4. In this Act, unless the contrary intention appears—

"banned contract" means—

(a) a contract or arrangement entered into before the appointed day and which pursuant to Part 2 is unlawful in whole or part; or

(b) a contract or arrangement which the Foundation considers there to have been a reasonable likelihood would have been entered into after the appointed day but for the passing of this Act and which pursuant to Part 2 would have been unlawful in whole or part but only where the potential parties to such contract or arrangement have prior to 24 August, 1989 been parties to a contract or arrangement which if it continued beyond the appointed day would pursuant to Part 2 be unlawful in whole or part;

"banned sponsorship" means a banned contract which pursuant to section 8 would be unlawful in whole or part;

"benefit" with respect to a banned contract or banned sponsorship means any benefit that would have flowed to a person other than a manufacturer or wholesaler of a tobacco product under or in connection with or as a result of a banned contract or banned sponsorship as the case may be;

"book" includes any printed material in any language;

"brand name" includes any part of a brand name;

"Chairperson" means Chairperson of the Foundation appointed under section 17 (1);

"function" has the meaning given by section 5 of the *Interpretation Act 1984*;

"member" means member of the Foundation appointed under or referred to in section 17 (1);

"newspaper" includes copy of any magazine, journal or periodical, or any other publication copies of which contain—

(a) news, intelligence, information or reports of occurrences;

or

(b) remarks, observations or comments in relation to any news, intelligence, information or occurrences or to any other matter of interest to the public or any section of the public,

which are printed in any language and published at regular or irregular intervals;

"objective" means objective of the Foundation set out in section 22;

"package", in relation to a tobacco product, means package—

(a) in which the tobacco product is packed by the manufacturer of; and

(b) which immediately contains,

the tobacco product;

"public place" includes place to which the public or a section thereof ordinarily has access, whether by payment or not or by invitation or not;

"racing" means horse racing and pacing, dog racing and motor car and motorcycle racing;

"sell" includes—

(a) barter or exchange;

(b) offer or expose for sale, barter or exchange;

(c) supply, or offer to supply, in circumstances in which the supplier derives, or would derive, a direct or indirect pecuniary benefit; and

(d) supply, or offer to supply, gratuitously but with a view to gaining or maintaining custom or otherwise with a view to commercial gain;

"sponsorship" includes—

(a) scholarship, prize, gift or other like benefit; and

(b) financial arrangement (other than *bona fide* contract of employment or *bona fide* contract for services) for the direct promotion or publicization of one or more of the matters referred to in section 8 (1) (a) and (b) through the medium of sporting, arts, youth, educational or other like activities;

"sporting" includes recreational and other such activities but does not include racing;

"the appointed day" means the day referred to in section 2 (1);

"the Commissioner of Health" has the meaning given by the *Health Act 1911*;

"the Foundation" means the Western Australian Health Promotion Foundation established by section 15 (1);

"the Fund" means the Western Australian Health Promotion Fund referred to in section 26 (3);

"the Minister for Racing and Gaming" means the Minister to whom the administration of the *Casino Control Act 1984* is for the time being committed by the Governor;

"the Minister for Sport and Recreation" means the Minister to whom the administration of the *Western Australian Sports Centre Trust Act 1986* is for the time being committed by the Governor;

"the Minister for the Arts" means the Minister to whom the administration of the *Art Gallery Act 1959* is for the time being committed by the Governor;

"tobacco advertisement" means writing, still or moving picture, sign, symbol or other visual image or message, or audible message, designed to promote or publicize a tobacco product;

"tobacco product" means tobacco, cigarette or cigar or any other product the main, or a substantial, ingredient of which is tobacco and which is designed for human consumption or use, but excludes nicotine or a product containing nicotine insofar as the *Poisons Act 1964* applies to or in relation to nicotine or a product containing nicotine;

"trademark" includes part of a trademark;

"vending machine" means machine, device or contrivance that is constructed to contain tobacco products that can be obtained from it by an operation which involves—

(a) the insertion in that machine, device or contrivance of a coin, token or similar object; or

(b) any other action taken without the assistance of the vendor or his or her employee or agent.

PART 2—CONTROLS RELATING TO TOBACCO PRODUCTS

Certain advertising prohibited

5. (1) A person who in Western Australia for any direct or indirect benefit displays a tobacco advertisement in, or so that it can be seen or heard from, a public place commits an offence.

(2) A person who in Western Australia—

(a) distributes to the public any unsolicited object; or

(b) sells, hires or supplies for any direct or indirect benefit any object,

that constitutes or contains a tobacco advertisement commits an offence.

(3) This section does not apply in relation to—

(a) anything done by means of a radio or television broadcast;

(b) a tobacco advertisement in or on—

(i) a newspaper or book printed or published outside Western Australia, the sole or main purpose of which newspaper or book is a purpose other than the promotion or publicization of—

(A) the purchase or use; or

(B) a trademark or brand name,

of a tobacco product; or

(ii) a package or carton containing a tobacco product;

(c) a tobacco advertisement that is an incidental accompaniment to the subject of a film or video tape (not being a film or video tape which is wholly or mainly concerned with the promotion of tobacco products);

(d) a tobacco advertisement that is displayed inside a shop or other retail outlet where tobacco products are offered or exposed for sale, that is directly adjacent to a place where all or any of those tobacco products are offered or exposed for sale and that complies with any regulations made under section 33(1) (c);

(e) an invoice, statement, order, letterhead, business card, cheque, manual or other document that is ordinarily used in the course of business; or

(f) anything to which this section does not apply by virtue of an exemption granted under section 14.

(4) In any proceedings for an offence under subsection (1), it shall be presumed that, if there is present in the relevant tobacco advertisement—

(a) the name of a person who manufactures or distributes any tobacco product;

(b) a trademark, of which a person who manufactures or distributes any tobacco product is the registered proprietor or the registered user within the meaning of the *Trade Marks Act 1955* of the Commonwealth; or

(c) a brand name, used by a person who manufactures or distributes any tobacco product, that person displayed that tobacco advertisement for a direct or indirect benefit, until the contrary is proved.

(5) In any proceedings for an offence under this section where the thing that is alleged to constitute a tobacco advertisement contains the trademark or brand name of a tobacco product it shall be presumed to be designed to promote or publicize the tobacco product to which it relates until the contrary is proved.

Competitions

6. (1) A person who, in connection with the sale of a tobacco product or for the purpose of promoting the sale of a tobacco product—

(a) supplies (whether from inside or outside Western Australia) to the purchaser, or any other person, in Western Australia—

(i) a prize, gift or other benefit; or

(ii) a stamp, coupon, token, voucher, ticket or other thing by virtue of which the purchaser or any other person may become entitled to, or may qualify for, a prize, gift or other benefit (whether that entitlement or qualification is absolute or conditional);

or

(b) conducts (whether from inside or outside Western Australia) a scheme—

(i) prescribed to be a scheme to promote the sale of a tobacco product or to promote smoking generally; and

(ii) the whole or any part of which is implemented in Western Australia,

commits an offence.

(2) It is a defence in proceedings for an offence under subsection (1) to prove that the benefit or thing supplied, or participation in the relevant scheme, was only incidentally connected with the purchase

of a tobacco product and that equal opportunity to receive that benefit or thing, or to participate in that scheme, and to buy products other than tobacco products, was afforded generally to persons who purchased products, whether or not they were tobacco products.

Free samples

7. A person who, for the purpose of inducing or promoting the sale of a tobacco product, offers, gives or distributes (whether from inside or outside Western Australia) to a member of the public within Western Australia a free sample of a tobacco product commits an offence.

Prohibition of sponsorships

8. (1) A person who promotes or publicizes, or agrees to promote or publicize, in Western Australia—

(a) a tobacco product or a trademark or brand name, or part of a trademark or brand name, of a tobacco product; or

(b) the name or interests of a manufacturer or distributor of a tobacco product (whether or not that manufacturer or distributor also manufactures or distributes a product other than the tobacco product) in association directly or indirectly with the tobacco product,

under a contract, or an arrangement (whether or not legally binding), under which a sponsorship is provided, or to be provided, by another person commits an offence.

(2) A person (whether inside or outside Western Australia) who provides, or agrees to provide, in Western Australia a sponsorship under a contract or arrangement of a kind referred to in subsection (1) commits an offence.

(3) For the purposes of subsection (1) (b), the name or interests of a manufacturer or distributor of a tobacco product shall be deemed to be in association directly or indirectly with the tobacco product if that name or those interests are commonly associated by members of the public in Western Australia with the tobacco product.

(4) This section does not apply in relation to—

(a) a contract or arrangement of a kind referred to in subsection

(1), which contract or arrangement was entered into before the appointed day, during the period of 12 months commencing on the appointed day; or

(b) anything to which this section does not apply by virtue of an exemption granted under section 14.

Labelling of packaged tobacco

9. A person who sells in Western Australia any tobacco prepared for smoking that is in a package that is not labelled—

(a) in accordance with any regulations made under section 33 with a prescribed statement and warning (if any) applicable to packages of the class to which that package belongs;

(b) with the prescribed statement (if any) applicable to packages of the class to which that package belongs and giving the tar content of that tobacco; or

(c) with any other prescribed information applicable to packages of the class to which that package belongs,

commits an offence.

Supplying tobacco to persons under 18 years

10. (1) A person who sells or supplies in Western Australia a tobacco product to a person under the age of 18 years commits an offence.

(2) A person who permits, or whose employee or agent permits, a person under the age of 18 years to obtain a tobacco product from a vending machine situated on premises in Western Australia occupied by the firstmentioned person commits an offence.

(3) It is a defence in proceedings for an offence under subsection (1) to prove that the defendant—

(a) had honest and reasonable cause to believe that the person to whom the tobacco product concerned was sold or supplied was not under the age of 18 years; or

(b) had taken all precautions that were reasonably required to ensure that the tobacco product concerned was not sold or supplied to a person under the age of 18 years.

(4) It is a defence in proceedings for an offence under subsection (2) to prove that—

(a) in the case of proceedings against the person occupying the premises concerned for himself or herself having permitted a person under the age of 18 years to obtain a tobacco product from a vending machine situated on those premises, the firstmentioned person—

(i) had honest and reasonable cause to believe that the secondmentioned person was not under the age of 18 years; or

(ii) had taken all precautions that were reasonably required to ensure that the tobacco product was not so obtained by a person under the age of 18 years;

or

(b) in the case of proceedings against the person occupying the premises concerned for his or her employee or agent having permitted a person under the age of 18 years to obtain a tobacco product from a vending machine situated on those premises, that employee or agent—

(i) had honest and reasonable cause to believe that the secondmentioned person was not under the age of 18 years; or

(ii) had taken all precautions that were reasonably required to ensure that the tobacco product was not so obtained by a person under the age of 18 years.

Vending machines

11. (1) A person who places, or causes or permits to be placed, in any premises in Western Australia a vending machine for operation by members of the public commits an offence unless the premises are—

(a) licensed premises within the meaning of the *Liquor Licensing Act 1988*; or

(b) premises set aside by an employer as a staff amenity area.

(2) A person who—

(a) owns or is the lessee of a vending machine in Western Australia; and

(b) does not ensure that a statement in the prescribed form is kept conspicuously displayed on the front of the vending machine referred to in paragraph (a),

commits an offence.

Packages of cigarettes

12. A person who sells in Western Australia cigarettes—

(a) in a package containing less than 20 cigarettes; or

(b) otherwise than in a package,

commits an offence.

Smokeless tobacco

13. (1) A person who manufactures or sells in Western Australia a tobacco product other than a tobacco product prepared for smoking commits an offence.

(2) Subsection (1) does not apply in relation to the manufacture or sale of prescribed tobacco products in prescribed circumstances.

Exemptions

14. (1) Subject to this section, the Minister may, by notice published in the *Gazette*—

(a) exempt a person or class of persons either wholly or in part from the operation of section 5 or 8 subject to such conditions (if any) as are set out in that notice or prescribed for the purposes of this paragraph; or

(b) amend or repeal an exemption granted under this section.

(2) An exemption may only be granted under this section—

(a) after consultation between the Minister and the appropriate Minister, and having regard to the nature and background of the event, function or series concerned and to the purposes of this Act, to facilitate the promotion and conduct of—

(i) a sporting, racing or arts event or function; or

(ii) a series of sporting, racing or arts events or functions,

of national or international significance;

(b) in the case of the operation of section 5, to allow the performance during the period of 12 months commencing on the appointed day of a contract entered into before that day if significant hardship to persons other than manufacturers or wholesalers of tobacco might result if the exemption is not granted; or

(c) in any other case of significant hardship to persons other than manufacturers or wholesalers of tobacco.

(3) For the purposes of subsection (2) (a), the appropriate Minister is—

(a) in relation to an exemption to facilitate the promotion and conduct of a sporting or racing event or function or a series of such events or functions—

(i) which is a racing event or function not involving motor car or motorcycle racing the Minister for Racing and Gaming;

or

(ii) which is a sporting event or function or a motor car or motorcycle racing event or function, the Minister for Sport and Recreation;

or

(b) in relation to an exemption to facilitate the promotion and conduct of a arts event or function or a series of such events or functions, the Minister for the Arts.

(4) The Minister shall, when deciding whether or not to grant an exemption under this section for the purpose referred to in subsection (2) (a), have regard to—

(a) any substantial connection between the relevant event or function or series of events or functions and other significant events or functions outside the State; and

(b) any reasonable efforts that have been made to obtain sufficient financial or other support for the relevant event or function or series of events or functions from sources other than the advertising of tobacco products to render the exemption unnecessary.

(5) An exemption granted under this section for the purpose referred to in subsection (2) (c) shall not have effect after 30 June 1994.

PART 3—WESTERN AUSTRALIAN HEALTH PROMOTION FOUNDATION

Establishment of Foundation

15. (1) The Western Australian Health Promotion Foundation is established.

(2) The Foundation is—

(a) a body corporate with perpetual succession and shall have a common seal;

(b) capable of suing and being sued in its corporate name and of acquiring, holding, dealing with and disposing of real and personal property;

(c) capable of acquiring or incurring any other rights or liabilities and of doing and suffering all such acts and things as bodies corporate may lawfully do and suffer; and

(d) an agency of, and holds its property on behalf of, the Crown.

(3) The common seal of the Foundation shall be in a form determined by the Foundation, shall be kept in such custody as the Foundation directs and shall not, subject to subsection (4), be used except as authorized by the Foundation.

(4) A document is duly executed by the Foundation if it is sealed with the common seal of the Foundation and signed by 2 members.

(5) A document apparently executed by the Foundation shall be presumed in any legal proceedings, in the absence of proof to the contrary, to have been duly executed.

(6) For the purposes of this Act, the Foundation may make use of a facsimile of the common seal of the Foundation and a document purporting to create or evidence an obligation on the part of the Foundation and to be endorsed with such a facsimile seal shall, until the contrary is proved, be deemed to have been sealed by the Foundation.

Provision of information to Minister

16. The Foundation shall provide the Minister with such information and reports concerning the activities of the Foundation as the Minister may from time to time require.

Constitution of Foundation

17. (1) The Foundation shall consist of 11 members, of whom—

(a) one shall be appointed by the Minister on the nomination of the Premier and shall be the Chairperson of the Foundation;

(b) one shall be appointed by the Minister on the nomination of the body known as the Australian Medical Association Western Australian Branch;

(c) one shall be appointed by the Minister on the nomination of the body known as the Western Australian Sports Federation;

(d) one shall be appointed by the Minister on the nomination of the body known as the Western Australian Sports Council;

(e) one shall be appointed by the Minister on the nomination of the body known as the Country Shire Councils' Association to represent country sporting interests;

(f) one shall be appointed by the Minister on the nomination of the body known as the WA Association of Professional Performing Arts;

(g) one shall be appointed by the Minister on the nomination of the body known as the Australian Council on Smoking and Health;

(h) one shall be the person for the time being holding or acting in the office of the Commissioner of Health or the nominee of that person;

(i) one shall be the chief executive officer of the department principally assisting the Minister for Sport and Recreation or the nominee of that chief executive officer;

(j) one shall be the chief executive officer of the department principally assisting the Minister for the Arts or the nominee of that chief executive officer; and

(k) one shall be the principal employee for the time being of the body known as the Office of the Family or the nominee of that principal employee.

(2) The Premier shall, before making a nomination for the purposes of subsection (1) (a), consult with the parliamentary leader of each party in the Parliament.

(3) A nomination referred to in subsection (1) (a), (b), (c), (d), (e), (f) or (g) shall—

(a) be submitted in writing to the Minister at his or her request;

and

(b) be in respect of a person who is willing to accept appointment as a member.

(4) If at any time—

(a) the Premier; or

(b) the body referred to in subsection (1) (b), (c), (d), (e), (f) or (g),

does not submit a nomination within 30 days after the making of the relevant request referred to in subsection (3) (a), the Minister may, without the submission of that nomination, appoint a person to be the member concerned to represent the interests of the Premier or body in default until—

(c) the relevant nomination is submitted and a member is appointed on that nomination; or

(d) the expiry of the period (being a period not exceeding 3 years) specified in the instrument of the appointment under this subsection,

whichever is the sooner.

(5) A person appointed, and holding office as a member, under subsection (4) shall for all purposes be deemed to be duly appointed a member and to be the representative of the Premier or body in default.

(6) The Minister shall, before making an appointment under subsection (4) representative of the interests of the Premier, consult with the parliamentary leader of each party in the Parliament.

(7) The members shall, at the first meeting of the Foundation after the appointed day and thereafter at the first meeting of the Foundation after a Deputy Chairperson ceases to be a member, elect a Deputy Chairperson from among their number to preside, whilst he or she remains a member, over any meeting, or part of a meeting, of the Foundation from which the Chairperson is absent.

(8) A member, other than the member referred to in subsection (1) (a), may nominate by writing served on the person concerned and on the Chairperson a person—

(a) to be his or her deputy and to attend; and

(b) to represent the interests of the relevant body or of the Commissioner of Health or of the relevant department at,

any meeting, or part of a meeting, of the Foundation from which that member is absent.

(9) A deputy nominated under subsection (8) has, while attending a meeting, or part of a meeting, of the Foundation from which the member who nominated him or her is absent, all the functions of a member.

Term of appointment or nomination

18. (1) A member referred to in section 17 (1) (a), (b), (c), (d), (e), (f) or (g) shall, subject to section 52 of the *Interpretation Act 1984*, hold office for such period not exceeding 3 years as is specified in the instrument of his or her appointment and is eligible for reappointment.

(2) A deputy nominated under section 17 (8) shall, unless his or her nomination is earlier withdrawn by writing served on that deputy and on the Chairperson by the member who made that nomination, hold office for such period ending on or before the end of the period for which that member holds office as is specified in the relevant instrument of nomination.

Remuneration and allowances of members and deputies

19. A member and his or her deputy are each of them entitled to such remuneration and allowances (if any) as the Minister from time to time determines in his or her case on the recommendation of the Public Service Commissioner.

Resignation of members

20. A member referred to in section 17 (1) (a), (b), (c), (d), (e), (f) or (g) may resign his or her office by notice in writing signed by the member and delivered to the Minister.

Further provisions relating to constitution, etc., of Foundation

21. Further provisions governing the constitution, proceedings and operations of the Foundation are set out in the Schedule.

Objectives of Foundation

22. (1) The objectives of the Foundation are—

(a) to fund activities related to the promotion of good health in general, with particular emphasis on young people;

(b) to offer an alternative source of funds for sporting and arts activities currently supported by manufacturers or wholesalers of tobacco products;

(c) to support sporting and arts activities which encourage healthy lifestyles and advance health promotion programmes;

(d) to provide funds to replace tobacco advertising with health promotion advertising;

(e) to provide grants to organizations engaged in health promotion programmes;

(f) to fund research relevant to health promotion;

(g) to raise funds by soliciting donations and grants and, subject to subsection (2), engaging in the production or marketing or both referred to in section 23 (2) (d) in order to support the work of the Foundation;

(h) to evaluate and report on the effectiveness of the performance of the Foundation in achieving health promotion activities; and

(i) generally to fulfil the purposes set out in section 3.

(2) It is not an objective of the Foundation to make a profit by engaging in the production or marketing or both referred to in section 23 (2) (d), but any surplus of revenue over expenditure arising as a result of that engagement shall be paid into and to the credit of the Fund.

(3) In providing funds or grants under this Act, the Foundation may impose such conditions as it considers desirable to fulfil the purposes set out in section 3.

Powers of Foundation

23. (1) The Foundation has power to do all things necessary or convenient to be done for or in connection with the achievement of its objectives.

(2) Without limiting the generality of subsection (1), the Foundation may, in its absolute discretion—

(a) after consultation with the Minister, make grants from the Fund to persons other than manufacturers or wholesalers of tobacco products who have suffered hardship as a result of the loss of benefits under a banned contract entered into before the appointed day; or

(b) make grants for the purpose of providing support to persons who have lost or who will lose benefits under a banned sponsorship;

(c) make grants to—

(i) sporting organizations;

(ii) arts organizations;

(iii) health organizations;

(iv) community organizations;

(v) research organizations;

(vi) youth organizations; and

(vii) racing organizations;

(d) engage in the production or marketing or both of goods and services which themselves constitute or form part of health promotion activities in order—

(i) to promote the purposes of this Act and the objectives of the Foundation; and

(ii) by generating revenue to cover the cost of that production or marketing or both;

and

(e) do anything necessary or desirable for implementing the capacity conferred on it by section 15 (2).

(3) For the period of five years from the appointed day the Foundation shall give priority to applicants for grants—

(a) firstly pursuant to subsection (2) (a); and

(b) secondly pursuant to subsection (2) (b),

up to the full amount of any loss of benefit.

Ministerial directions

24. (1) The Minister may give directions in writing to the Foundation with respect to the exercise or performance of its functions, either generally or in relation to a particular matter, and the Foundation shall give effect to any such direction.

(2) The text of any direction given under subsection (1) shall be included in the annual report submitted by the accountable authority of the Foundation under section 66 of the *Financial Administration and Audit Act 1985* and shall also be tabled in both Houses of Parliament within 6 sitting days.

Staff of Foundation

25. (1) The Foundation may, subject to any relevant industrial agreement or award, appoint and employ, either on a permanent full time basis or otherwise and on such terms and conditions as the Foundation determines, a Director of the Foundation and such other persons as the Foundation considers necessary to assist that Director and to enable the Foundation to achieve its objectives.

(2) The Foundation shall not appoint or employ any person except in accordance with an establishment scheme from time to time approved by the Minister which shall set out—

(a) the numbers of staff which may be employed and the general functions each is intended to perform; and

(b) the salary range for each such person.

(3) With the consent of the Minister or within a budget approved by the Minister, the Foundation may engage under a contract for services or other arrangement any consultant or person to provide such administrative, professional, technical or other assistance as the Foundation considers necessary to enable it to achieve its objectives.

(4) The Foundation may, by arrangement made between it and the Minister concerned, and on such terms and conditions as may be mutually arranged by it with that Minister and, if appropriate, with the Public Service Commissioner, make use, either full time or part time, of—

(a) the services of any officer or employee employed in the Public Service of the State or in a State agency or instrumentality or otherwise in the service of the Crown in right of the State; or

(b) any facilities of a department of the Public Service of the State or of a State agency or instrumentality.

(5) The appointment and employment or engagement of a person under subsection (1) or (3) does not—

(a) render the provisions of the *Public Service Act 1978* or of any Act applying to persons as officers of the Public Service of the State applicable to the person; or

(b) affect or prejudice the application to the person of the provisions referred to in paragraph (a) if they applied to him or her at the time of his or her appointment or engagement.

Funds of Foundation

26. (1) The funds available for the purpose of enabling the Foundation to achieve its objectives and to exercise and perform its functions consist of—

(a) moneys paid to the Foundation under subsection (2);

(b) moneys from time to time appropriated by Parliament and paid to the Foundation; and

(c) any moneys, other than moneys referred to in paragraphs (a) and (b), lawfully received by, made available to or payable to the Foundation.

(2) There shall in respect of the financial year commencing on—

(a) 1 July 1990 be paid to the Foundation an amount equal to 10 per cent; and

(b) 1 July 1991 and of each subsequent financial year be paid to the Foundation an amount equal to 10 per cent, or to such greater percentage as the Minister may determine by notice published in the *Gazette*,

of the total amount of fees paid under the *Business Franchise (Tobacco) Act 1975* to the Commissioner of State Taxation during that financial year, and the Consolidated Revenue Fund is hereby appropriated to the extent necessary for the making of each such payment.

(3) The funds referred to in subsection (1) shall be paid into and placed to the credit of an account at the Treasury to be called the "Western Australian Health Promotion Fund".

(4) There shall be paid from the moneys from time to time in and standing to the credit of the Fund—

(a) the remuneration and allowances payable to members and their deputies and to persons employed under section 25 (1);

(b) expenditure incurred by the Foundation in achieving its objectives and exercising and performing its functions and in complying with subsection (8); and

(c) all expenditure, other than expenditure referred to in paragraphs (a) and (b), lawfully incurred by the Foundation for the purposes of, and in meeting the costs and expenses of the administration of, this Act.

(5) A publication, pamphlet or advertisement that is paid for, wholly or in part, from the moneys from time to time in and standing to the credit of the Fund shall not contain any picture of, statement by or reference to any Member of Parliament, other than any statement or reference of that kind—

(a) required by law; or

(b) necessary or desirable for a proper understanding of the subject matter of that publication, pamphlet or advertisement,

nor shall any such moneys be paid under subsection (4) in such a manner that any Member of Parliament is, or appears to be, associated with that payment.

(6) The Fund shall not decide nor announce any decision to disburse any part of the Fund, pursuant to section 23 (2) (c) of the Act during the period from the issue of the writs for a general election to be held within the State, whether State or Federal until the close of voting in that election.

(7) All moneys in and standing to the credit of the Fund immediately before the commencement of a financial year shall, subject to subsection (4), remain in and standing to the credit of the Fund after that commencement.

(8) The Foundation shall endeavour to ensure that, in each financial year—

(a) not less than 30% of the moneys paid under subsection (4) in any one financial year are disbursed to sporting organizations;

(b) not less than 15% of the moneys paid under subsection (4) in any one financial year are disbursed to arts organizations; and

(c) not more than 50% of the moneys paid under subsection (4) in any one financial year are disbursed to any one of the following categories of organizations—

(i) sporting organizations;

(ii) arts organizations;

(iii) health organizations;

(iv) community organizations;

(v) research organizations; or

(vi) racing organizations,

which the Foundation is satisfied are promoting, or will promote, the objectives of the Foundation.

(9) The Foundation shall endeavour to disburse the funds received from the State by it for the objectives of the Foundation within the year they are received or reasonably soon thereafter and shall include in its annual report the reason for any accumulation beyond that year.

(10) Any amount of funds received by the Foundation from the State which have not been disbursed within 4 months of the end of the financial year for which they have been allocated or 4 months of receipt if received outside the financial year shall be returned to Consolidated Revenue.

Temporary investment of moneys in Fund

27. All moneys recorded as standing to the credit of the Fund may, until required by the Foundation for the purposes of this Act, be temporarily invested as the Treasurer directs in any securities in which money standing to the credit of the Public Bank Account, as constituted under the *Financial Administration and Audit Act 1985*, may lawfully be invested and the Treasurer shall cause all interest derived from that investment to be paid to the credit of the Fund.

Application of *Financial Administration and Audit Act 1985*

28. Subject to this Part, the provisions of the *Financial Administration and Audit Act 1985* regulating the financial administration, audit and reporting of statutory authorities apply to and in respect of the Foundation and its operations.

PART 4—ENFORCEMENT

Consent required for prosecutions

29. Proceedings for an offence under this Act shall not be commenced without the consent in writing of the Commissioner of Health or a person authorized by him or her in writing for the purpose of this section.

Penalties

30. (1) A person who commits an offence under a provision of this Act specified in the Table to this subsection is liable—

(a) in the case of an individual, to a penalty of—

(i) $5 000 for a first offence; or

(ii) $10 000 for a second or subsequent offence;

or

(b) in the case of a body corporate, to a penalty of—

(i) $20 000 for a first offence; or

(ii) $40 000 for a second or subsequent offence.

TABLE

Sections 5 (1), and (2), 6 (1), 7, 8 (1) and (2), 9, 10 (1) and (2), 11 (1) and (2), 12 and 13 (1).

(2) If a continuing state of affairs is created by an offence referred to in subsection (1), the offender is liable to a penalty of—

(a) $5 000 in the case of an individual; or

(b) $20 000 in the case of a body corporate,

in respect of each day on which that offence continues, in addition to the penalty specified in that subsection.

Offences by bodies corporate

31. (1) When a body corporate commits an offence under this Act, every officer of the body corporate commits the like offence unless he or she proves that—

(a) that offence was committed without his or her consent or connivance; and

(b) he or she exercised all such due diligence to prevent the commission of that offence as he or she ought to have exercised, having regard to the nature of his or her functions in that capacity and to all the circumstances.

(2) In subsection (1)—

"officer", in relation to a body corporate, means—

(a) a director, secretary or executive officer of the body corporate;

(b) a receiver, or receiver and manager, of property of the body corporate, or any other authorized person who enters into possession or assumes control of property of the body corporate for the purpose of enforcing any charge;

(c) an official manager or a deputy official manager of the body corporate;

(d) a liquidator of the body corporate; and

(e) a trustee or other person administering a compromise or arrangement made between the body corporate and another person or other persons,

and any other person, by whatever name called and whether or not a director of the body corporate, who is concerned, or takes part, in the management of the body corporate.

PART 5—GENERAL

Certain civil proceedings barred

32. An action does not lie against a person for—

(a) the omission to do any thing the doing of which; or

(b) the doing of any thing the omission to do which,

would constitute an offence under this Act.

Regulations

33. (1) The Governor may make regulations prescribing all matters that are required or permitted by this Act to be prescribed, or are necessary or convenient to be prescribed for giving effect to the purposes of this Act, and, in particular—

(a) prescribing the labelling of packages containing tobacco, including the position of labels on packages and the size, colour, style and nature of labels or labelling;

(b) prescribing statements or warnings for the purpose of labelling packages;

(c) prescribing the size, colour, style, position and nature of tobacco advertisements displayed inside shops and other retail outlets where tobacco products are offered or exposed for sale, and any statements or warnings to be included in those tobacco advertisements;

(d) prescribing the labelling of vending machines containing tobacco products;

(e) prescribing the duty of persons packing, or causing other persons to pack, specified tobacco products prepared for smoking to label those tobacco products in a specified manner;

(f) prohibiting the sale of packages containing specified tobacco products prepared for smoking unless those packages are labelled in a specified manner; and

(g) creating offences and providing in respect of any such offence a penalty not exceeding $1 000.

(2) In subsection (1)—

"specified" means specified in regulations made under this section.

Review of Act

34. (1) Within a period of 12 months commencing on the third anniversary of the appointed day, the Minister shall cause an investigation and review to be conducted, and a report prepared, concerning—

(a) the operation of this Act;

(b) the operation of the Foundation; and

(c) the need for this Act to continue in operation.

(2) The Minister shall cause a copy of the report referred to in subsection (1) to be laid before each House of Parliament as soon as is practicable after the completion of that report.

PART 6—AMENDMENTS, REPEAL AND TRANSITIONAL

Amendment and modification of *Constitution Acts Amendment Act 1899*

35. (1) Schedule V to the *Constitution Acts Amendment Act 1899** is amended in Part 3 by inserting in the appropriate alphabetical position the following item—

" The Western Australian Health Promotion Foundation established by the *Tobacco Control Act 1990.* ".

(2) Section 37 (1) (b) of the *Constitution Acts Amendment Act 1899** shall have effect in relation to the Foundation as if the reference to "member" included a reference to a deputy of a member.

[**Reprinted as at 16 March 1989 and amended by Acts Nos. 75 of 1988 and 19 of 1989.*]

Amendment of *Financial Administration and Audit Act 1985*

36. Schedule 1 to the *Financial Administration and Audit Act 1985** is amended by inserting in the appropriate alphabetical position the following—

" Western Australian Health Promotion Foundation. ".

[**Reprinted as at 4 March 1987 and amended by Acts Nos. 94 of 1986, 9, 32, 65, 88, 89, 91, 99 and 113 of 1987, 4, 19, 21 and 52 of 1988 and 5, 31 and 48 of 1989.*]

Amendment of *Government Employees Superannuation Act 1987*

37. Schedule 1 to the *Government Employees Superannuation Act 1987** is amended by inserting in Part B in the appropriate alphabetical position the following—

" Western Australian Health Promotion Foundation ".

[**Act No. 25 of 1987 as amended by Acts Nos. 83 and 91 of 1987, 52 of 1988 and 5, 44 and 48 of 1989.*]

Amendment of *Health Act 1911* and transitional

38. (1) Section 3 (1) of the *Health Act 1911** is amended in the definition of "Drug" by deleting "tobacco,".

(2) The *Tobacco (Warning Labels) Regulations 1987* as in force under the *Health Act 1911** immediately before the appointed day shall be deemed to have been made and to be in force under section 33 and may be amended or repealed accordingly.

[**Reprinted as approved 14 May 1981 and amended by Acts Nos. 63 of 1981, 30 and 116 of 1982, 28 of 1984, 26, 53, 57, 98 and 109 of 1985, 93 of 1986 and 80 of 1987.*]

Amendment of *Parliamentary Commissioner Act 1971*

39. The Schedule to the *Parliamentary Commissioner Act 1971** is amended by inserting in the appropriate alphabetical position the following—

" Western Australian Health Promotion Foundation established by the *Tobacco Control Act 1990*. ".

[**Reprinted as at 31 March 1989 and amended by Acts Nos. 75 of 1988 and 31 of 1989.*]

Repeal of *Sale of Tobacco Act 1916*

40. The *Sale of Tobacco Act 1916** is repealed.

[**Reprinted as at 17 February 1987.*]

THE SCHEDULE (Section 21)

FURTHER PROVISIONS RELATING TO WESTERN AUSTRALIAN HEALTH PROMOTION FOUNDATION

Interpretation

1. (1) In this Schedule—

"committee" means committee established under clause 5.

(2) A reference in this Schedule to a member includes, unless the contrary intention appears, a reference to the deputy of a member.

Meetings and procedure

2. (1) Five members constitute a quorum of the Foundation.

(2) A decision carried by the votes of a majority of the members present at a meeting of the Foundation is a decision of the Foundation.

(3) Each member present at a meeting of the Foundation is entitled to one vote on a matter arising for determination at that meeting and the presiding member has, in the event of an equality of votes, a second or casting vote.

(4) The Foundation shall cause accurate minutes to be kept of its proceedings.

(5) Subject to this Act, the business of the Foundation may be conducted in a manner determined by the Foundation.

Disclosure of interest

3. (1) A member who has a direct or indirect pecuniary or other personal interest in a matter under consideration by the Foundation—

(a) shall disclose the nature of that interest to the Foundation; and

(b) shall not take part in any deliberation or decision of the Foundation with respect to that matter.

Penalty: $2 500.

(2) A disclosure under this clause shall be recorded in the minutes of the Foundation.

Delegation by Foundation

4. (1) Subject to this clause, the Foundation may, by instrument in writing, delegate any of its functions—

(a) to a member or employee of the Foundation; or

(b) to a committee.

(2) The Foundation shall not delegate its function of determining to whom or in what amounts financial support may be provided from the Fund.

(3) A function delegated under this clause may, if the instrument of delegation so provides, be subdelegated.

(4) When a delegation is made to a committee under this clause—

(a) the instrument of delegation may regulate the procedures to be followed by the committee when acting under the delegation; and

(b) the committee may, if the instrument of delegation so provides, act by a majority of the members present at a meeting of the committee.

(5) A person to whom, or a member of a committee to which, a function is delegated under this clause is disqualified from acting under the delegation in relation to any matter in which that person or member of a committee has a direct or indirect pecuniary interest or other personal interest.

Committees

5. (1) The Foundation may establish one or more Committees to advise or assist it in the exercise or performance of its functions. In any event, the Foundation shall establish three advisory Committees to advise on—

(1) the Arts;

(2) Sport; and

(3) Racing;

each of which shall include a reasonable number of country representatives.

(2) A committee established under subclause (1) may act in relation to any matter referred or delegated to it by the Foundation and shall be governed in its proceedings by rules approved by the Foundation.

(3) A member of a committee established under subclause (1) is entitled to such allowances and expenses (if any) as the Minister may determine.

Duty to act honestly

6. A member, or officer of the Foundation shall at all times act honestly and exercise a reasonable degree of care and diligence in the exercise of his or her powers or the performance of his or her duties.

Penalty—$5 000.

Non-disclosure of information

7. A member, member of a committee or employee of the Foundation shall not disclose any information declared in writing by the Foundation to be confidential, to which information he or she has had access in the course of official duties, unless that disclosure is made—

(a) with the consent of the person from whom the information was obtained;

(b) in connection with the administration of this Act; or

(c) for the purposes of any legal proceedings arising out of the administration of this Act.

Penalty: $2 500.

BELGIUM

BELGIUM. Crown Order of 28 December 1979 on the manufacture and marketing of tobacco, tobacco products, and similar products. (*Bulletin du Ministère de la Santé Publique et de la Famille*, 1980, No. 1, pp. 86-98)
Belg. 81.25

The following are among the principal provisions of this Order, which has been made in pursuance of the Law of 24 January 1977 on the protection of the health of consumers with regard to foods and other products (see *IDHL*, 1978, **29**, 528) and repeals the Crown Order of 15 June 1971 prohibiting the offering for sale, sale, or supply against payment or without charge of tobacco, its derivatives, or similar products to which substances considered to be toxic or harmful to health have been added (see *ibid.*, 1972, **23**, 460) and the Law of 3 April 1975 concerning protection against the hazards of cigarette smoking (see *ibid.*, 1976, **27**, 529).

Sec. 1 defines a number of terms, including "tobacco products" (products manufactured using at least 75% tobacco, to which natural tobacco extracts and the substances listed in the Annex may be added, including cigarettes, cigars and cigarillos, smoking tobacco, chewing tobacco, and snuff) and "similar products" (tobacco substitutes, i.e. products manufactured using less than 75% tobacco, to which the substances listed in the Annex may be added and which may be used for the same purposes in place of tobacco products, but excluding chewing gum, and accessories intended for the preparation of cigarettes, cigars, or cigarillos, i.e. cigarette papers and paper tubes, filters, and mouthpieces).

Sec. 2 prohibits the manufacture or marketing of tobacco products or similar products which, *inter alia*, contain substances other than those listed in the Annex to this Order or that contain levels of substances exceeding those specified in the Annex. Such products are declared to be harmful within the meaning of Sec. 18 of the Law.

Sec. 3 prohibits the marketing of, *inter alia*: tobacco products that do not display the warning "Tobacco is harmful to health" (the word "tobacco" is to be replaced by "snuff" or "chewing tobacco" in appropriate cases); cigarettes which do not display the words "Per cigarette: tar: ...mg; nicotine... mg; carbon monoxide" (provision is made for a tolerance of 15%); cigars, cigarillos, and pipe tobacco which do not display the following statement: "The smoke contains tar, nicotine, and carbon monoxide"; snuff and chewing tobacco which do not display the following statement: "Contains nicotine"; and tobacco substitutes which do not display the health warning prescribed above and the words "Tobacco substitute". The above particulars must appear in conspicuous, legible, and indelible characters on packages, containers, or labels or on tax labels. The health warning and the details of the tar and nicotine levels and the presence of carbon monoxide must not be hidden, obscured, or interrupted by any other words or pictures. All of the above particulars must appear in all three official languages (Dutch, French, and German).

Sec. 4 prohibits the use of automatic vending machines for the distribution of tobacco products and tobacco substitutes; however, this prohibition does not apply to machines located on premises which are accessible to the consumer and in which such products are also marketed in a traditional manner.

Sec. 5 requires the addition of new substances or changes in the level of substances authorized in the products covered by this Order to be licensed by the Food Inspectorate of the Ministry of Public Health and the Family. The Minister or a person delegated by him may request the applicant to provide additional information. The application is forwarded to the Higher Council of Health, which must submit its views to the Minister or the person delegated by him.

BELGIUM. Crown Order of 5 March 1980 on advertising for tobacco, tobacco products, and similar products. (*Bulletin du Ministère de la Santé Publique et de la Famille*, 1980, No. 1, pp. 99-101) **Belg. 81.27**

Sec. 1 of this Order, which has been made in pursuance of the Law of 24 January 1977 on the protection of the health of consumers with regard to foods and other products (see *IDHL*, 1978, **29**, 528), defines, *inter alia*, "advertising" (any communication disseminated with the direct or indirect intention of promoting sales, irrespective of the place or means of communication used). Sec. 2 prohibits the advertising of tobacco, tobacco products, and similar products: (1) on radio or television; (2) by means of aircraft or ships; (3) by means of films, slides, or other visual projection in public places; (4) by means of posters or hoardings, other than on premises where such products are marketed normally; (5) by means of illuminated signs, except inside or outside premises where such products are marketed normally; (6) through the distribution or door-to-door delivery of stickers or leaflets; (7) by oral recommendations in public; (8) through the distribution of free samples of tobacco, tobacco products, or similar products; (9) through the use of the brand symbol or brand name of the tobacco, tobacco product, or similar product or the use of any other pictorial or verbal material referring to such products on consumer goods other than those directly connected with smoking; and (10) in children's periodicals. Sec. 3 prohibits the following in advertisements for tobacco, tobacco products, or similar products: (1) the use of pictures of living persons familiar to the general public; (2) the use of attestations or texts concerning any person other than the inventor of the manufacturing process of the product concerned; (3) the publication of extracts from scientific texts; (4) the use of texts relating to hygiene or health; (5) the organization of competitions or raffles; and (6) the use of more than half a page per brand in daily newspapers or more than one page per brand in periodicals. Sec. 4 requires all advertisements for cigarettes, cigars, cigarillos, and pipe tobacco to include the warning: "Tobacco is harmful to health" in the language in which the advertisement appears. The warning must appear in conspicuous, legible black characters on a white background, and may not be hidden, obscured, or interrupted by any other words or pictures. This Section does not however, apply to illuminated signs or sports equipment.

BELGIUM. Crown Order of 22 September 1980 amending the Crown Order of 5 March 1980 on advertising for tobacco, tobacco products, and similar products. (*Bulletin du Ministère de la Santé publique et de la Famille*, 1980, No. 4, pp. 780-781) **Belg. 82.22**

Subsection 9 of Sec. 2 of the Crown Order of 5 March 1980 (see *IDHL*, 1981, **32**, 86) now exceptionally authorizes the advertising of tobacco, tobacco products, and similar products on equipment belonging to persons participating in sports competitions, while subsection 3 of Sec. 4 extends the exemption from the health warning requirement to include consumer goods directly connected with smoking.

BELGIUM. Crown Order of 30 March 1981 amending the Crown Order of 28 December 1979 on the manufacture and marketing of tobacco, tobacco products, and similar products. (*Bulletin du Ministère de la Santé publique et de la Famille*, 1981, No. 1, pp. 27-28) **Belg. 82.37**

Under the amended provisions of Sec. 3 of the Crown Order of 28 December 1979 (see *IDHL*, 1981, **32**, 85), the marketing of, *inter alia*, the following is prohibited: tobacco products that do not display the warning "Tobacco is harmful to health"; cigarettes which do not display details of the tar level (in mg) and the nicotine level (in mg and tenths of an mg) per cigarette, using the following words: "Tar: ... mg; nicotine: ... mg" (provision is made for a tolerance of 15%; however, in the case of cigarettes containing less than 7 mg of tar or 0.7 mg of nicotine per cigarette, the tolerance is 1 mg in the case of tar and 0.1 mg in the case of nicotine; and tobacco substitutes which do not display the words "Tobacco substitute". The above particulars must appear on packages and containers in conspicuous, legible, and indelible characters in the language of the Region in which the products are offered for sale. The health warning and details of the tar and nicotine levels must not be hidden, obscured, or interrupted by any other words or pictures. Tax labels affixed to cigars and cigarillos must display the warning "Tobacco is harmful" in Dutch, French, and German.

BELGIUM. Crown Order of 21 January 1982 amending the Crown Order of 5 March 1980 on advertising for tobacco, tobacco products, and similar products. (*Bulletin du Ministère de la Santé publique et de la Famille*, 1982, No. 1, pp. 119-120) **Belg. 83.11**

The Crown Order of 5 March 1980 (see *IDHL*, 1981, **32**, 86, **Belg. 81.27**), as amended, is further amended by the insertion of a new Sec. 4 *bis*, reading as follows:

"**4** *bis*. Without prejudice to the provisions of Section 4 of this Order, advertising in the form of bills or posters, under the conditions laid down in subsection 4 of Section 2 of this Order, shall be limited to the following particulars:

(*a*) the name and address of the manufacturer, importer, or distributor;

(*b*) the brand name and its symbol;

(*c*) a representation of products and of consumer goods directly associated with smoking; and

(*d*) the tar and nicotine levels."

BELGIUM. Decree of 2 December 1982 on the control of smoking. (*Bulletin du Ministère de la Santé publique et de la Famille*, 1983, No. 1, pp. 80-83) **Belg. 86.3**

The Council of the French Community has adopted, and the Executive approved, the following:

"Division 1

The prohibition of smoking

1. Smoking shall be prohibited on public premises if they fail to comply with the ventilation standards laid down by the member of the Executive of the French Community who is responsible for Health.

The member of the Executive of the French Community who is responsible for Health shall in addition take all steps to prohibit smoking on other premises where it may have consequences which are dangerous for health.

2. Without prejudice to prohibitions laid down by administrative authority, smoking shall be prohibited on premises where pupils are present in kindergardens, and establishments providing primary, special, and artistic schooling, full time and of a vocational nature [*de promotion sociale*].

3. Smoking shall be prohibited on all premises for the reception, care, and accommodation of patients in hospital and care establishments, homes for the elderly, and in all other public and private health establishments.

4. Smoking shall be prohibited on premises where food is stored, handled, prepared for consumption, or offered for sale. Nevertheless, this prohibition shall not apply to premises which are principally concerned with the consumption of food *in situ.*

5. Smoking shall be prohibited in:

(*a*) vehicles for collective transport, on a regular or special basis, for the transport of pupils attending the teaching establishments referred to in Section 2 or of persons less than 16 years of age; and

(*b*) urban public transport vehicles.

Without prejudice to any prohibitions laid down by transport operators, public or private vehicles for collective transport shall, after 1 January 1985, contain an area reserved for non-smokers protected by proper equipment preventing the diffusion of smoke; this area shall extend to not less than half of the available seats.

The criteria to be met by the equipment preventing the diffusion of smoke shall be determined by the member of the Executive of the French Community who is responsible for Health.

6. Smoking shall be prohibited in lifts for collective use.

7. The prohibitions on smoking laid down in pursuance of this Decree shall be displayed clearly on the premises and in the vehicles or parts of vehicles to which they apply.

Division 2

Information on the dangers of the consumption of tobacco

8. The member of the Executive of the French Community who is responsible for Education shall, with the assent of the member of the Executive of the French Community who is responsible for Health, take all the steps necessary to organize annually, in kindergartens, and establishments providing primary, special, and artistic schooling, full time and of a vocational nature, an information compaign on the dangers of tobacco consumption.

9. The member of the Executive of the French Community who is responsible for Health shall organize annually an information day on the dangers of tobacco consumption. He shall associate the Belgian French-speaking radio and television services with this campaign.

10. The dangers of tobacco consumption shall be clearly publicized:

1. on premises principally intended for the collective leisure activities of persons less than 16 years of age, and

2. on the residential premises of centres for leisure activities and holidays when persons less than 16 years of age have been admitted.

These provisions shall not derogate from the rights and duties of the organizers of such leisure activities and of the local authorities.

The member of the Executive of the French Community who is responsible for Health shall determine the conditions which must be fulfilled in order that such publication may be considered effective.

11. Packets of cigarettes, cigars, cigarillos, and other tobacco products shall carry a printed statement with a clear indication of the tar and nicotine contents.

Sellers of tobacco products shall display on their sales premises a notice with a clear indication of the danger of the tar and nicotine contents of such products.

The member of the Executive of the French Community who is responsible for Health shall lay down, by order, detailed procedures applicable to such publications.

Division 3

Prohibition of publicity or advertising for tobacco

12. For the purposes of this Division, 'tobacco products' means products intended to be smoked if they are made from tobacco, even partially.

13. The provisions of Sections 2-6 of the Crown Order of 5 March 1980 on the advertising of tobacco, tobacco products, and similar products [see *IDHL*, 1981, **32**, 86, **Belg. 81.27**], as amended by the Crown Order of 22 September 1980 [see *ibid.*, 1982, **33**, 32, **Belg. 82.22**] and by the Crown Order of 21 January 1982 [see *ibid.*, 1983, **34**, 767, **Belg. 83.11**], shall have the status of a decree.

Division 4

Final provisions

14. The provisions laid down in Section 1 shall not apply to existing public premises whose management has fulfilled the duties concerning fire prevention laid down by law and regulations before the entry into force of this Decree.

15. Without prejudice to subsection 2 of Section 5 of this Decree and to Section 6 of the Crown Order of 5 March 1980, this Decree shall enter into force on the day of its publication in the *Moniteur belge*."

BELGIUM. Crown Order of 20 December 1982 amending the Crown Order of 28 December 1979 on the manufacture and marketing of tobacco, tobacco products, and similar products. (*Bulletin du Ministère de la Santé Publique et de la Famille*, 1982, No. 4, pp. 622-624) **Belg. 85.13**

A number of amendments, including some relating to the definitions given in Sec. 1, are made to the Crown Order of 28 December 1979 (see *IDHL*, 1981, **32**, 85, **Belg. 81.25**), as amended by the Crown Order of 30 March 1981 (see *ibid.*, 1982, **33**, 32, **Belg. 82.37**).

BELGIUM. Crown Order of 20 December 1982 on the advertising of tobacco, tobacco products, and similar products. (*Bulletin du Ministère de la Santé Publique et de la Famille*, 1982, No. 4, pp. 620-622) **Belg. 85.12**

This Order repeals the Crown Order of 5 March 1980 on the same subject (see *IDHL*, 1981, **32**, 86, **Belg. 81.27**), as amended by the Crown Order of 21 January 1982 (see *ibid.*, 1983, **34**, 767, **Belg. 83.11**).

"Advertising" is defined in Sec. 1 in the same terms as in the 1980 Order. Sec. 2 prohibits the advertising of tobacco, tobacco products, and similar products: (1) on radio or television; (2) by means of aircraft, boats, or vehicles other than those participating in competitions or used for the transportation of tobacco, tobacco products, or similar products; (3) by means of films, video cassettes, slides, or other visual projections; (4) by the distribution or door-to-door delivery of stickers or leaflets; (5) by oral recommendations in public; (6) by the free distribution of tobacco, tobacco products, or similar products; (7) by the use on consumer goods of the brand name or brand symbol of the tobacco, tobacco product, or similar product or by the use of any other representation or statement which could refer to such products (this provision does not apply to consumer goods directly associated with smoking or to the equipment of participants in sports competitions or of the technical team accompanying them); and (8) in children's periodicals. Sec. 3 reads as follows:

"**3.** The advertising of tobacco, tobacco products, and similar products shall be authorized only under the conditions indicated below.

(1) Without prejudice to the provisions of Section 4, advertising shall be limited to the following particulars:

(*a*) the name and address of the manufacturer, importer, or distributor;

(*b*) the name and nature of the product;

(*c*) the brand name and its symbol;

(*d*) representations of products and consumer goods directly associated with smoking;

(*e*) the tar and nicotine levels; and

(*f*) information on price and quantity.

(2) In the case of advertising by means of bills and posters:

(*a*) the surface area must not exceed 16 m^2 per poster and per brand; and

(*b*) only a single poster may be used for any one brand in a given visual field.

(3) It shall be prohibited to use more than half a page in newspapers and more than one page per brand in periodicals."

Under Sec. 4, all advertisements for cigarettes, cigars, cigarillos, and pipe tobacco in newspapers and periodicals and in bills and posters must include the warning "Tobacco is harmful to health" in the language in which the advertisement appears. The conditions governing the manner in which this warning is to appear are the same as in the 1980 Order.

BELGIUM. Crown Order of 31 March 1987 prohibiting smoking in certain public places. (*Moniteur belge*, 14 April 1987, No. 73, pp. 5444-5445) **Belg. 87.94**

This Order has been made in pursuance of, *inter alia*, certain provisions of Sec. 7 of the Law of 24 January 1977 on the protection of the health of consumers with regards to foods and other products (see *IDHL*, 1978, **29**, 528). Secs. 1-4 of the Order read as follows:

"**1.** For the purposes of this Order, the following definitions shall apply:

1. 'premises' — a place separated from the ambient environment by walls and having a ceiling;

2. 'smoking' — the act of smoking tobacco, products produced from tobacco, or similar products; and

3. 'no-smoking sign' — the symbol given in an Annex hereto.

2. Smoking shall be prohibited in the following public places which form part of the buildings, parts of buildings, or establishments mentioned in the second paragraph:

1. halls;
2. corridors;
3. staircases;
4. lifts;
5. waiting-rooms;
6. toilets;
7. conference rooms generally accessible to the public;
8. premises in which services are provided to the public, and which are accessible to the public, whether or not against payment;
9. premises in which patients or elderly persons are received or cared for;
10. premises in which children or persons of school age are received, lodged, or cared for;
11. premises in which preventive or curative health care is provided;
12. premises in which teaching is provided;
13. premises in which live entertainment is provided;
14. premises in which exhibitions are organized; and
15. premises and covered areas where sports are practised.

The following constitute the buildings, parts of buildings, or establishments referred to in the first paragraph:

1. those in which the State or another legal person governed by public law enjoys a right of use or in which a public service is provided;
2. those in which children or young persons of school age are received or lodged;
3. those containing hospitals, rest-homes, or nursing homes, or old people's homes, or in which elderly persons are received or lodged;
4. those in which teaching is provided;
5. those in which cultural centres are located;
6. those in which musical, dance, theatrical, cinematographic, or other performances take place; and
7. those constituting sports facilities.

3. If, in a building, part of a building, or an establishment, there are a number of premises of the type referred to in item 5 of the first paragraph of Section 2 intended for the same group of members of the public, the management may authorize smoking on not more than one of them. On these latter premises, the public shall be notified of the availability of other premises for the same purpose where smoking is prohibited.

If the service to the public consists in the provision of meals or beverages, the management of the premises referred to in item 8 of the first paragraph of Section 2 may authorize smoking on part of these premises. That part shall be clearly demarcated. Nevertheless, that authorization may not be given if such premises form part of buildings or parts of buildings in which teaching is provided for children or pupils, or where such persons are received, lodged, or cared for.

4. The management of places where smoking is prohibited in accordance with this Order, shall display in these places one or more no-smoking signs so that all persons in these places are aware of that prohibition."

A model of the no-smoking sign referred to in Sec. 1 is given in an Annex.

BERMUDA

BERMUDA. The Tobacco Products (Public Health) Act 1987. Act No. 2 of 1987. Operative date: 1 April 1988. (5 pp.) **Berm. 89.1**

This Act includes provisions dealing with: health warnings and tar designation on cigarette packets (Sec. 3); health warnings when tobacco or tobacco products are sold (Sec. 4); restrictions on the advertising of cigarettes and tobacco products (Sec. 6); health warnings when cigarette and other tobacco product advertisements are displayed (Sec. 7); and a number of interpretative provisions (Secs. 8-9). Sec. 11 empowers the competent Minister to make regulations for the implementation of this Act.

BERMUDA. The Tobacco Products (Public Health) Regulations 1988. B.R. 23/88. Dated 24 March 1988. (*Official Gazette*, 4-31 March 1988, Vol. 86, No. 3, 1 p.) **Berm. 89.2**

These Regulations had been made by the Acting Minister of Health in pursuance of Sec. 11 of the Tobacco Products (Public Health) Act 1987 (see *supra*). Reg. 3 (Cigarette packets) indicates that the health warning required to be borne on packets under Sec. 3 of the Act is to be the warning required to be placed thereon by: (*a*) the country of origin of the cigarettes for the consumption therein of the cigarettes; or (*b*) the country from which the tobacco or tobacco products are exported. Corresponding provisions in respect of tobacco or tobacco products are laid down in Reg. 4. Reg. 5 deals with cigarette and tobacco product advertising, it being specified that the health warning is to be that set out in the Schedule (''Health Warning: Smoking is Hazardous to Your Health'').

BOLIVIA

BOLIVIA. Decree-Law No. 15629 of 18 July 1978 promulgating the Health Code. (*Código de Salud de la República de Bolivia y Disposiciones Reglamentarias*, Ministry of Social Welfare and Public Health, La Paz, 1981, pp. 1-29) **Bol. 83.1**

The following are among the principal provisions of the Code approved by this Decree-Law, which repeals all earlier contrary provisions, including the Health Code approved by Supreme Decree No. 05006 of 24 July 1958 and ratified by Decree-Law No. 07155 of 8 May 1965.

Chapter II. Family health (Secs. 15-21). Sec. 15 requires the Health Authority to lay down provisions regarding maternal and child health programmes. Under the provisions of Sec. 16, women undergoing antenatal and postnatal examinations, as well as children, are to be given priority in the form of special health services in all institutions in the health sector.

Chapter IX. Tobacco (Secs. 123-124). Sec. 123 prescribes that the Health Authority is the sole agency authorized to regulate all aspects of public health protection with regard to tobacco and tobacco products.

Sec. 124 prohibits advertising that encourages tobacco consumption on grounds of wellbeing or health, as well as the use of children and adolescents in tobacco advertisements or the association of tobacco in advertisements with sporting, domestic, or occupational situations.

BOLIVIA. Regulations on the use of tobacco. Dated 15 March 1982. (3 pp.) **Bol. 83.23**

Sec. 1 of these Regulations defines the term "tobacco" to include all products manufactured from the plant *Nicotiana tabacum* that are smoked, chewed, or inhaled by humans.

Under the provisions of Sec. 2, the Health Authority (the Ministry of Social Welfare and Public Health), acting through the Health Education Division, is to draw up mass education programmes to counteract the harmful effects of the use of tobacco. Sec. 3 requires the Health Education Division to supervise the use of mass communications media (television, radio, press, etc.) for tobacco advertising campaigns in order to prevent indiscriminate promotion of tobacco consumption.

Sec. 4 prescribes that smoking in school or health premises is an offence. Sec. 5 prohibits smoking in indoor public places and public transport vehicles. Sec. 6 requires indoor public places to provide separate, special smoking areas.

Under the provisions of Sec. 7, labels and advertisements for tobacco must be licensed by the Authority, subject to the condition that the labels of containers in which the tobacco is supplied must bear the following clear, conspicuous statement: "This product is harmful to your health". Sec. 8 requires advertisements for tobacco to refer simply to the quality, origin, and purity of the product; they may not encourage tobacco consumption on grounds of stimulation, wellbeing, or health, show persons inhaling or exhaling smoke (whether actually or apparently) in front of the public, make use of adolescents, pregnant women, or children, or in any way be associated with sporting, domestic, or occupational activities. Sec. 9 prescribes that licences for tobacco advertising are to be issued by the Ministry of Social Welfare and Public Health through its Health Education Division. Sec. 10 stresses that submission of an application for a licence does not in itself authorize the applicant to carry out advertisements for tobacco.

Details are given in Secs. 11-13 of the penalties applicable to offenders against these Regulations (for example, Sec. 13 prescribes that communications media that fail to comply with the Regulations are to receive first a warning and subsequently a fine that is three times the value of the advertising space concerned).

BRAZIL

BRAZIL. Law No. 7488 of 11 June 1986 establishing a National Anti-Smoking Day. (*Diário Oficial*, Section I, 12 June 1986, No. 109, p. 8531) **Braz. 89.1**

Sec. 1 of this Law, which repeals all earlier contrary provisions, lays down that the National Anti-Smoking Day is to be commemorated on 29 August each year. The Executive Power, acting through the Minister of Health, is made responsible for promoting a national campaign during the week preceding 29 August, aimed at alerting the population to the adverse effects of smoking.

BRAZIL. Order No. 490 of 25 August 1988. (*Diário Oficial*, Section I, 29 August 1988, pp. 16524-16525) **Braz. 89.4**

Sec. I of this Order, which has been made by the Minister of State for Health, recommends that the Secretariats for Health of the States, the Federal District, and the territories, as well as other administrative agencies and entities of the Federal, State, and Municipal Administrations, adopt or encourage measures aimed at limiting smoking or holding lighted cigarettes, cigars, cigarillos, or pipes in enclosed public places, that lack adequate ventilation. Sec. II requires manufacturers throughout the national territory to print the following legend on cigarette packets, boxes of cigarillos, and boxes, etc. containing cigars, pipe tobacco, and rolling tobacco: "WARNING FROM THE MINISTRY OF HEALTH: SMOKING IS HARMFUL TO HEALTH". This legend must be clear and legible, in contrasting colours, and without any reference to any legal or regulatory provisions. It must be separate from any other information carried on the container. Sec. III lays down that the provisions of Sec. II do not apply to cigarettes intended for export. Sec. IV requires the warning to appear on the packages of free samples. Sec. V indicates the graphic requirements applicable to advertising messages disseminated through the various media and in public places.

Without prejudice to the provisions of Secs. II, IV, and V, Sec. VIII lays down that advertising for the products referred to above by any means whatsoever must meet the following criteria: (1) it must not incite to excessive or irresponsible consumption, allude to well-being or health, or make allusion to civil or religious holidays; (2) it must not incite to the consumption of tobacco, by attributing to tobacco products calming or stimulating properties, or the ability to reduce fatigue or tension, or any other such effect; (3) there must be no association of ideas or images of increased success from the standpoint of sexuality, implying an increase in the virility or femininity of smokers; (4) it must not suggest or encourage smoking in places or situations where this is illegal or dangerous; (5) injunctions that incite directly to smoking must not be used; and (6) either by image or sound, there must be no reference to children or adolescents and advertising must not be addressed to them.

Sec. IX lays down the following restrictions, in addition to the requirements referred to above, applicable to advertising on television, or in cinemas and theatres: (1) advertising messages may appear on television only between 9 p.m. and 6 a.m.; and (2) no advertising messages may be disseminated in cinemas, theatres, etc. before 8 p.m. if persons under 18 years of age can attend.

Penalties for contraventions of this Order are laid down in Secs. 10 and 11.

BRAZIL (RIO GRANDE DO SUL). Order No. 1/80-SSMA of 8 April 1980. (1 p.)
Braz. (RGS) 81.1

This Order, which has been made by the Secretary of State for Health and the Environment, prohibits smoking by health professionals and other personnel in those parts of health units, hospitals, and other working premises attached to the Secretariat for Health and the Environment that are used for care of the general public. In addition, it is recommended that smoking be avoided in any enclosed premises, particularly work premises, and health services and hospitals in general, and that the sale of tobacco be avoided in hospitals and health services of any kind.

BRAZIL (RIO GRANDE DO SUL). Law No. 7813 of 21 September 1983 laying down provisions on smoking, and other provisions. (2 pp.)
Braz. (RGS) 83.1

Sec. 1 of this Law prohibits smoking in the following premises: (1) closed areas of public educational establishments; (2) halls used for meetings, entertainment events, and lectures, and museums and libraries, either administered or subsidized by the State; (3) public health establishments; (4) gymnasia or any other closed premises used for sports activities, either maintained or subsidized by the State; and (5) inter-city passenger transport vehicles.

Under Sec. 2, it is prohibited to market cigarettes and similar products in any establishment that is administered or subsidized by the State, including the buildings of the Legislative Assembly. Sec. 3 prescribes that any person working in the public service who fails to comply with the provisions of this Law is guilty of professional misconduct, and is liable to the penalties laid down in the relevant legislation; any other person failing to comply with the provisions of this Law is requested to leave the premises referred to in Sec. 1.

BURKINA FASO

BURKINA FASO. Order No. AN V—81 FP.SAN.CAPRO.DP of 29 February 1988. (*Journal officiel du Burkina Faso*, 3 March 1988, No. 9, p. 167) **BF 90.3**

This Order, which repeals all earlier contrary provisions, contains a number of measures aimed at the control of smoking.

Advertising for tobacco, cigarettes, cigars and cigarillos is prohibited on advertising billboards and on screens. It is prohibited to smoke in various types of premises, including health establishments, kindergartens, and places that accommodate children.

Cigarette packets, etc. must henceforth indicate the tar and nicotine content and the following warning: "Attention, for your own health".

CANADA

CANADA. Aeronautics Act: Air Regulations, amendment. SOR/87-554. Dated 10 September 1987. (*The Canada Gazette*, Part II, Vol. 121, No. 20, 30 September 1987, pp. 3701-3704) **Can. 88.12**

The purpose of these Regulations is stated to be "to prohibit smoking on commercial flights of Canadian aircraft that carry passengers on a unit toll basis and last two hours or less. The ban also applies to any segment of a longer flight where that segment is two hours or less; however the ban does not apply to a segment of certain international flights originating outside Canada where the only passengers on board the aircraft are those who boarded at the point of origin of the flight. The Regulations also require air carriers to post signs that smoking is prohibited and require the crew to request smokers to stop doing so" (the quotation is from the Regulatory Impact Analysis Statement appended to the Regulations).

CANADA. An Act (C-51) to prohibit the advertising and promotion and respecting the labelling and manufacturing of tobacco products. Dated 31 May 1988. (The Tobacco Products Control Act.) (*The Canada Gazette*, Part III, Vol. 11, No. 4, 2 September 1988, pp. 393-405) **Can. 88.19**

The following are among the principal provisions of this Act.

Interpretation (Sec. 2). Definitions are given of various terms, including "package" ("any pack, carton, wrapping or other container in which tobacco products are customarily sold at retail"), and "tobacco product" ("any product manufactured from tobacco and intended for use by smoking, inhalation or mastication, and includes nasal and oral snuff").

Purpose (Sec. 3). This Section reads as follows:

"**3.** The purpose of this Act is to provide a legislative response to a national public health problem of substantial and pressing concern and, in particular,

(*a*) to protect the health of Canadians in the light of conclusive evidence implicating tobacco use in the incidence of numerous debilitating and fatal diseases;

(*b*) to protect young persons and others, to the extent that is reasonable in a free and democratic society, from inducements to use tobacco products and consequent dependence on them; and

(*c*) to enhance public awareness of the hazards of tobacco use by ensuring the effective communication of pertinent information to consumers of tobacco products."

Advertising (Secs. 4-5). Subsections 1-4 of Sec. 4 read as follows:

"**4.** (1) No person shall advertise any tobacco product offered for sale in Canada.

(2) No person shall, for consideration, publish, broadcast or otherwise disseminate, on behalf of another person, an advertisement for any tobacco product offered for sale in Canada.

(3) For greater certainty, subsection (2) does not apply in respect of the distribution for sale of publications imported into Canada or the retransmission of radio or television broadcasts originating outside Canada.

(4) No person in Canada shall advertise a tobacco product by means of a publication published outside Canada or a radio or television broadcast originating outside Canada primarily for the purpose of promoting the sale in Canada of a tobacco product."

The remaining subsections are as follows: (5) Transitional: signs; and (6) Definition of "sign". Sec. 5 deals with retail displays and vending machines.

Promotion (Secs. 6-8). This rubric comprises Sections dealing with: permitted sponsorships (Sec. 6); free distribution and rewards and contests (Sec. 7); and trademarks on non-tobacco goods and related matters (Sec. 8).

Labelling (Sec. 9); and *Reporting (Sec. 10).* Sec. 9 and Sec. 10(1) and (2) read as follows:

"**9.** (1) No distributor shall sell or offer for sale a tobacco product unless

(*a*) the package containing the product displays, in accordance with the regulations, messages pertaining to the health effects of the product and a list of toxic constituents of the product and, where applicable, of the smoke produced from its combustion indicating the quantities of those constituents present therein; and

(*b*) if and as required by the regulations, a leaflet furnishing information relative to the health effects of the product has been placed inside the package containing the product.

(2) No distributor shall sell or offer for sale a tobacco product if the package in which it is contained displays any writing other than the name, brand name and any trade marks of the tobacco product, the messages and list referred to in subsection (1), the label required by the *Consumer Packaging and Labelling Act* and the stamp and information required by sections 203 and 204 of the *Excise Act.*

(3) This section does not affect any obligation of a distributor, at common law or under any Act of Parliament or of a provincial legislature, to warn purchasers of tobacco products of the health effects of those products.

10. (1) Subject to any regulations made under paragraph 17(*h*), every manufacturer or importer of tobacco products of a class prescribed for the purposes of this subsection shall provide to the Minister, in the prescribed form and manner and at the prescribed intervals, reports identifying the constituents of those products and, where applicable, of the smoke produced from their combustion and indicating the quantities of those constituents present therein.

(2) Every manufacturer or importer of tobacco products of a class prescribed for the purposes of this subsection shall provide to the Minister, in the prescribed form and manner and at the prescribed intervals, reports indicating the quantity of those tobacco products manufactured or imported by that manufacturer or importer and the quantity thereof sold by that manufacturer or importer."

Enforcement (Secs. 11-16). Sec. 11 deals, with *inter alia*, the appointment of tobacco product inspectors and tobacco product analysts. The remaining provisions deal with inspection and enforcement procedures, and related matters.

Regulations (Sec. 17). Details are given of the matters in respect to which the Governor in Council may make regulations for the implementation of this Act.

Offences and punishments (Secs. 18-19). Details are given of the penalties to which persons are liable for offences under this Act.

Coming into force (Sec. 20). This Act is to come into force on 1 January 1989.

CANADA. An Act (C-204) to regulate smoking in the federal workplace and on common carriers and to amend the Hazardous Products Act in relation to cigarette advertising. Dated 31 May 1988. (The Non-smokers' Health Act). (*The Canada Gazette*, Part III, Vol. 11, No. 4, 2 September 1988, pp. 407-413) Can. 88.20

The following is an outline of the principal provisions of this Act; most of the provisions are to come into force on a date or dates to be fixed by proclamation.

Sec. 2 (Definitions) defines various terms, including "designated smoking area" ("a separate space set aside for use by smokers and clearly identified as such, and meeting such criteria as the Governor in Council may prescribe by regulation, but does not include an area normally occupied by non-smokers"), "designated smoking room", "smoke-free", or "smoke-free environment" ("in respect of an enclosed area, an environment where: (*a*) smoking is not permitted, and (*b*) concentrations of by-products of tobacco combustion are no higher than those prescribed by the Governor in Council"), "smoking" and "to smoke" (these terms include holding or having control over any ignited tobacco product or any device containing an ignited tobacco product), and "tobacco product" (the term includes any cigarette, cigar, tobacco, or tobacco derivative).

Secs. 3-4 read as follows:

"**3.** (1) Every employer shall provide a smoke-free environment where all employees may perform the duties that are directly or indirectly related to their employment.

(2) Nothing in this section shall prevent an employer from providing a designated smoking room for use by smokers.

(3) Notwithstanding subsection (1), an employee may, because of the nature of the employee's duties, be required by an employer to perform his or her duties from time to time in a designated smoking room.

(4) Every employer shall make reasonable efforts to ensure that a designated smoking room is independently ventilated.

(5) The Governor in Council may make regulations exempting employers from the application of subsection (4) in cases where significant structural modifications are required or the cost of compliance is prohibitive.

(6) Nothing in this Act affects any rights to protection from tobacco smoke at common law or under any Act of Parliament or of a provincial legislature.

4. No person shall smoke in any office or other enclosed work space provided by an employer, outside of a designated smoking room or a designated smoking area."

Sec. 5 imposes restrictions on smoking in enclosed spaces in or on passenger transport vehicles (as defined). Sec. 6 indicates the fines to be imposed on persons guilty of offences under Secs. 4 or 5. Sec. 7 empowers the Governor in Council to make regulations: prescribing criteria for the designation of smoking areas and smoking rooms; prescribing rules for the location, identification, and ventilation of designated smoking rooms and designated smoking areas; prescribing the maximum concentration of by-products of tobacco combustion that is permissible for purposes of a smoke-free environment; exempting employers, subject to this Act, from their obligation to provide independent ventilation in designated smoking rooms; etc.

Sec. 9 amends Part II of Schedule I to the Hazardous Products Act (see *IDHL*, 1988, **39**, 466, **Can. 88.18**), as amended, by the addition of the following item:

"**5.** Products manufactured from tobacco and intended for use by smoking, inhalation or mastication, including nasal and oral snuff."

CANADA. An Act (Chapter 7) to amend the Non-smokers' Health Act. Dated 29 June 1989. (*Canada Gazette*, Part III, Vol. 12, No. 1, 6 September 1989, pp. 79-88) **Can. 90.3**

The following are among the principal provisions of this Act, which amends the Non-smokers' Health Act (see *IDHL*, 1988, **39**, 859, **Can. 88.20**).

Revised versions are introduced of Secs. 2-8. Sec. 2 (Definitions) now defines "designated smoking area" to mean "an area, other than an enclosed room, that is designated for smoking under subsection 3(2)", while "tobacco product" is defined as "any product manufactured from tobacco and intended for use by smoking". Revised definitions are likewise introduced of various other terms. This Section also includes provisions dealing with: the application of the Act outside Canada; non-application of the Act to "foreign carriers"; and non-application of the Act to commuter trains.

Secs. 3-4 read as follows:

"**3.** (1) Every employer, and any person acting on behalf of an employer, shall ensure that persons refrain from smoking in any work space under the control of the employer.

(2) An employer may, to the extent permitted by the regulations, designate for smoking

(*a*) enclosed rooms under the control of the employer other than rooms normally occupied by non-smokers; and

(*b*) areas under the control of the employer on an aircraft, train, motor vehicle or ship or in an airport passenger terminal, railway passenger station, interurban bus station or marine passenger terminal other than areas normally occupied by non-smokers.

(3) Notwithstanding subsection (1), an employer may require employees, by reason of the nature of their duties, to perform those duties in a room or area designated for smoking under subsection (2).

(4) Where an employer has designated a room for smoking under subsection (2) in a building or portion of a building the construction of which commenced before January 1, 1990, the employer shall, to the extent reasonably practicable, ensure that the room conforms to any requirements of the regulations respecting independent ventilation of designated smoking rooms.

(5) No employer shall designate a room for smoking under subsection (2) in a building or portion of a building the construction of which commenced after Decem-

ber 31, 1989 if the room fails to conform to any requirements of the regulations respecting independent ventilation of designated smoking rooms.

(6) No employer shall designate a room or area for smoking under subsection (2) in a work place, other than on an aircraft, train, motor vehicle or ship that is carrying passengers, until after the employer has consulted with the safety and health committee or safety and health representative in respect of that work place or, if there is no such committee or representative, with the employees employed there.

(7) In subsection (6), the expressions 'safety and health committee', 'safety and health representative' and 'work place' have the same meaning as in Part II of the *Canada Labour Code*.

4. (1) No person shall smoke in any work space under the control of an employer except in a designated smoking room or designated smoking area.

(2) An employer shall, to the extent and in the manner required by the regulations, inform employees and members of the public of the prohibition imposed by subsection (1) and of the location of designated smoking rooms and designated smoking areas under the control of the employer."

Sec. 5 imposes restrictions on smoking on aircraft and on trains. Under Sec. 6, nothing in Secs. 4 or 5 "affects the operation of any other Act of Parliament or regulations thereunder or any rule of law in relation to the protection of persons from exposure to tobacco smoke". Sec. 7 redesignates the matters in respect of which the Governor General in Council may make regulations for the implementation of this Act. Most of the other provisions deal with penal and administrative matters.

CANADA. Regulations respecting the health of non-smokers. SOR/ 90-21. Dated 14 December 1989. (The Non-smokers' Health Regulations).[a] (*Canada Gazette*, Part II, Vol. 124, No. 1, 3 January 1990, pp. 121-136) **Can. 90.14**

These Regulations have been made in pursuance of subsection 7(1) of the Non-smokers' Health Act (see *IDHL*, 1988, **39**, 859, **Can. 88.20**), as amended by an Act of 29 June 1989 (see *supra*). They lay down detailed provisions, notably in respect of "designated smoking rooms and designated smoking areas" (Secs. 3-5) and "notices of smoking restrictions" (Secs. 6-7).

There are also provisions dealing with smoking on trains, ships, and aircraft and in terminals and stations. Models of various signs (prohibiting or, as appropriate, permitting smoking) are given in Schedule I, while Schedule II lists the fines imposed under Sec. 14 of the Act. There is a particularly detailed Regulatory Impact Analysis Statement.

---

[a] These Regulations were amended by Order in Council P.C. 1989-2614 of 28 December 1989 (SOR/90-70; *Canada Gazette*, Part II, Vol. 124, 5 January 1990, Extra No. 1, pp. 1-3). The amendment allows Canadian air carriers to designate smoking areas on board aircraft for international flights that have a duration of longer than six hours; this amendment will cease to be in effect on 1 July 1990, after which smoking will not be allowed on such flights. — ED.

CANADA (ONTARIO). An Act (Chapter 48, Statutes of Ontario, 1989) to restrict smoking in workplaces. Date of Royal Assent: 26 July 1989. (The Smoking in the Workplace Act).[b] (4 pp.)

Can. (Ont) 90.3

The following are among the highlights of this Act.

• The Act prohibits smoking in enclosed workplaces. An 'enclosed workplace' means a partially or fully completed building, mine or tunnel that is separated from the outdoors.

• Vehicles, such as buses or the cabs of trucks, are not considered to be workplaces. However, a mobile library or health unit located in a trailer, for example, would be considered a workplace and therefore is subject to this Act.

• Areas of a workplace used primarily by the public are also exempt from the Act. For example, shopping malls, the floor area of a store or service centre that is accessible to the public, restaurants and bars are exempt from this legislation. Areas of a workplace that are not accessible to the public, such as lunch rooms and the area behind counters, are subject to this Act. Many Ontario municipalities now have regulations in place restricting smoking in public areas.

• Employers may designate a smoking area in the workplace. If an employer does not designate a smoking area, smoking is banned in that workplace.

• If an employer chooses to designate a smoking area, this area (or areas) cannot exceed 25 per cent of the floor area of the workplace.

• Prior to designating the smoking area, an employer is required to consult with one of the following: 1) the joint health and safety committee; 2) a similar committee in which employees participate; or 3) the workers' health and safety representative.

• If an employee asks to work in a place away from a designated smoking area, the employer is obliged to make every reasonable effort to accommodate that request.

• The Smoking in the Workplace Act recognizes that there now exist workplace smoking restrictions in some municipalities and in federally regulated workplaces. In order to work effectively with other statutes and by-laws that restrict workplace smoking, the Act states that the more restrictive provision, whether it is a municipal by-law or other Act or regulation, will prevail."

CANADA (QUEBEC). An Act respecting the protection of non-smokers in certain public places. Dated 18 June 1986. (9 pp.)

Can. (Queb) 87.1

The following are the principal provisions of this Act, which came into force on 1 January 1987.

Chapter I. Application and interpretation (Secs. 1-7)

Under Sec. 1, the object of this Act is to "regulate the use of tobacco in certain public places with a view to ensuring better protection for the health and well-being of non-smokers". "Smoking" is defined in Sec. 2 to mean the "fact of having lighted tobacco in one's possession". The term "public bodies" is interpreted in Sec. 3 to include Government agencies, municipal bodies, school bodies, and health

[b] This summary is based on "A Guide to Ontario's Workplace Smoking Law", issued by the Ontario Ministry of Labour. No editorial emendations have been made. — ED.

and social services establishments. Interpretations of these terms are given in Secs. 4-7.

Chapter II. Protection of non-smokers (Secs. 8-17)

Division I. Public bodies (Secs. 8-11). Sec. 8 imposes stringent restrictions on smoking in premises occupied by Government agencies, municipal bodies, etc. Sec. 9 prohibits smoking in premises occupied by a health and social services establishment. This provision does not however apply to: (1) quarters restricted to the personnel; (2) a smoking room; or (3) any area designated by the person who is the highest authority within the establishment. Under Sec. 10, public bodies required by law to produce an annual report of activities are required to report on the application of this Act in the premises occupied by them. In the report of the activities of his Department, that the Minister of the Environment tables every year before the National Assembly, the Minister is to present an assessment of the application of this Act by all public bodies. Sec. 11 requires the person who is the highest authority within a public body to take every appropriate measure to ensure that this Act is enforced in premises occupied by the public body. This function may be delegated, in accordance with the procedures laid down.

Division II. Public transportation (Secs. 12-14). Sec. 12 prohibits smoking in ambulances, subway cars, buses used for the transportation of schoolchildren or handicapped persons, and buses used for urban transportation or for transportation to and from airports. Further restrictions on smoking in certain categories of transportation services are laid down in Secs. 13-14.

Division III. Miscellaneous places (Secs. 15-17). Sec. 15 prohibits (except in the circumstances indicated) smoking in enclosed premises used for religious, sports, judicial, cultural, or artistic activities while these activities are in progress. Sec. 16 prohibits smoking in premises used to provide child day care in day care centres, "stop over centres", or nursery schools, or in school premises, while Sec. 17 prohibits smoking in the waiting rooms of private consulting offices of health professionals, etc.

The remaining Chapters are as follows: III. Powers and duties of municipalities (Secs. 18-19); IV. Posting of signs (Secs. 20-22); V. Inspection (Secs. 23-26); VI. Offences and penalties (Secs. 27-35); and VII. Final provisions (Secs. 36-38) (Sec. 36 lays down that the Minister of the Environment is responsible for the administration of this Act).

CAYMAN ISLANDS

CAYMAN ISLANDS. A Law (No. 21 of 1986) to make provision for the display of a health warning in connection with the advertisement of tobacco products; to provide for the control of advertising of tobacco products and intoxicating liquor; and for purposes connected therewith and incidental thereto. Dated 24 November 1986. (The Tobacco Product and Intoxicating Liquor Advertising Law, 1986). (3 pp.)

Cay. Is. 89.1

CHILE

CHILE. Decree No. 106 of 8 April 1981 prescribing a warning in connexion with the marketing and advertising of tobacco.[a] (*Diario Oficial de la República de Chile*, 19 May 1981, No. 30968, pp. 2392-2393)
Chile 82.13

Under the terms of Sec. 1 of this Decree, which has been made in pursuance of, *inter alia*, certain Sections of the Health Code promulgated by Decree No. 725 of 11 December 1967 (see *IDHL*, 1969, **20**, 47), tobacco is declared to be a toxic, irritant, and harmful substance which is liable to produce health disorders in persons who inhale its combustion products. Sec. 2 prohibits the sale of tobacco, either alone or in combination with other substances, in the form of cigars, cigarettes, or mixtures for pipes, etc. unless the packaging is conspicuously labelled with the following warning in black characters on a white background or *vice versa*, in a box occupying not less than 10% of the surface of the principal face of the packaging: "WARNING: Tobacco is harmful to health. Ministry of Health". However, in the case of cigarette packets, the warning may appear on one of the side faces of the packaging, which may retain its basic colour provided that the letters are of a colour which stands out from it; in such cases, the warning must cover the entire surface of that face of the packaging, and no other words or characters must appear on it. Sec. 3 prescribes that the same warning must appear in advertisements for tobacco products appearing in newspapers or magazines or on television or radio, and in general in any advertising or promotion of the use or consumption of tobacco by any communications media. In the case of television or cinema advertising, the warning must be displayed on the entire screen, after the advertisement, for not less than five seconds.

CHILE. Decree No. 01 of 2 January 1986 establishing a National Commission for Smoking Control. (3 pp.) **Chile 86.9**

Sec. 1 of this Presidential Decree provides for the establishment of a National Commission for Smoking Control, its task being to study matters related to tobacco and to propose measures designed to control and reduce smoking. Sec. 2 reads as follows:

"**2.** The specific functions of the Commission shall be as follows:

— to undertake an assessment of the smoking situation and to keep it under continuous review, with particular reference to:

(*a*) the place of the tobacco industry in the economy, and as regards employment;

(*b*) coordinating its activities and information with the National Institute of Statistics and other agencies and bodies, with a view to

[a] Account has been taken of amendments introduced by Decree No. 156 of 2 June 1981 (*Diario Oficial de la República de Chile*, 23 June 1981, No. 30997, p. 2917). — ED.

monitoring throughout the country the prevalence of smoking among the population;

(*c*) determining the effects of smoking on mortality and morbidity levels in the population and on absenteeism and unfitness for work;

(*d*) identifying the resources available in the public and private sectors for developing informational, educational, and care activities; and

(*e*) analysing constitutional, legal, and regulatory texts, particularly those related to health, with a view to enacting measures that will form a legal basis for the implementation of anti-smoking activities;

— to propose a policy for smoking control; and

— to design and evaluate a programme of medium- and long-term smoking control activities based on strategies in the fields of education, information, regulation, and evaluation."

Details are given in Sec. 3 of the composition of the Commission. This is chaired by the Minister of Health; the other members include the Under-Secretary for the Interior, the Under-Secretary for Economic Affairs, Development and Public Works, the Under-Secretary for Finance, the Under-Secretary for Education, the Under-Secretary for Agriculture, the Under-Secretary for Labour, the Under-Secretary for Transport and Telecommunications, and the Under-Secretary for Justice.

The remaining Sections deal with administrative matters.

CHILE. Decree No. 1 of 2 January 1986 establishing the National Commission for the Control of Smoking. (*Diario Oficial de la República de Chile*, 2 June 1986, No. 32485, p. 2722) **Chile 87.19**

Sec. 1 of this Decree, which has been made in pursuance of, *inter alia*, Decree Law No. 2763 of 11 July 1979 (see *IDHL*, 1982, **33**, 671, **Chile 82.1**), establishes the Commission referred to in the title. The objectives of the Commission are to study tobacco-related problems and propose measures for the control and reduction of smoking. Under Sec. 2, the specific functions of the Commission are: 1. to supplement and update the diagnosis of the position concerning smoking, in particular in relation to (*a*) assessing the importance of the activities of the tobacco industry in the economy and the labour market, (*b*) coordinating its activities and information with the National Statistical Institute and other agencies and services in monitoring the level of smoking in the population of the country, (*c*) determining the effects of smoking on the mortality and morbidity rates of the population and on absenteeism from and accidents at work, (*d*) identifying resources available in the public and private sectors for informational, educational, and care activities, and (*e*) analysing the constitutional, legal, and regulatory provisions, in particular from the health standpoint, concerning the development of an anti-smoking strategy by legislative means; 2. to put forward a smoking control policy; and 3. to outline and assess a medium- and long-term programme on the basis of strategies in relation to the following matters — education, information, regulations, and evaluation. Secs. 3-8 deal with the membership and working procedures of the Commission.

CHILE. Decree No. 164 of 4 June 1986 prescribing a new warning for use in the marketing and advertising of tobacco. (*Diario Oficial de la República de Chile*, 13 August 1986, No. 32547, p. 3990) **Chile 87.25**

Sec. 1 of this Decree replaces the warning referred to in Sec. 2 of Supreme Decree No. 106 of 8 April 1981 on the same subject (see *IDHL*, 1982, **33**, 732, **Chile 82.13**), as amended by Supreme Decree No. 156 of 2 June 1981 (see *ibid.*, footnote), by the following warning: "WARNING: TOBACCO MAY CAUSE CANCER – MINISTRY OF HEALTH, CHILE". Sec. 2 lays down that the warning is to appear on the screen for at least five seconds in advertising for tobacco products on television or in cinemas. At the same time, the sound-track provided by the Ministry of Health is to be played; the sound-track is also to be played in conjunction with advertising on the radio or other broadcast media.

COSTA RICA

COSTA RICA. Decree No. 17377-S of 13 January 1987. (*La Gaceta*, 5 February 1987, No. 25, p. 1) **Costa R. 87.10**

This Decree amends Sec. 1 of Executive Decree No. 1520-SPPS of 24 February 1971 (see *IDHL*, 1974, **25**, 61), as amended, to read as follows:

"Every importer or manufacturer of cigarettes intended for consumption on the domestic market shall be required to print the following warning on every packet offered to the public: 'Warning: Cigarette smoke contains carbon monoxide'."

COSTA RICA. Decree No. 17967-S of 4 February 1988. (*La Gaceta*, 25 February 1988, No. 39, p. 3) **Costa R. 89.9**

Sec. 1 of this Decree prohibits the sale of cigarettes to minors in all commercial establishments. Under Sec. 2, the owners, administrators, or persons in charge of such establishments are required to ensure compliance with this probibition. Sec. 3 lays down that persons contravening the above provisions are liable to judicial proceedings, in pursuance of Sec. 378 of the General Health Law promulgated by Decree No. 5395 of 30 October 1973 (see *IDHL*, 1976, **27**, 312).

COSTA RICA. Decree No. 17969-S of 4 February 1988. (*La Gaceta*, 25 February 1988, No. 39, p. 4) **Costa R. 89.11**

Sec. 1 of this Decree, which has been made in the light of the appeal launched by WHO to its Member States during the Fortieth World Health Assembly in May 1987 [in resolution WHA40.38], declares 7 April each year to be "No-Smoking Day". Sec. 2 urges all natural persons, or public or private legal persons, to undertake campaigns and activities aimed at marking this occasion; emphasis is to be placed on the injury to health caused by cigarette smoking.

COSTA RICA. Decree No. 18216-S-TSS of 23 June 1988. (*La Gaceta*, 11 July 1988, No. 131, p. 3) **Costa R. 89.18**

Sec. 1 of this Decree imposes a formal ban on smoking in workplaces. Sec. 2 requires the director of the workplace, or his representative, to ensure strict compliance with this prohibition. Under Sec. 3, the director or his representative is required to post at least one copy of the full text of this Decree in a conspicuous position at the workplace. Sec. 4 lays down that an area may be reserved at the workplace for smokers, to the extent that this is possible. Under Sec. 5, directors or workers committing breaches of the provisions of this Decree are liable to prosecution and/or a penalty in accordance with the applicable legislation.

COSTA RICA. Decree No. 18248-MOPT-S of 23 June 1988. (*La Gaceta*, 21 July 1988, No. 139, p. 1) **Costa R. 89.19**

Sec. 1 of this Decree imposes a further ban on smoking in all means of public transport (motor vehicles and railways). Under Sec. 2, drivers of these vehicles are entitled to call on the assistance of the authorities to ensure compliance with these provisions, and are directly responsible to the State for any contraventions committed by users. Sec. 3 lays down that if, in spite of a request to stop, a user persists in smoking, the driver may refuse to continue the service and may seek the assistance of the authorities.

Sec. 4 lays down that the penalties laid down by the applicable legislation are to be imposed in the event of any breach of the provisions of this Decree, without prejudice to any applicable administrative measures and sanctions. Sec. 5 lays down that, in the case of railways, a carriage specifically marked for this purpose may be reserved for smokers as far as this is possible. Under Sec. 6, every vehicle intended for any of the public services covered by this Decree is required to carry, in a conspicuous place, at least one copy of the full text of this Decree; any breach of this provision is punishable in accordance with the applicable legislation.

CUBA

CUBA. Ministerial Resolution No. 165 of 17 August 1981. (3 pp.)
Cuba 89.1

Sec. 1 of this Resolution, which has been issued by the Minister of Public Health prohibits all members of the staff of the National Health System from smoking, or holding any lighted tobacco product during the discharge of their duties other than in open premises and spaces and during meal-breaks, in accordance with the labour law in force.

Sec. 2 lays down that a breach of the general prohibition is particularly serious in the following circumstances: (*a*) any kind of a meeting, held in roofed premises, of an administrative, political, educational, scientific, or similar nature, and in the waiting rooms, cafeterias, and refectories of these premises; (*b*) teaching activities at all levels, whether the smoking is by teachers or students; and (*c*) where it may affect the health of patients, whether during consultations or visits, in the rooms, laboratories, corridors, and other areas not reserved for smokers. This prohibition applies to all health personnel and patients, persons in their company, visitors, or any other person permanently or from time to time present in the units of the National Health System.

Under Sec. 3, administrators, officials, and workers within the National Health System, in addition to complying with the provisions of this Resolution, are required to take advantage of all opportunities to provide information and persuade other workers, and the population in general, of the harmfulness of tobacco and its hazards to health. Sec. 4 makes provision for penalties for breaches of this Resolution.

CYPRUS

CYPRUS. Law No. 51 of 1980 on the adoption of measures to restrict smoking. (The Health Protection (Smoking Control) Law of 1980). (*Episêmos Ephêmeris tês Kypriakês Dêmokratias*, 1 August 1980, Supplement No. 1 to No. 1620, pp. 1175-1179) **Cypr. 81.5**

Sec. 2 of this Law contains a number of definitions, including "public place" ("any place which the public is entitled or authorized to enter, whether free of charge or against payment, that is defined by regulations issued under this Law"), and "tobacco" ("industrially manufactured tobacco or other tobacco, whatever its characteristics, nature, or form of packaging").

Sec. 3 makes it an offence to supply tobacco to persons under 18 years of age (however, if it can be shown that the tobacco was supplied other than for use by the adolescent or another adolescent, such an act is not deemed to be an offence).

Sec. 4 establishes the Tobacco Advertising Control Commission, whose members are to be appointed by the Council of Ministers, at the proposal of the Minister of Health. The Commission is responsible for examining all tobacco advertisements submitted to it under Sec. 5 and may amend and lay down conditions governing all such advertisements. The Commission is also to advise the Minister on general matters concerning tobacco advertising. Sec. 5 prohibits all radio or television advertising of tobacco. Commencing six months after the entry into force of this Law, all tobacco advertisements in newspapers, magazines, and other printed publications circulating in Cyprus, as well as on cinema screens, must be submitted in advance to the above-mentioned Commission for approval (however, this does not apply to advertisements contained in imported foreign magazines or newspapers, provided that these do not solely or principally contain tobacco advertisements). Under the provisions of Sec. 6, no tobacco advertisement submitted to the Commission may be approved if: (*a*) it is likely to result in the impression being created among members of the public that smoking leads to professional success or success in other areas of human activity; or (*b*) it in any other way encourages nonsmokers to smoke. Any advertisement approved by the Commission must in addition contain a notice, of a type determined by the Commission, to the effect that smoking can adversely affect smokers' health. Sec. 7 lays down provisions concerning appeals against decisions by the Commission.

Sec. 8 requires the warning referred to in Sec. 6 to appear on every package of tobacco offered for sale (the manufacturer, packager, or importer are made responsible for ensuring that this is done).

Sec. 9 makes it an offence for any person: (*a*) to have under his supervision or in his possession any automatic tobacco vending machine, or to allow any such machine to be installed or used on any premises under his supervision or in his possession; (*b*) to use or operate any such vending machine in any place; or (*c*) to import or manufacture any such machine.

Sec. 10 prohibits smoking in such public places as may be defined. Persons responsible for such places are deemed to have violated the provisions of this Section if they cannot be shown to have taken all reasonable measures to prevent smoking in the place concerned.

Sec. 11 prescribes that levels of nicotine, tar, and other potentially harmful constituents present in tobacco products offered for consumption may not exceed the limits to be laid down in the regulations issued in pursuance of this Law.

Under the provisions of Sec. 14, the Council of Ministers is empowered to issue regulations for the implementation of this Law (however, the regulations must first be submitted to the House of Representatives, which may amend them within 30 days).

CYPRUS. The Health Protection (Smoking Control) Regulations of 1988. No. 152. (*Episêmos Ephêmeris tês Kypriakês Dêmokratias*, 27 May 1988, No. 2327, Supplement No. 3, pp. 467-470) **Cypr. 89.1**

These Regulations have been made in pursuance of Sec. 14 of the Health Protection (Smoking Control) Law of 1980 (see *IDHL*, 1981, **32**, 731, **Cypr. 81.5**). Sec. 2 defines various terms, including "public place" (i.e., theatres, cinemas, etc.; health care establishments, including the waiting rooms; museums; cultural centres; public libraries; food premises; educational establishments; elevators; etc.) and "public vehicle".

A fine may be imposed in the case of smoking in public places, other than in rooms specially reserved for smokers (Sec. 3) or in buses, taxis, and hired vehicles transporting passengers (Sec. 4).

Under Sec. 5, notices carrying the ban on smoking are required to be posted in public places and public vehicles. Notices carrying the following warning must be posted in cafés and restaurants: "CAUTION smoking is seriously harmful to your health: Ministry of Health".[a] Under Secs. 7 and 8, a legend carrying the same warning must appear on tobacco packets and on advertisements for tobacco products. Provision is made for penalties in the event of breaches of these Regulations.

---

[a] This is the English version given in the original text. — ED.

DENMARK

DENMARK. Law No. 398 of 10 June 1987 on the Council on Prevention and the Council on Tobacco-induced Damage to Health. (*Lovtidende for Kongeriget Denmark, 1987*, Part A, 17 June 1987, No. 45, pp. 1332-1333) **Den. 88.23**

Sec. 1 of this Law, which repeals Law No. 217 of 23 May 1979 on the Council on Prevention (see *IDHL*, 1979, **30**, 766), lays down that, with a view to promoting health and preventing diseases and accidents, both in the health and other sectors, the Council on Prevention is responsible for the following, in particular: (1) advising the national and communal authorities on measures to be taken to promote health and to prevent diseases and accidents; (2) reinforcing measures of this nature adopted at the local level, through cooperation with the local councils on prevention and by means of support given to local activities in the fields of research and development; (3) taking the initiative for analyses and inquiries undertaken within the framework of overall preventive activities, or for the evaluation of existing measures for the promotion of health and the prevention of diseases and accidents; and (4) stimulating research in the prevention sector.

Details are given in Sec. 2 of the membership of the Council.

Sec. 3 provides for the appointment, by the Minister of the Interior, of an independent Council on Tobacco-induced Damage to Health. It is composed of nine members, comprising two members of the Council on Prevention and seven members who are technically expert in the fields of medicine, law, sociology, statistics and epidemiology, pedagogy, psychology, and information. Details are given of the working procedures of the Council, which is responsible for strengthening activities aimed at limiting the prejudicial effects caused by smoking and the harm it causes to the health of both active and passive smokers.

Sec. 4 lays down that the Council on Prevention may have recourse to the assistance of expert committees in carrying out its functions.

DENMARK. Circular of 23 March 1988 of the Ministry of Health on the provision of nonsmoking environments on public premises, means of transport, etc. (2 pp.) **Den. 89.1**

This Circular indicates that individual Ministers are required to introduce, by 1 July 1988, in the areas for which they are responsible, nonsmoking environments on public premises, in means of transport, etc., in accordance with the following guidelines:

"**1.** (1) Smoking shall not be permitted in workplaces that constitute a place of work for more than one person, and in rooms for general occupation, etc., by employees.

(2) Nevertheless, smoking on the premises mentioned in subsection 1 shall be permitted if the employees having places of work on the same premises declare it acceptable or if effective measures are adopted to ensure that no employee is inconvenienced by smoke.

(3) Smoking shall also be permitted on special premises specifically intended for smoking. In cases where it is unduly expensive to establish special premises for smoking, smoking shall be permitted in specially marked areas provided that effective measures are adopted to prevent inconvenience to nonsmokers.

2. Smoking shall not be permitted during meetings in the field of public administration (including meetings of public councils, boards, and commissions) unless all participants agree to permit smoking.

3. (1) Smoking shall not be permitted on premises to which the public has access.

(2) Nevertheless, smoking shall be permitted on premises specially established for smokers.

4. (1) Smoking shall not be permitted in public hospitals, day-care and day-and-night care institutions, and educational establishments.

(2) Nevertheless, smoking shall be permitted on premises specially established for smokers. Patients in hospital, etc. who cannot use the special premises for smokers, shall be permitted to smoke on other premises provided that at the same time measures are adopted to prevent the smoke inconveniencing other patients.

5. (1) Smoking shall not be permitted in means of public transport on fixed routes within Denmark.

(2) Nevertheless, smoking shall be permitted in such means of transport provided that measures are adopted to ensure that no-one is compelled to suffer inconvenience from smoke.

6. Notwithstanding the provisions of Sections 1-5, smoking shall be permitted as an exception if there are special grounds for not prohibiting smoking, provided that no inconvenience is thereby caused to nonsmokers.

7. Steps shall be taken to ensure that the competent authorities provide information in the form of signs, etc., on the rules on smoking on the premises and in the means of transport in question."

DENMARK. Order No. 441 of 26 July 1988 on advertisements through local radio services. (*Lovtidende, 1988*, Part A, 29 July 1988, No. 65, pp. 1549-1551) **Den. 89.16**

Sec. 1 of this Order, which has been made by the Ministry of Transport and Communications, lays down that, for the purposes of this Order, "advertising" means recommendations for and references to goods, services, and undertakings for commercial purposes, whether or not the broadcast is paid for. Sec. 9 of Chapter 4 (Special rules applicable to specified products) reads as follows:

"**9.** (1) Alcoholic beverages (beer, wine, spirits, and similar products having an alcohol content of 2.25% and more) may not be advertised.

(2) Tobacco products or goods primarily used in connection with tobacco smoking may not be advertised.

(3) Medicaments may not be advertised unless the National Board of Health has issued a licence to that effect."

EGYPT

EGYPT. Law No. 52 of 20 June 1981 on protection against the harmful effects of smoking. (*Al-Jarida Al-Rasmiya*, 25 June 1981, Supplement No. 26) **Eg. 81.1**

Sec. 1 of this Law prohibits the import, export, production, sale, or possession with a view to sale of cigarettes or tobacco which fail to comply with the conditions laid down in a decision to be issued by the Minister of State for Health in consultation with the Minister of Industry. The conditions are to include a requirement that tar levels do not exceed 20 mg per cigarette (this level may be reduced by decision of the Minister of State for Health in consultation with the Minister of Industry). Sec. 3 requires all packages of domestic or imported cigarettes or tobacco to give details of the tar and nicotine levels as well as the levels of any other substances specified in a decision issued by the Minister of State for Health. The Minister may likewise issue a decision requiring other particulars to appear on the packaging of cigarettes and tobacco. All such packaging must, in addition, bear the following warning: "Smoking is very harmful to health".

Sec. 4 prohibits all advertising or promotion of the sale of cigarettes or other tobacco products by State agencies, public corporate bodies, public sector units, cinemas, theatres, and sports clubs, subject to the provision of the regulations made in pursuance of this Law. Sec. 5 prescribes that advertisements for cigarettes and tobacco products in other cases must be limited to the shape, contents, and price of the package, and that all such advertisements must conspicuously display the warning referred to in Sec. 3, subject to the provisions of the regulations made in pursuance of this Law.

Sec. 6 prohibits smoking in public transport vehicles and enclosed public places, to be defined by the Minister.

Sec. 9 empowers the Minister to issue a decision laying down regulations for the implementation of this Law as well as other decisions necessary for its implementation.

EL SALVADOR

EL SALVADOR. Decree No. 955 of 11 May 1988 promulgating the Health Code. (*Diario Oficial*, 11 May 1988, No. 86) **El Salv. 90.1**

Division 41. Activities for the control of alcoholism, tobacco use, and drug dependence (Secs. 186-190). Sec. 186 requires the Ministry to adopt the measures necessary to prevent and control alcoholism and drug dependence, drawing up programmes for scientific counselling on the effects of the consumption of drugs, alcohol, and tobacco on health and social relationships, and encouraging cultural, civil, and sports activities that help to prevent such consumption. Sec. 187 lays down that radio and television programmes and cinemas may only feature advertising for beer, wine, spirits, or tobacco products in programmes which are not intended for children. Sec. 188 lays down that the surveillance, treatment, and detoxification of alcoholics and drug-dependent persons is to be carried out in public establishments specified by the Ministry or in private establishments licensed by the Council. Under Sec. 189, packets of tobacco products, whether of national or foreign origin, must carry the following warning: "TOBACCO MAY HARM YOUR HEALTH. Ministry of Public Health and Social Welfare". Sec. 190 prohibits the possession of the seeds of various species of cannabis, poppy, coca, and other plants from which dependence-producing drugs or their derivatives can be obtained, and further prohibits the sowing, cultivation, or harvesting of such species, or their introduction into El Salvador.

FEDERAL REPUBLIC OF GERMANY

FEDERAL REPUBLIC OF GERMANY. First Ordinance of 26 October 1982 amending the Tobacco Ordinance. (*Bundesgesetzblatt*, Part I, 30 October 1982, No. 40, pp. 1444-1445) **FRG 82.42**

This Ordinance introduces a number of amendments to the Tobacco Ordinance of 20 December 1977 (see *IDHL*, 1978, **29**, 737). In particular, a new Sec. 3*a* is introduced. Under this Section, tobacco products within the meaning of subsection 1 of Sec. 3 of the Foods and Consumer Goods Law of 15 August 1974 (see *ibid.*, 1975, **26**, 524) may be commercially marketed in packages intended for supply to the consumer only if they bear the following health warning: "The Federal Minister of Health: smoking endangers your health". In addition, cigarettes may be sold only if the nicotine and condensate levels are indicated as follows: "The smoke of a cigarette of this brand, as tested in accordance with DIN Standards, contains on an average ...mg of nicotine and on average ...mg of condensate (tar)". The above particulars are required to be displayed conspicuously, legibly, and indelibly on the packaging.

FINLAND

FINLAND. Decree No. 130 of 11 February 1982 of the Council of State on the maximum levels of harmful substances in tobacco products approved for sale and the classification of factory-manufactured cigarettes. (*Finlands Författningssamling*, 16 February 1982, Nos. 118-131, pp. 230-231) **Fin. 82.22**

Sec. 1 of this Decree, which repeals Decree No. 747 of 26 September 1979 on the same subject (see *IDHL*, 1980, **31**, 307), prescribes that the maximum permitted level of nicotine in tobacco products, as referred to in Sec. 5 of Law No. 693 of 13 August 1976 on measures to restrict smoking (see *ibid.*, 1977, **28**, 486) and Sec. 8 of Ordinance No. 225 of 25 February 1977 on the same subject (see *ibid.*, 489), is 50 mg in 1 g of the dry matter of the tobacco product. Sec. 2 prescribes that the maximum permitted levels of harmful substances in factory-manufactured cigarettes are henceforth as follows: tar (smoke condensate) — 18 (previously 23) mg per cigarette when smoked; carbon monoxide — 14 (previously 20) mg per cigarette when smoked; nicotine — 1.3 (previously 1.6) mg per cigarette when smoked. Under the provisions of Sec. 3, such cigarettes are to be classified as "harmful" if their smoke contains up to 10 (previously 12) mg of tar, up to 8 (previously 10) mg of carbon monoxide, and up to 0.7 (previously 0.8) mg of nicotine when smoked, and as "extremely harmful" if these levels are exceeded.

Sec. 4 lists various approved methods of determining the above levels.

Sec. 6 prescribes that the quantities of tar, nicotine, and carbon monoxide indicated in the certificate of approval may not be exceeded by more than 15%, or 1.5 mg in the case of tar and carbon monoxide and 0.15 mg in the case of nicotine (whichever is the greater).

FINLAND. Decree No. 770 of 15 November 1984 of the Council of State on the maximum levels of harmful substances in tobacco products approved for sale and the classification of factory-manufactured cigarettes. (*Finlands Författningssamling*, 21 November 1984, Nos. 764-770, pp. 1547-1548) **Fin. 85.6**

This Decree, which has been made in pursuance of certain provisions of Secs. 5 and 6 of Law No. 693 of 13 August 1976 on measures to reduce smoking (see *IDHL*, 1977, **28**, 486), repeals Decree No. 130 of 11 February 1982 of the Council of State on the same subject (see *ibid.*, 1982, **33**, 498, **Fin. 82.22**). The following are among the principal provisions.

Sec. 2 lays down the following maximum permissible levels in harmful substances for factory-manufactured cigarettes: tar (condensates) — 15 mg (previously 18 mg) per cigarette smoked; carbon monoxide — 12 mg (previously 14 mg) per cigarette smoked; nicotine — 1.2 mg (previously 1.3 mg) per cigarette smoked. The other values set out in Secs. 3 and 6 are identical to those in the corresponding Sections of the repealed Decree.

FRANCE

FRANCE. Order of 16 July 1984 on the additives permitted in the manufacture of tobacco products and their substitutes. (*Journal officiel de la République française, Lois et Décrets*, 9 September 1984, Supplementary issue No. 211, pp. 8215-8217) **Fr. 85.28**

This Order has been made in pursuance of, *inter alia*, Law No. 76-616 of 9 July 1976 concerning measures to combat smoking (see *IDHL*, 1976, **27**, 817) and Decree No. 78-1108 of 23 November 1978 for the implementation of the Law of 1 August 1905 on fraudulent practices and misbranding with regard to products or services in respect of tobacco, tobacco products, and tobacco substitutes (see *ibid.*, 1979, **30**, 785). It evidently supersedes the Order of 5 June 1979 on the same subject (see *ibid.*, 786).

Annex I lists the additives (flavouring agents, texture agents, preservatives, and colouring matters) permitted in the manufacture of tobacco products and their substitutes, while Annex II prescribes maximum permitted levels and purity criteria for such additives.

FRANCE. Circular No. 231 of 13 January 1988 on the control of tobacco consumption in hospital establishments. (*Bulletin officiel du Ministère des Affaires sociales et de l'Emploi et du Ministère chargé de la Santé et de la Famille*, 1 April 1988, No. 88/7, Text No. 11059, pp. 143-145) **Fr. 89.32**

This Circular is addressed by the Minister *délégué* responsible for Health and Family Affairs to the regional and departmental authorities responsibles for health and social affairs. It notes a failure in certain hospitals to observe the prohibition on smoking laid down by Decree No. 77-1042 of 12 September 1977 on the prohibition of smoking in certain places intended for use by groups of persons where this practice may have harmful effects upon health (see *IDHL*, 1978, **29**, 352) and emphasizes the need to observe the provisions of the law, in order to reduce the consumption of tobacco products in hospital establishments in particular. The role of the medical profession in educating patients is stressed.

FRANCE. Law No. 91-32 of 10 January 1991 on measures to combat tobacco use and alcoholism. (*Journal officiel de la République française, Lois et Décrets*, 12 January 1991, No. 10, pp. 615–618) Fr. 91.

Among other provisions, this Law repeals Secs. 13–15 of Law No. 76-616 of 9 July 1976 on measures to combat tobacco use (see *IDHL*, 1976, **27**, 732), as well as, with effect from 1 January 1993, Secs. 4, 5, 7, 8, 10, and 11 of that Law. It amends Article L. 192 of Title II (School and university health) of Book II (Health protection of the family and children) of the Public Health Code, which now reads as follows:

"**Article L. 192.** All members of the staff of teaching and educational establishments, whether public or private, and all persons in regular contact with pupils and students within such establishments, shall be required to undergo, periodically, and at least once every two years, a medical examination aimed at the detection of infectious diseases.

On this occasion, they shall be provided by the school physician with information concerning the causes, consequences, and means for the treatment and control of tobacco use, alcoholism, and drug dependence."

Sec. 1 of the present Law reads as follows:

"**1.** With effect from 1 January 1992, it shall be prohibited to take into account the price of tobacco in calculating consumer price indexes, published by the State administrations and in particular the National Institute of Statistics and Economic Studies."

The following is a summary of some of the other principal amendments introduced by this Law to existing legislation.

Title I. Provisions on measures to combat tobacco use (Secs. 3–9)

Under Sec. 3, Sec. 2 of the 1976 Law, as amended, is to remain in force until 1 January 1993. As from that date, that Section (i.e. Articles L. 355-24 of a new Title VIII (Control of tobacco use) (Articles L. 355-24 – L. 355-32) of Book III (Control of social scourges) of the Public Health Code) is to read as follows:

"**2.** Any advertising, whether direct or indirect, for tobacco or tobacco products, as well as any form of free distribution thereof, shall be prohibited.

These provisions shall not apply to signs in tobacco retail shops, nor to small posters displayed inside such establishments that are not visible from the outside, provided that such signs or small posters conform to the characteristics defined by interministerial Order. Any form of sponsorship shall be prohibited if its objective or purpose is direct or indirect advertising for tobacco or tobacco products."

Under Sec. 4, Secs. 1, 3, 9, 12, 16, and 18 of the Law become Articles L. 355-25, L. 355-26, L. 355-27, L. 355-31, L. 355-28, and L. 355-32, respectively, of Title VIII (as

"**1.** The following shall be considered to be tobacco products:
products intended to be smoked, snuffed, chewed, or sucked, insofar as they are constituted, even partially, of tobacco, as well as products intended to be smoked even if they do not contain tobacco ...".

"**3.** The following shall be considered to be indirect advertising:
any advertising for an agency, service, activity, product, or article other than tobacco or a tobacco product whenever, on account of its logo, its presentation, or the use of a trade mark, advertising symbol, or any other distinctive sign, it is suggestive of tobacco or a tobacco product.

Notwithstanding the above, these provisions shall not be applicable to advertising for a product other than tobacco or a tobacco product that was marketed before 1 January 1990 by an undertaking that is legally and financially distinct from any undertaking engaged in the manufacture, importation, or marketing of tobacco or a tobacco product. The establishment of any legal or financial link between such undertakings shall render this exemption null and void."

"**9.** (I) The maximum contents of tar in cigarettes shall be laid down by an Order of the Minister responsible for Health.

(II) Every packaging unit of tobacco or tobacco products shall bear the following legend, in accordance with the arrangements established by an Order of the Minister responsible for Health: 'Seriously harmful to health'.

(III) Every packet of cigarettes shall indicate:

1. the full composition except, where appropriate, the composition of the filters; and
2. the average content of tar and nicotine.

An Order of the Minister responsible for Health shall lay down the arrangements governing the marking of these obligatory legends, the analytical methods for measuring the levels of nicotine and tar, and the methods for the verification of the accuracy of legends carried on the packets.

In addition, every packet of cigarettes shall carry a 'health message' [*message de caractère sanitaire*], under conditions laid down by an Order of the Minister responsible for Health.

(IV) Packaging units of tobacco and tobacco products produced prior to 31 December 1991 which are not in conformity with the provisions of subsections II and III above may be marketed until 31 December 1992 in the case of cigarettes, and up to 31 December 1993 in the case of other tobacco products, subject to the condition that, on the one hand, they indicate the complete composition except, where appropriate, the composition of the filters, and the average content of tar and nicotine, and, in additon, carry the following legend in conspicuous characters: 'Abuse is dangerous'."

"**12.** [*Penal provisions*]".

"**16.** It shall be prohibited to smoke in premises that are assigned for community use, and in particular scholastic use, as well as in public transport vehicles, other than in places that are specifically reserved for smokers.

A decree made with the assent of the *Conseil d'Etat* shall lay down the conditions for the implementation of the preceding paragraph."

"**18.** [*Provisions applicable to associations whose terms of reference include combating tobacco use*]"

Secs. 6-7 of the Law read as follows:

"**6.** (I) Until 31 December 1992, all advertising for tobacco or tobacco products shall be accompanied by a health message, under conditions to be laid down by an Order of the Minister responsible for Health.

(II) The space annually allotted in the written press to advertising for tobacco or tobacco products shall be one-third less in 1991, and two-thirds less in 1992 than that allocated, on average, during the years 1974 and 1975. In this connection, Section 8 of the above-mentioned Law No. 76-616 of 9 July 1976, shall be applicable.

The above provisions shall apply to existing contracts that are in the course of implementation on the date of promulgation of this Law.

"**7.** The Government shall lay down, by decree, the date of an annual event entitled 'No-Tobacco Day'."

Title II. Provisions on measures to combat alcoholism (Secs. 10-13)

Among other amendments introduced to the Code on Licensed Premises [*débits de boissons*] and Measures Against Alcoholism, Articles L. 13, L. 17 (as from 1 January 1993), L. 17-1 (new), L. 18, L. 49-1-2 (new), L. 80, L. 85, and L. 97-1 (new) are amended or introduced, and read substantially as follows:

"**Artical L. 13.** The supply of alcoholic beverages by means of automatic vending machines shall be prohibited."

"**Article L. 17.** Advertising, whether direct or indirect, for alcoholic beverages whose manufacture and sale are not prohibited shall be authorized solely in/on:

1.-7 [*various advertising media, etc.*]

Any form of sponsorship shall be prohibited if its objective or purpose is direct or indirect advertising for alcoholic beverages.

Article L. 17-1. The following shall be considered to be indirect advertising:
any advertising for an angency, service, activity, product, or article other than an alcoholic beverage which, on account of its logo, its presentation, use of a name, trade mark, advertising symbol, or any other distinctive sign, is suggestive of an alcoholic beverage.

Notwithstanding the above, these provisions shall not be applicable to advertising for a product other than an alcoholic beverage that was marketed before 1 January 1991 by an undertaking that is legally and financially distinct from any undertaking engaged in the manufacture, importation, or marketing of an alcoholic beverage.

Article L. 18. [*Content of authorized advertising for alcoholic beverages*]

Any advertising for alcoholic beverages, with the exception of commercial brochures intended for persons acting on a professional basis, shall be accompanied by a health message stipulating that alcohol abuse is dangerous to health.

"**Article L. 49-1-2.** [*Prohibitions on the sale and distribution of certain categories of alcoholic beverages in establishments engaging in physical education and sports activities*]".

"**Article L. 80.** In licensed premises, and in all public commercial establishments or places, it shall be prohibited to sell alcoholic beverages (to be consumed *in situ* or to be taken away) to persons under 16 years of age."

"**Article L. 85.** [*Prohibition on the admission of unaccompanied young persons, as specified, to licensed premises*]".

"**Article 97-1.** Information campaigns conducted within the framework of measures to combat alcohol consumption shall contain messages aimed at prevention and education. Such messages may not be of a discriminatory nature with regard to different products."

FRENCH POLYNESIA

FRENCH POLYNESIA. Deliberation No. 82-11 of 18 February 1982 of the Territorial Assembly of French Polynesia on the organization of the control of tobacco abuse and tobacco dependence in the Territory.

Fr. Poly. 82.1

This Deliberation, which was brought into force by Order No. 1586/AA of 19 March 1982, lays down similar provisions, *mutatis mutandis*, to those contained in the French Law No. 76-616 of 9 July 1976 concerning measures to combat smoking (see *IDHL*, 1976, **27**, 732). The following are the principal provisions which diverge from those of the French Law: provision is made in Sec. 7 for not less than 1% of the revenue from tobacco taxes to be used for a health education campaign through the press, posters, etc.; Sec. 8 prohibits all advertising and promotion of tobacco, tobacco products, and smokers' accessories in publications produced or printed in French Polynesia; Sec. 9 extends to all tobacco products the requirement concerning the indication of composition and substances released (tar and nicotine levels, however, are required to appear only on cigarette packages); the same Section prescribes that the health warning, which must appear in both French and Tahitian, is to read "Smoking is dangerous"; and Sec. 10 extends the prohibition concerning sponsoring by producers, manufacturers, and importers of, and dealers in, tobacco and tobacco products to all public meetings, entertainments, and cultural, sporting, and charitable events.

GAMBIA

GAMBIA. An Act (No. 1 of 1986) to control advertisements of tobacco products and for matters connected therewith. Dated 3 March 1986. (The Tobacco Products (Control of Advertisements) Act, 1985). (*The Gambia Gazette*, No. 8, 3 March 1986, Supplement C, pp. 1-4) **Gamb. 86.1**

Sec. 1 of this Act defines various terms, including "advertisement" and "tobacco product" ("any form of tobacco intended for smoking or chewing including cigarettes and smoking mixtures intended as a substitute for tobacco"). Secs. 3 (Prohibition on certain advertisements of tobacco products) and 4 (Power of Minister to make orders) read as follows:

"**3.** With effect from the date of coming into operation of this Act, advertisements of tobacco products—

(*a*) by transmission over radio or television;

(*b*) by the exhibition of photographic or cinematographic films;

(*c*) by the display or distribution, as the case may be, of notices, signs, posters, models, placards, leaflets, labels or showcards;

(*d*) on any structure or apparatus erected, used or adapted for use, for the display of such advertisements; or

(*e*) by conducting a lottery or any other game,

are hereby prohibited.

4. The Minister may, by Order published in the Gazette, provide for the control or prohibition of advertisements of tobacco products by any means other than those referred to in section 3 of this Act."

Penal provisions are laid down in Sec. 5.

GREECE

GREECE. Ministerial Decision No. A2g/Ec. 1989 of 12 April 1979 prohibiting smoking in hospital establishments and private nursing homes. (1 p.) **Gr. 81.1**

Under the provisions of Sec. 1 of this Decision of the Minister of Social Services, smoking is prohibited in public and private hospitals and private nursing homes. Sec. 2 requires a smoking room, reserved for hospital personnel and visitors, to be provided on every floor of the establishment having an area of up to 200 m^2 (the number of such rooms must be increased in accordance with the area of the establishment). Smokers may only smoke in these rooms.

GREECE. Ministerial Decision No. A2/ik. 6139 of 23 December 1988 on the labelling of tobacco products with regard to the harmful effect of tobacco on health. (*Ephêmeris tês Kybernêseôs tês Hellênikês Dêmokratias*, Part II, 29 December 1988, No. 928, pp. 8687-8788) **Gr. 89.13**

This Decision, which has been made by the Minister of Health, Welfare and Social Security, is stated to have been made having regard to, *inter alia*, WHO policy in this area. It lays down that all packets of tobacco products marketed in any form on Greek territory must carry the following warning in Greek: "Warning by the Ministry of Health: Tobacco seriously harms health". For the purposes of this Decision, the term "tobacco products" is defined to mean products consisting wholly or in part of tobacco intended for smoking, sucking, sniffing, or chewing. Detailed rules are laid down concerning the positioning, dimensions, etc. of the warning.[a]

---

[a] These rules were amended by Ministerial Decision No. A2/ik. 797 of 17 February 1989 (*Ephêmeris tês Kybernêseôs tês Hellênikês Dêmokratias*, Part II, 28 February 1989, No. 153, p. 1309). — ED.

HONG KONG

HONG KONG. An Ordinance (No. 58 of 1982) to prohibit smoking in certain areas, to provide for the display of a health warning and other information on cigarette packets and in cigarette advertisements and for matters incidental thereto including the amendment of the Places of Public Entertainment Ordinance. (The Smoking (Public Health) Ordinance 1982). Dated 29 July 1982. (*Hong Kong Government Gazette*, Vol. 124, Legal Supplement No. 1 to No. 30, 30 July 1982, pp. A279-A287) **HK 82.6**

The following are among the principal provisions of this Ordinance.

Part I. Preliminary (Secs. 1-2). Sec. 1 (Short title and commencement) prescribes that the Ordinance is to come into operation on a day or days to be appointed by the Governor by notice in the *Gazette*.[a] Sec. 2 (Interpretation) includes a number of definitions, including "advertisement" ("any announcement to the public made or to be made in any manner", cf. Sec. 14 below), and "public transport vehicle" (a ferry vessel, a land vehicle, or train which is transporting members of the public, but excluding a taxi cab, private hire vehicle, or other vehicle or vessel hired or chartered to an individual whether on his own behalf or that of a number of persons).

Part II. No smoking areas (Secs. 3-7). Sec. 3 (Prohibition on smoking in no smoking areas) reads as follows:

"**3.** No person shall smoke or carry a lighted cigarette, cigar or pipe in—

(*a*) any area demarcated as a no smoking area under section 4;

(*b*) any public lift;

(*c*) any land vehicle, being a public transport vehicle, having only one deck;

(*d*) the lower deck of a land vehicle, being a public transport vehicle, having more than one deck."

Sec. 4 (Setting aside of no smoking areas) requires managers of cinemas, theatres, or concert halls, and managers of public transport services (other than those covered by items (*c*) and (*d*) of Sec. 3), to designate not less than 50% of each class of their seating accommodation as a no smoking area, and empowers them to so designate all such accommodation. Seating accommodation identified by signs placed in compliance, or purported compliance, with Sec. 5 is deemed to be a no smoking area under this Section. Sec. 5 (Display of signs in no smoking areas) requires managers to place in a prominent position in each no smoking area a sufficient number of signs in English and Chinese indicating that smoking is prohibited. The signs must be of the prescribed description and must be maintained in legible condition and good order. Sec. 6 (Powers exercisable in relation to persons

---

[a] Under the terms of the Smoking (Public Health) Ordinance 1982 (Commencement) Notice 1982 (*Hong Kong Government Gazette*, Vol. 124, Legal Supplement No. 2 to No. 32, 13 August 1982, p. B767), all of the provisions of the Ordinance are due to have come into operation by 15 August 1983. — ED.

smoking in no smoking area) empowers managers (or ticket collectors, ushers, etc. authorized by managers) to require persons smoking in a no smoking area to cease smoking immediately or to give their name and address and produce proof of identity. Persons who fail to comply with such a requirement are deemed to be trespassing.

Part III. Sales of cigarettes and cigarette tobacco (Secs. 8-10). Secs. 8 and 9 read as follows:

"*Health warnings and tar group designation when cigarettes sold*

8. (1) No person shall sell, offer for sale or possess for the purposes of sale any cigarettes unless the packets thereof and, if the packets are within a retail container, the container also, bear in the prescribed form and manner—

(*a*) a health warning;

(*b*) the tar group designation of the cigarettes.

(2) Nothing in this section or section 9 shall apply to anything done in relation to cigarettes which are held—

(*a*) in bond; or

(*b*) by a manufacturer of tobacco products, for export from Hong Kong.

Health warnings when cigarette tobacco is sold

9. No person shall sell, offer for sale or possess for the purposes of sale any cigarette tobacco unless the container thereof bears a health warning in the prescribed form and manner."

Sec. 10 (Offences under Part III) designates various offences regarding incorrect or misleading tar group labelling.

Part IV. Cigarette advertising (Secs. 11-15). Secs. 11-14 read as follows:

"*Cigarette advertisements in printed publications*

11. (1) No person shall print or publish a cigarette advertisement in a printed publication to which this section applies unless the advertisement bears, in the prescribed form and manner—

(*a*) a health warning;

(*b*) the tar group designation of the cigarettes advertised.

(2) This section applies to—

(*a*) any local newspaper;

(*b*) any printed document published or distributed in Hong Kong, not being a newspaper or an advertisement published or distributed for the purpose of display.

(3) Nothing in this section or section 12 shall apply in relation to a cigarette advertisement in a printed publication—

(*a*) being a local newspaper—

(i) not less than 80 *per cent* of whose circulation is outside Hong Kong;

(ii) published for the passengers of any airline or shipping company;

(iii) published for the tobacco trade or as the 'in house' magazine of any company engaged in that trade;

(*b*) in such circumstances as may be prescribed.

Health warning when cigarette advertisement displayed

12. (1) No person shall—

(*a*) display;

(*b*) publish or distribute for the purpose of display,

any cigarette advertisement in writing or other permanent or semi-permanent form unless the advertisement has a health warning in the prescribed form and manner.

(2) Nothing in this section shall apply in relation to a cigarette advertisement—

(*a*) on any—

(i) small portable object, being of a decorative nature or for personal, domestic or business use;

(ii) object worn on the person;

(iii) umbrella,

if that object or umbrella carries a cigarette advertisement only because it bears the name or trade name of a person associated with the marketing of cigarettes or cigarette tobacco or a brand name of cigarettes or cigarette tobacco and additionally or alternatively any pictorial device commonly associated therewith, but which does not illustrate or mention cigarette tobacco or cigarettes or their packages or qualities or smoking;

(*b*) in or upon that part of the premises of any manufacturer of tobacco or tobacco products or any dealer (whether by way of wholesale or retail) in cigarettes or cigarette tobacco which is used for the manufacture of cigarettes or cigarette tobacco or for the purpose of dealing in cigarettes or cigarette tobacco;

(*c*) upon a commercial vehicle registered in the name of a person who is a manufacturer or distributor of, or wholesale dealer in, cigarettes or cigarette tobacco;

(*d*) broadcast by television;

(*e*) of such other categories as may be prescribed.

Cigarette advertisements on radio

13. (1) The Television Authority appointed under the Television Ordinance may from time to time issue Codes of Practice relating to cigarette advertisements broadcast by radio.

(2) Any Code of Practice issued under subsection (1) shall not be inconsistent with any prescribed conditions relating to the broadcast by radio of any cigarette advertisement.

(3) A Code of Practice issued under this section shall provide that when a cigarette advertisement is broadcast by radio a health warning shall also be broadcast in such manner and at such time as the Code may specify.

(4) No person shall broadcast by radio a cigarette advertisement which does not comply with a Code of Practice issued under this section or fail to broadcast a health warning in the manner and at the time specified in such a Code of Practice.

Meaning of cigarette advertisement

14. (1) For the purposes of this Part an advertisement is a cigarette advertisement if it—

(*a*) contains any express or implied inducement, suggestion or request to purchase or smoke cigarettes or cigarette tobacco; or (*b*) relates to smoking in terms which are calculated, expressly or impliedly, to promote or encourage the use of cigarettes or cigarette tobacco.

(2) An advertisement which mentions the name or trade name of any person associated with the marketing of cigarettes or cigarette tobacco or a brand name of cigarettes or cigarette tobacco or any pictorial device commonly associated therewith or which illustrates or mentions smoking or cigarettes or cigarette tobacco or their packages or qualities shall be deemed to be a cigarette advertisement unless the contrary is proved.

(3) Notwithstanding subsection (2), no advertisement shall be deemed to be a cigarette advertisement only because it uses the name or trade name or a brand name of, or otherwise identifies, a person associated with the manufacture or marketing of cigarettes or cigarette tobacco as the sponsor of an event as congratulating another person or thing on an achievement of, or event relating to, such person or thing.''

Part V. Supplementary (Secs. 16-18). Sec. 16 (Evidence of tar group) empowers the Government Chemist to analyse any cigarette for the purpose of determining the tar group to which it belongs and to publish the result of any such analysis. This result is deemed to be evidence of the tar group of the brand of cigarettes concerned.

Under Sec. 18 (Regulations and Orders), the Governor in Council is empowered to make regulations for the implementation of this Ordinance, and the Secretary for Social Services is empowered to prescribe by order in the *Gazette* the form of notices prohibiting smoking, health warnings, or tar group designations required or permitted under the Ordinance, and the manner in which they are to be displayed.

HONG KONG. The Smoking (Public Health) (Notices) Order 1982. L.N. 313 of 1982. Dated 10 August 1982. (*Hong Kong Government Gazette*, Vol. 124, Legal Supplement No. 2 to No. 32, 13 August 1982, pp. B762-B766) **HK 82.10**

Paragraphs 2-5 and 7 of this Order, which has been made in pursuance of the Smoking (Public Health) Ordinance 1982 (see p. 733, **HK 82.6**), read substantially as follows:

''*No smoking signs*

2. No smoking signs placed under section 5(1) of the Ordinance shall—

(*a*) read 'No Smoking' or 'Smoking Prohibited' and [*Chinese equivalent*];

(*b*) be in plain and readily legible letters or characters;

(*c*) be on a background of contrasting colour.

Cigarette packets and retail containers

3. (1) The form of the health warning and tar group designation which is to be borne on the packets of cigarettes containing less than 20 cigarettes shall be as set out in Part I of the Schedule.

(2) The form of the health warning and tar group designation which is to be borne on the packets of cigarettes containing 20 or more cigarettes and on the retail containers of cigarette packets, irrespective of the size of those packets, shall be as set out in Part II of the Schedule.

(3) The lettering and characters of any health warning and tar group designation prescribed in the Schedule shall be of a colour which contrasts with the colour

of the background upon which they are printed and, subject to this Order, the area within which the warning or designation is displayed, as indicated in the Schedule, shall not contain anything other than the warning and designation.

(4) [*Provisions concerning size of typeface*]

(5) The area within which any health warning or tar group designation is displayed shall be rectangular in shape, as indicated in the Schedule, and, although reasonable variations in the dimensions of the area shall be permissible, the sides of the area, and any line demarcating such sides, shall not touch any letter or character within the area.

(6) No health warning or tar group designation shall be printed—

(*a*) upon more than one face of the packet or container on which it appears; or

(*b*) across any opening in the packet or container or upon any part of a packet which is removed when it is opened;

(*c*) except on the outside of a packet or container.

Cigarette tobacco

4. Paragraphs 3(2), 3(3), 3(4)(*b*), 3(5), 3(6) and Part II of the Schedule shall apply in the case of the health warning to be borne by containers of cigarette tobacco, save that such containers shall not bear a tar group designation.

Advertisements

5. (1) The provisions of this paragraph shall apply to any advertisement which is required to carry a health warning under the provisions of Part IV of the Ordinance.

(2) In this paragraph and paragraph 6 'the prescribed particulars' mean the health warning, as prescribed under sub-paragraph (3), and the tar group designation, where the advertisement is one to which section 11 of the Ordinance applies, as determined in accordance with the Smoking (Public Health) Regulations 1982 [see *supra*] as read with paragraph 7.

(3) The health warning shall be as set out in Part III of the Schedule.

(4) The prescribed particulars shall be—

(*a*) placed in a separate panel within the advertisement which—

(i) is distinguished from the remainder of the advertisement by means either of a line or by being of a different colour;

(ii) occupies not less than 10 *per cent* of the surface of the advertisement;

(iii) subject to this Order, contains nothing other than the prescribed particulars;

(*b*) in a colour which contrasts with the background upon which they appear, being black or a colour used elsewhere in the advertisement;

(*c*) in the language of the advertisement;

(*d*) if in English, in capital letters;

(*e*) properly displayed in a manner appropriate to the size and shape of the panel in which they are displayed.

(5) Where both a health warning and a tar group designation appear, they shall be in words or characters of the same size and style."

"*Additional provisions applying to tar group designations*

7. (1) [*Chinese equivalents of tar group designations*]

(2) The tar group designation may be followed by the word 'Group' in English or [*Chinese equivalent*].

(3) In the case of an advertisement appearing in a printed publication to which section 11 of the Ordinance applies, where the tar group designation has been determined under regulation 4 of the Smoking (Public Health) Regulations 1982 the words 'Manufacturers Estimate' in English and [*Chinese equivalent*] shall appear immediately after the words or characters indicative of the tar group designation and may appear after the tar group designation on cigarette packets and retail containers.

(4) Where more than one brand of cigarettes is illustrated in or referred to in an advertisement appearing in a printed publication to which section 11 of the Ordinance applies and the brands have different tar group designations, the designation of each brand shall be stated and each designation shall be given equal prominence."

The health warning, as set out in the various Schedules to the Order, reads as follows:

"HK GOVERNMENT HEALTH WARNING: CIGARETTE SMOKING IS HAZARDOUS TO YOUR HEALTH."

HONG KONG. The Smoking (Public Health) Regulations 1982. L.N. 311 of 1982. Dated 10 August 1982. (*Hong Kong Government Gazette*, Vol. 124, Legal Supplement No. 2 to No. 32, 13 August 1982, pp. B758-B760) **HK 82.9**

Reg. 2 of these Regulations, which have been made in pursuance of the Smoking (Public Health) Ordinance 1982 (see *supra*), prescribes that the tar group designations for cigarettes under the terms of the Ordinance are as follows (the figures indicate the tar content in mg per cigarette): 0-10 — low tar; 11-16 — low to middle tar; 17-22 — middle tar; 23-28 — middle to high tar; and 29 and over — high tar. Reg. 3 (Determination by the Government Chemist) prescribes that, where the Government Chemist has published a determination under Sec. 16 of the Ordinance, the brand of cigarettes concerned is to be designated as belonging to the tar group indicated by that determination. Reg. 4 (Determination by the proprietor of the brand) prescribes that, where there has been no determination by the Government Chemist or where the manufacturer has altered the tar content and thereby rendered the previous designation incorrect, the tar group is to be determined by the proprietor of the brand or his agent. Reg. 6 (Notification of retail sales) requires wholesale distributors of cigarettes to notify the Director of Medical and Health Services within two days following the first offer for sale by retail of cigarettes bearing on their packets or retail containers a tar group designation determined under Reg. 4.

HONG KONG. The Smoking (Public Health) (Notices) (Amendment) Order 1983. L.N. 61 of 1983. Dated 22 February 1983. (*Hong Kong Government Gazette*, Vol. 125, Legal Supplement No. 2 to No. 8, 25 February 1983, pp. B145-B147) **HK 83.3**

A number of amendments are made to the Smoking (Public Health) (Notices) Order 1982 (see *IDHL*, 1982, **33**, 736, **HK 82.10**).

The following new sub-paragraph 7 is inserted in paragraph 3 (Cigarette packets and retail containers):

"(7) The health warning and tar group designation which is to be borne on packets of cigarettes and on the retail containers of cigarette packets may be printed on a label securely affixed to the packets or containers—

(*a*) if the packets or containers are of metal or are plastic drums;

(*b*) with the approval of the Commissioner of Customs and Excise where he is satisfied—

(i) the circumstances in which the packets or containers are in Hong Kong, or are to be brought to Hong Kong, are such that they could not reasonably be expected to have had printed on them a warning and designation at the time of their manufacture; and

(ii) the approval is required for a limited period of time or in relation to a particular consignment of cigarettes only."

Paragraph 5 (Advertisements) is amended by the insertion of new sub-paragraphs 6-8; these "deal with problems created by advertisements lacking a written message other than the brand name, by advertisements on more than one plane and by neon signs" (the quotation is from the Explanatory Note appended to the Order). In addition, the Schedule is amended by the introduction of an alternative form of health warning and tar group designation for use on packets containing 20 or more cigarettes.

HONG KONG. An Ordinance (No. 26 of 1984) to amend the Smoking (Public Health) Ordinance. Dated 18 May 1984. (The Smoking (Public Health) (Amendment) Ordinance 1984). (*Hong Kong Government Gazette*, Vol. 126, Legal Supplement No. 1 to No. 20, 18 May 1984, p. A242) **HK 84.7**

This Ordinance was originally presented to the Legislative Council as the Smoking (Public Health) (Amendment) Bill. The Explanatory Memorandum appended to the Bill reads substantially as follows:

"This Bill makes certain amendments to the Smoking (Public Health) Ordinance [see *IDHL*, 1982, **33**, 733, **HK 82.6**] in relation to cigarette advertising.

2. Under section 11 of the Ordinance cigarette advertisements in a locally printed newspaper need not bear a health warning or tar group designation if not less than 80% of the newspaper's circulation is outside Hong Kong. Clause 2 of the Bill amends section 11 to add a further requirement that for such advertisements to be exempt, the newspaper's circulation *within* Hong Kong must not exceed a figure from time to time specified by the Governor in Council by notice. Other specific exemptions relating to the passenger magazines of airline and shipping companies and the 'in house' magazines of the tobacco trade remain unchanged.

3. Under section 12 of the Ordinance cigarette advertisements for display are required to bear a health warning, unless the advertisements are in a category specifically exempted. Clause 3 amends section 12 to remove the following exempted categories—

(*a*) advertisements on small portable objects, clothing and umbrellas, which consist only of a brand name or logo;

(*b*) advertisements in or upon the premises of a manufacturer of, or dealer in, tobacco products; and

(*c*) advertisements on the commercial vehicles of a manufacturer or distributor of, or wholesale dealer in, cigarettes or cigarette tobacco.

It is intended that the exemption of categories (*a*) and (*b*) above will be re-enacted in regulations and will continue for the present time, although category (*b*) will be in modified form.

4. .....''

HONG KONG. The Smoking (Public Health) (Specification of Newspaper Circulation) Notice 1984. L.N. 156 of 1984. Dated 12 June 1984. (*Hong Kong Government Gazette*, Vol. 126, Legal Supplement No. 2 to No. 24, 15 June 1984, p. B377) **HK 84.9**

The Explanatory Note appended to this Notice reads as follows:

"Under section 11 of the Smoking (Public Health) Ordinance [see *supra*], cigarette advertisements in a locally printed newspaper need not bear a health warning or tar group designation if the circulation of the newspaper within Hong Kong is not more than 20 *per cent* of total circulation and does not exceed a figure specified by the Governor in Council. This notice specifies a figure of 10,000."

HONG KONG. The Smoking (Public Health) (Amendment) Regulations 1984. L.N. 155 of 1984. Dated 12 June 1984. (*Hong Kong Government Gazette*, Vol. 126, Legal Supplement No. 2 to No. 24, 15 June 1984, pp. B375-B376) **HK 84.8**

The Explanatory Note appended to these Regulations reads as follows:

"These regulations amend the principal regulations to prescribe two categories of cigarette advertisements which are exempt from the requirement to carry a health warning as provided by section 12 of the Smoking (Public Health) Ordinance [see *IDHL*, 1982, **33**, 733, **HK 82.6**].

2. Both exemptions were formerly prescribed in the Ordinance. However, the exemption relating to cigarette manufacturers' and dealers' premises has now been modified to exclude retailers' premises, and is further restricted to advertisements which are not visible from outside the premises of the manufacturer or wholesale dealer."

HONG KONG. An Ordinance (No. 62 of 1986) to amend the Public Health and Municipal Services Ordinance. Dated 14 November 1986. (The Public Health and Municipal Services (Amendment) (No. 2) Ordinance 1986). (*Hong Kong Government Gazette*, Vol. 128, Legal Supplement No. 1 to No. 46, 14 November 1986, pp. A379-A380) **HK 87.12**

The following are the principal amendments introduced to the principal Ordinance.

Sec. 2(*a*) amends Sec. 2(1) by deleting the existing definition of "food" and substituting a new definition that includes smokeless tobacco products. Sec. 2(*b*) amends Sec. 2(1) of the principal Ordinance by inserting a definition of "smokeless tobacco product". The definition includes chewing tobacco and moist snuff but excludes tobacco subject to combustion and dry snuff taken by inhalation. Sec. 3 amends Sec. 51(1) of the principal Ordinance by deleting the existing paragraph (*b*) and substituting a new version therefor. The existing text, insofar as it relates to food and drugs which "may be prejudicial to public health", only provides for regulations to be made prohibiting, restricting, or regulating the "importation" of such food and drugs. The new paragraph (*b*) provides that such prohibition or regulation may, in addition to importation, extend to the manufacture, sale, possession for sale, offer or exposure for sale, or consignment or delivery of such food or drugs.

HONG KONG. The Smokeless Tobacco Products (Prohibition) Regulations 1987. L.N. 9 of 1987. Dated 6 January 1987. (*Hong Kong Government Gazette*, Vol. 129, Legal Supplement No. 2 to No. 3, January 1987, p. B39) **HK 87.13**

These Regulations have been made by the Governor in Council under Sec. 55 of the Public Health and Municipal Services Ordinance, as amended by Ordinance No. 62 of 1986 (see *supra*). They prescribe (in Reg. 3) that no person may import, manufacture, sell, possess for sale, offer or expose for sale, consign, or deliver any smokeless tobacco product.

HONG KONG. An Ordinance (No. 56 of 1987) to establish the Hong Kong Council on Smoking and Health, to define its functions and powers, to negative personal liability of members and employees, and to provide for matters incidental thereto or connected therewith. Dated 16 July 1987. (The Hong Kong Council on Smoking and Health Ordinance 1987). (*Hong Kong Government Gazette*, Vol. 129, Legal Supplement No. 1 to No. 29, 17 July 1987, pp. A 405-A413) **HK 88.5**

This Ordinance is to come into operation on a date to be appointed by the Governor by notice in the *Gazette*. Sec. 3 provides for the establishment of the Council referred to in the title. Its purposes are laid down in Sec. 3(2), which reads as follows:

"(2) The purposes of the Council are to—

(*a*) protect and to improve the health of the community by acquiring and disseminating, and assisting others to acquire and to disseminate, information concerning the causes, prevention and cure of tobacco dependence in human beings and its adverse effects and related diseases;

(*b*) engage in research into the causes, prevention and cure of tobacco dependence in human beings and its adverse effects and related diseases and to promote and to assist such research by other individuals and organizations, and to publish the results of such research;

(*c*) advance the education of the public concerning the effects of the smoking of tobacco and other forms of usage of tobacco and its effects on the health of the community and the individual;

(*d*) take such action as it thinks justified by information in its possession including giving advice to the Government, to any public body, to any public officer, to community health organizations, or to the public on the causes, prevention and cure of tobacco dependence in human beings and its adverse effects and related diseases;

(*e*) engage in such other activities, and to perform such other functions, as the Governor may, after consultation with the Council, permit or assign to it by order published in the *Gazette*."

ICELAND

ICELAND. Law No. 74 of 28 May 1984 on the prevention of the use of tobacco.[a] (*Stjórnartídindi*, 1984, Part A, 4 pp.) **Icel. 84.1**

The following are among the principal provisions of this Law, which repeals Law No. 27 of 11 May 1977 prescribing measures to reduce smoking (see *IDHL*, 1979, **30**, 570).

Chapter I. Objectives, scope, and administration (Secs. 1-5). Sec. 1.1 prescribes that the purpose of this Law is to reduce the consumption of tobacco, thereby limiting its damage to health, and to protect persons against the effects of tobacco smoke. Secs 2.1-2.2 provide a detailed interpretation of the term "tobacco". It is laid down (in Sec. 2.3) that the Law does not apply to tobacco used as a drug in accordance with the Pharmaceuticals Law (No. 49) of 1978 (see *ibid*, 1980, **31**, 330) or as a toxic substance in accordance with Law No. 85 of 1968 on toxic and hazardous substances (see *ibid.*, 1971, **22**, 470). Sec. 3.1 defines the term "smokers' perquisites". Under Sec. 4.1, overall surveillance of the implementation of this Law is assigned to the Minister of Health and Social Security. Sec. 5.1 provides for the appointment by the Minister of a Committee for the Prevention of the Use of Tobacco, consisting of three members at least two of whom are to be experts on the harmful effects of tobacco or on measures to prevent its use. The principal functions of the Committee, as laid down in Sec. 5.2, are as follows: (1) to advise the Government, the Minister of Health and Social Security, the National Centre for Hygiene, Food Control, and Environmental Protection, the Directorate of Occupational Safety and Health, and other public agencies on all matters relating to the prevention of the use of tobacco; (2) to submit proposals to the authorities regarding measures to control the use of tobacco in accordance with this Law; (3) to encourage other parties to launch anti-smoking campaigns and endeavour to coordinate such activities; (4) to provide assistance and instruction on anti-smoking activities, for example by publishing and distributing informational literature and other related materials; (5) to keep records of the consumption of tobacco in the country; and (6) to utilize the experience and knowledge of other countries in the field of smoking control. Sec. 5.3 lays down that the Ministry of Finance is to consult the Committee on policy regarding the importation and pricing of tobacco. Under Sec. 5.4, the opinion of the Committee is to be sought on all regulations concerning the prevention of the use of tobacco and the sale of tobacco. Sec. 5.5 indicates that the Committee is to cooperate with various other bodies, while Sec. 5.6 empowers the Minister to issue further provisions, by way of regulations, concerning the duties and functions of the Committee.

Chapter II. Sale and advertising (Secs. 6-8). The provisions of this Chapter read as follows:

"*Section 6*

6.1 Tobacco may be sold or distributed only on condition that a warning as to the harmful effect of the product is printed on the packaging.

[a] This summary is based on an English translation prepared in Iceland. — ED.

6.2 The Minister shall lay down, by way of regulations, detailed provisions on the labelling of such packaging, for example on the warning notice, its size, type of lettering, and other relevant matters.

6.3 Tobacco manufacturers shall defray the costs of labelling required in accordance with this Section.

Section 7

7.1 Advertising of any kind for tobacco and smokers' perquisites shall be prohibited in the country. However, the foregoing sentence shall not apply to advertising in foreign publications by foreign persons, provided that the principal objective of the publications is not the advertising of such products.

7.2 Similarly, advertising or information relating to other kinds of products or services may not depict the use of tobacco or smokers' perquisites or carry any kind of display of such products.

7.3 For the purposes of this Law, advertising shall include, *inter alia*, all kinds of public announcements, replicas of tobacco products, signs and similar devices, window displays, and the use of the brand names and distinctive marks of tobacco.

Section 8

8.1 Tobacco may not be sold to persons under 16 years of age.

8.2 The sale of tobacco from automatic vending-machines shall be prohibited.

8.3 Tobacco may not be sold in schools or institutions for children and adolescents."

Chapter III. Restrictions on tobacco smoking (Secs. 9-13). Sec. 9.1 prescribes that tobacco smoking is prohibited in those parts of the premises of institutions and undertakings and the like that are accessible to the public in connection with the services provided by such institutions and undertakings. This does not apply to restaurants and places of entertainment; however, such establishments must at all times reserve for their guests a specified number of tables at which smoking is prohibited, this being indicated by conspicuous notices. Sec. 10.1 prohibits smoking: (1) in basic schools and day nurseries, and on premises primarily intended for the social and leisure activities of children and adolescents under 16 years of age; (2) at indoor public meetings for children and adolescents if the age of admission is under 16; and (3) in health centres. Sec. 10.2 empowers the persons in charge of the above-mentioned institutions, etc. to permit smoking by personnel in those parts of the premises that are specifically intended for personnel (care must be taken to ensure that no inconvenience is caused thereby to non-smoking personnel). Under Sec. 10.3, smoking may be permitted in hospitals only in specific places where non-smokers are not inconvenienced. Sec. 11.1 authorizes persons in charge of premises accessible to the public but to which Secs. 9 and 10 do not apply to decide on their own initiative to restrict smoking on the premises. Any such decision is to be conspicuously displayed on the premises and notified to the authorities indicated. Sec. 12.1 lays down that tobacco smoking in workplaces other than those mentioned in Secs. 9 and 10 is to be conditional upon the adoption of further regulations in consultation with the Directorate of Occupational Safety and Health. Particular care must be taken to ensure that non-smokers are not inconvenienced. Sec. 13.1 prohibits smoking in the passenger sections of public transport vehicles carrying fare-paying passengers. Under Sec. 13.2, aircraft operators may permit smoking in parts of the passenger section during international commercial flights; however, care must always be taken to ensure that non-smokers are not inconvenienced. Sec. 13.3 lays down that special regulations governing smoking on board ship are to be adopted in consultation with the State Directorate of Shipping.

Chapter IV. Information activities (Sec. 14). The provisions of this Section read as follows:

"14.1 The Ministry of Education, in consultation with the Ministry of Health and Social Security, shall arrange for regular instruction concerning the harmful effects of the use of tobacco:

1. in the country's schools. Particular emphasis shall be laid on such instruction in basic schools and institutions preparing persons for work in the fields of education, teaching, and health care; and
2. in State-owned media.

14.2 The Ministry of Health and Social Security shall provide support to persons wishing to give up smoking:

1. through health centres; and
2. by means of courses given in cooperation with societies, institutions, and undertakings."

Chapter V. General provisions (Secs. 15-16). Sec. 15.1 prescribes that 0.2% of the proceeds from the gross sales of tobacco is to be spent on anti-smoking activities. Under Sec. 15.2, the Committee for the Prevention of the Use of Tobacco is to submit proposals to the Minister for the utilization of the proceeds. Sec. 16.1 empowers the Minister to issue further provisions, by way of regulations, for the implementation of this Law.

Chapter VI. Supervision and penalties (Secs. 17-21). Various penal and administrative matters connected with the implementation of the Law are laid down.

Chapter VII. Entry into force (Sec. 22). This Law entered into force on 1 January 1985.

Transitional provisions. It is laid down, *inter alia*, that regulations under Sec. 6.2 regarding the labelling of tobacco are to be drawn up forthwith and are to come into effect on the same date as the Law.

ICELAND. Regulations No. 499 of 28 December 1984 concerning warnings on tobacco products.[a] (2 pp.) **Icel. 86.15**

These Regulations have been made by the Ministry of Health and Social Security in pursuance of Sec. 6 of Law No. 74 of 28 May 1984, on the prevention of the use of tobacco (see *IDHL*, 1984, **35**, 772, **Icel. 84.1**).

Sec. 1 prescribes that tobacco may be sold or distributed by the State Wine, Spirit and Tobacco Monopoly only on condition that a warning of the harmful effects of the product is printed on each package. Provision is made in Sec. 2 for a series of alternative warnings (to be used with equal frequency), details being given of the way they are to appear on cigarette packets, the packaging of cigars and pipe tobacco, and the packaging of snuff and chewing-tobacco. Provision is likewise made for the Minister of Health and Social Security, acting on the proposal of the Committee for the Prevention of the Use of Tobacco, to alter the warnings.

Secs. 3 and 4 deal with financial and penal matters respectively, while transitional provisions are laid down in a concluding (unnumbered) paragraph.

---

[a] The Icelandic version of these Regulations was not available. This summary is based on a translation prepared in Iceland. — ED.

The alternative warnings, given in an Annex, are as follows (the words "Director General of Public Health" appear after each legend): 1. Smoking during pregnancy endangers the health of mother and child; 2. Smoking may damage your arteries and cause heart attacks; 3. Protect children from tobacco smoke; 4. If you stop smoking you improve your health; 5. Smoking is a health problem you can help to solve; 6. Hundreds of Icelanders die each year due to smoking; 7. Tobacco smoke pollutes the air and is a health hazard; and 8. Snuff and chewing-tobacco may damage the mucous membranes.

Warnings 1-6 are to be used for cigarettes, 3 and 7 for cigars and pipe tobacco, and 8 for snuff and chewing-tobacco.

INDIA

INDIA. No. 27/1/3/90–Cab. GOVERNMENT OF INDIA (BHARAT SARKAR). CABINET SECRETARIAT (MANTRIMANDAL SACHIVALAYA). New Delhi, the 7th May, 1990. 17 Vaisakha, 1912(S).

OFFICE MEMORANDUM

Subject: Prohibition of tobacco smoking in Public Places.

1. The Central Government have been viewing with concern the increasing scientific evidence of non-smoking public being exposed to serious health hazards due to exposure to passive smoking in the proximity of tobacco smokers. There has been a widespread public demand that measures be taken to protect this majority of non-smoking public from the polluting impact of tobacco smoking by a small minority. Further, there is a need to save smokers from their own excesses.
2. In order to protect the non-smoking public from the hazards of passive smoking, at least in Public Places where large number of people are expected to be present for prolonged periods, it has been decided to prohibit tobacco smoking to start with, in a few selected places, namely, hospitals, dispensaries and other health care establishments, educational institutions, conference rooms, domestic airflights, airconditioned chaircars and air-conditioned sleeper coaches in trains, suburban trains and air-conditioned buses.
3. The ban, referred to above, will become into effect after 30 days from the issue of this Office Memorandum and will be strictly enforced.
4. Ministries and Departments may issue appropriate instructions to the various authorities under their control to ensure implementation of these orders. The authorities concerned should take steps to clearly identify the non-smoking areas/buildings. No ashtrays should be placed in non-smoking areas and all cigarette shops removed from the compound of buildings in which smoking is prohibited.
5. Copies of the orders issued may be endorsed to Cabinet Secretariat.

Secretary (Coordination)

To,

(All Ministries/Departments of Government of India).
Secretaries to the Govt. of India.

Copy to: (i) Secretary, Ministry of Environment and Forests, and
(ii) Secretary, Ministry of Health & Family Welfare, with the request that suitable campaign may be mounted regarding the risks and hazards of smoking and the pollutant effect on environment to enable the ban to be subsequently extended to all public places.

Accompaniment to Cabinet Secretariat's O.M. No. 27/1/3/90-Cab. dated 7th May, 1990

Guidelines for ban on smoking

(1) In every room of the office or institution a Board having the following words may be displayed in Hindi & English.

"NO SMOKING"

(2) Similar boards should be displayed on the wall outside every room of the institution or office, if there is ample vacant space available for example: Corridor, Out patient Department, Meeting Hall, etc., such boards in Hindi and English as above should be displayed at a distance of every 3 metres.

(3) At every entrance of the building, the following words should be displayed prominently in Hindi and English with suitable visuals:–
"Smoking strictly prohibited inside this building and compound".

(4) A similar board should also be displayed at the entrance of the compound of the building.

(5) All these boards should be of a permanent nature i.e. wooden, tin or plastic material. If some period is likely to be taken for preparation of the permanent boards, temporarily paper or card boards should be displayed.

(6) The boards on the wall should be at a minimum height of 1.5 meter.

(7) All ash-trays should be removed from the rooms and other places of the office/institution.

(8) All cigarette shops in the building or in the compound of the building, should be moved outside the compound of the building.

IRELAND

IRELAND. The Health (Restricted Article) Order, 1985. S.I. No. 429 of 1985. Dated 20 December 1985. (3 pp.) **Irel. 86.7**

The effect of this Order is to make "tobacco in the form of finely-cut, moist tobacco contained in sachets or pouches and intended for use by being placed in the mouth" a restricted article under Sec. 66 of the Health Act, 1947 (see *IDHL*, 1949, **1**, 245). Under this Section, it is an offence for a person, unless authorized by a permit granted by the Minister for Health, to import, manufacture, sell or otherwise dispose of, keep for sale or other disposal or advertise, a restricted article.

IRELAND. The Tobacco Products (Control of Advertising, Sponsorship and Sales Promotion) Regulations, 1986. S.I. No. 7 of 1986. Dated 17 January 1986. (15 pp.) **Irel. 86.8**

These Regulations have been made by the Minister for Health under powers conferred by Sec. 2 of the Tobacco Products (Control of Advertising, Sponsorship and Sales Promotion) Act 1978 (see *IDHL*, 1979, **30**, 806). The Explanatory Note appended to the Regulations reads as follows:

"These Regulations control the promotion of tobacco products by means of advertising, sponsorship and certain other promotional activities. They replace the Tobacco Products (Control of Advertising, Sponsorship and Sales Promotion) Regulations, 1979 [see *IDHL*, 1980, **31**, 537]. The effect of the Regulations is:—

— to restrict the media which may be used for tobacco advertising,

— to limit the content of advertisements of tobacco products,

— to require that advertisements for, and packages of, tobacco products display in rotation a number of health warnings,

— to provide for the curtailment of expenditure on advertising of tobacco products and sponsorship, by tobacco companies,

— to limit the form which advertising associated with sponsored events may take, and

— to prohibit the use of coupons, gifts, cut-price offers and sale promotions in relation to tobacco products.

The Regulations come into operation on the lst of July, 1986."

The following alternative approved statements are to appear on advertisements for, and packages of, cigarettes: (*a*) "SMOKING CAUSES CANCER"; (*b*) "SMOKERS DIE YOUNGER"; and (*c*) "SMOKING KILLS!". The corresponding statement in respect of advertisements for, and packages of, pipe tobacco, cigars, and cigarillos, is as follows: "SMOKING SERIOUSLY DAMAGES YOUR HEALTH". The corresponding statement in regard to advertisements for, and packages of, chewing-tobacco, is as follows: "THIS PRODUCT MAY CAUSE ORAL CANCER". Each of the above statements is to terminate on a separate line with the attribution "Government Warning".

IRELAND. The Tobacco Products (Control of Advertising, Sponsorship and Sales Promotion) (No. 2) Regulations, 1986. S.I. No. 107 of 1986. Dated 9 May 1986. (17 pp.) **Irel. 86.9**

The Explanatory Note appended to these Regulations reads as follows:

"These Regulations control the promotion of tobacco products by means of advertising, sponsorship and certain other promotional activities. They replace the Tobacco Products (Control of Advertising, Sponsorship and Sales Promotion) Regulations, 1979 [see *IDHL*, 1980, **31**, 537]. The effect of the Regulations is:—

— to restrict the media which may be used for tobacco advertising,

— to limit the content of advertisements of tobacco products,

— to require that advertisements for, and packages of, tobacco products display in rotation a number of health warnings,

— to provide for the curtailment of expenditure on advertising of tobacco products and sponsorship, by tobacco companies,

— to limit the form which advertising associated with sponsored events may take, and

— to prohibit the use of coupons, gifts, cut-price offers and sales promotions in relation to tobacco products.

The Regulations come into operation on the 1st of December, 1986."

IRELAND. An Act (No. 24 of 1988) to provide for the prohibition and restriction on the consumption of tobacco products in designated areas and facilities; to provide for the restriction on the sale of tobacco products to persons under the age of 16 years; to make provision in relation to the importation, manufacture and sale of certain tobacco products; to provide for the amendment of the Tobacco Products (Control of Advertising, Sponsorship and Sales Promotion) Act, 1978; and to provide for other connected matters. Dated 12 July 1988. (The Tobacco (Health Promotion and Protection) Act, 1988). (6 pp.)

Irel. 89.4

This Act includes substantive Sections dealing with the following matters: the imposition of prohibitions or restrictions on the consumption of tobacco products in designated areas or designated facilities (Sec. 2); restrictions on the sale of tobacco products to persons under 16 years of age (Sec. 3); restrictions on the sale of cigarettes other than in packets containing 10 or more cigarettes (Sec. 4); and amendments to the Tobacco Products (Control of Advertising, Sponsorship and Sales Promotion) Act, 1978 (see *IDHL*, 1979, **30**, 806) (Sec. 9).

Secs. 5 (Prohibition on use of specified constituents of tobacco products) and 6 (Prohibition on import etc. of oral smokeless tobacco products) read substantially as follows:

"**5.** (1) A person engaged in the manufacture of tobacco products shall, whenever the Minister so requests, notify the Minister of any constituent of the tobacco product, other than tobacco, water or reconstituted sheet made wholly from tobacco, and of the amount of such constituent, used in the manufacture of such products.

(2) Any person who imports a tobacco product shall, whenever the Minister so requests, notify the Minister of any constituent of the tobacco product, other than tobacco, water or reconstituted sheet made wholly from tobacco, and of the amount of such constituent which is contained in the tobacco product so imported.

(3) The Minister, after consulting with the tobacco manufacturer or tobacco importer concerned, may by regulations—

(*a*) control or prohibit the use in the manufacture of tobacco products of such constituent of the tobacco product (other than tobacco, water or reconstituted sheet made wholly from tobacco) as may be specified in the regulations.

(*b*) prohibit or restrict the importation of any tobacco product which contains such constituent (other than tobacco, water or reconstituted sheet made wholly from tobacco) as may be specified in the regulations.

(4) [*Penal provisions*]

6. (1) Any person who imports, manufactures, sells or otherwise disposes of, or offers for sale or other disposal, or advertises, an oral smokeless tobacco product shall be guilty of an offence and shall be liable—

(*a*) on summary conviction, to a fine not exceeding £1,000, or

(*b*) on conviction on indictment to a fine not exceeding £10,000.

(2) In this section 'oral smokeless tobacco product' means any product or substance, made wholly or partly from tobacco, which is intended for use, unlit, by being placed in the mouth and kept there for a period, or by being placed in the mouth and sucked or chewed."

IRELAND. The Tobacco (Health Promotion and Protection) Regulations, 1990. S.I. No. 39 of 1990. Dated 23 February 1990. (14 pp.) **Irel. 90.2**

These Regulations have been made by the Minister for Health under powers conferred by Sec. 2 of the Tobacco (Health Promotion and Protection) Act, 1988 (see *IDHL*, 1989, **40**, 103, **Irel. 89.4**). Their effect is to prohibit and/or restrict the consumption of tobacco products in various public areas and facilities, as indicated in the text.

ISRAEL

ISRAEL. The Restriction on Smoking (Public Places) Law, 1983. Dated 26 July 1983.[a] (*Sefer Ha-Chukkim*, No. 1090, 4 August 1983, p. 148) **Isr. 84.2**

Sec. 1. of this Law reads as follows:

"**1.** (*a*) No person may smoke in a place specified in the Schedule (hereinafter referred to as a 'public place').

(*b*) No person may hold a lighted cigarette, cigarillo, cigar, or pipe in a public place.

(*c*) The Minister of Health may amend the Schedule by order with the approval of the Labour and Social Affairs Committee of the Parliament [*Knesset*]".

Sec. 2 deals with the affixing of signs drawing attention to the prohibition of smoking in public places, etc. The Minister of Health is empowered to issue regulations on this matter.

Various administrative, enforcement, and penal provisions are laid down in Secs. 3-9. Sec. 10 prescribes that the provisions of this Law are in addition to and do not derogate from any provision as to the prohibition of smoking laid down by any other law. Sec. 13 assigns responsibility for the implementation of this Law to the Minister of Health, who may, with the approval of the above-mentioned Committee, make regulations for its implementation, including regulations as to procedures for supervising such implementation.

A list of public places as referred to in Sec. 1 is given in the Schedule. These include the following item: "Any place in a hospital or clinic building, except a place allocated by the hospital or clinic management where smoking is permitted, provided it is not a place intended for the accommodation, treatment, or examination of patients".

ISRAEL. The Criminal Procedure (Violations Subjects to a Fine — Smoking Restrictions in Public Places) Order, 1986.[a] (*Kovetz Hatakkanot*, 27 April 1986, No. 4928, pp. 826) **Isr. 88.7**

This Order establishes the procedure whereby "tickets" are served upon persons violating the law restricting smoking in public places and indicates the fines to which first offenders and repeat offenders are liable.[b]

---

[a] This summary is based on a translation prepared in Israel. — ED.

[a] This summary is based on an English summary prepared by the Ministry of Health, Jerusalem. — ED.

[b] WHO has been informed that Regulations are being prepared that would broaden the scope of the definition of "public places" and would include control of smoking in the workplace. — ED.

ISRAEL. The Aircraft (Operation of Aircraft and Flight Rules) (Amendment) Regulations, 1987.[c] (*Kovetz Hatakkanot*, 17 December 1987, No. 5071, pp. 263-264) **Isr. 88.18**

These Regulations, which have been made by the Minister of Transport, prohibit smoking on board Israeli aircraft, other than in certain circumstances (notably on commercial flights of more than two hours' duration, under the conditions indicated).

[c] This summary is based on an English translation prepared by the Ministry of Health, Jerusalem. — ED.

IVORY COAST

IVORY COAST. Decree No. 79-477 of 6 June 1979 prohibiting smoking in certain public premises. (*Journal officiel de la République de Côte d'Ivoire*, 21 June 1979, No. 30, p. 1344) **Iv. C. 81.1**

Sec. 1 of this Decree prohibits smoking in schools, places of entertainment, public or private hospitals, or health establishments, and lifts. Sec. 2 requires a certain number of seats to be reserved for non-smokers in all road or rail vehicles or aircraft. Sec. 3 requires no-smoking signs to be posted visibly in the above-mentioned places.

JORDAN

JORDAN. Rules No. 64 of 10 August 1977 on the protection of public health against the hazards of smoking. (2 pp.) **Jord. 82.1**

Sec. 2 of these Rules contains a number of definitions, including "public place" (any cinema, theatre, public library, public transport vehicle, or any other place which, by decision of the Minister of Health published in the official gazette, is declared to be a public place for the purposes of these Rules). Sec. 3 prohibits smoking in all public places during the hours in which such places are used by the public (however, a special smoking area may be designated in a public place in accordance with conditions laid down by the Minister). Sec. 4 prohibits the printing, display, or publication of any kind of advertisement for tobacco. Sec. 5 prohibits the manufacture or sale in Jordan, or the import into Jordan, of tobacco imitations (including cigarette candy). Sec. 6 requires manufacturers or importers of tobacco to affix in a conspicuous part of the package or container of the product as exhibited for sale a label containing such particulars as are specified by the Minister.

JORDAN. Ordinance No. 1 of 1980 of the Ministry of Health. (1 p.) **Jord. 82.2**

Under the terms of this Ordinance, which has been made in pursuance of Rules No. 64 of 10 August 1977 on the protection of public health against the hazards of smoking (see *supra*), the following health warning must appear in red in a conspicuous part of the package or container of any domestic or imported tobacco product that is exhibited for sale: "Smoking is a major cause of lung cancer and pulmonary and cardiovascular diseases."

KENYA

KENYA. The Public Health (Warning on Cigarette Smoking) Rules, 1984. Legal Notice No. 122. Dated 31 July 1984. (*Kenya Gazette Supplement No. 52 (Legislative Supplement No. 34)*, 10 August 1984, pp. 371-372) **Ken. 85.5**

These Rules have been made by the Minister for Health under powers conferred by Sec. 169 of the Public Health Act. Rule 2 lays down that no person may import or sell any cigarettes in Kenya unless there is printed on the packet a warning in English and Swahili in the form prescribed under Rule 3. Rule 3 reads as follows:

"**3.** The warning which shall be clearly and prominently printed on all cigarette packets shall be as follows—

MINISTRY OF HEALTH WARNING

CIGARETTE SMOKING CAN BE HARMFUL TO YOUR HEALTH

[*Swahili equivalent*]"

Under Rule 4, the information required to be printed on a cigarette packet must not be placed at the bottom or on top of the packet. Rule 5 deals with the manner in which the warning is to be displayed. Penal provisions are laid down in Rule 6.

KUWAIT

KUWAIT. Ministerial Resolution No. 25 of 1980 on the particulars to be stated on cigarette packages. (*Al-Kuwait Al-Youm*, Vol. 26, No. 1297, 20 April 1980, p. 5; corrigendum, *ibid.*, Vol. 26, No. 1299, 4 May 1980, p. 6)

Kuw. 81.1

Under the provisions of Sec. 1 of this Resolution, the packages of all cigarettes and cigars imported into Kuwait must bear the following warning: "Smoking is a leading cause of lung cancer and of pulmonary and cardiovascular diseases".[a]

KUWAIT. Ministerial Decree No. 180 of 28 April 1988 laying down detailed provisions on the analysis of the components of imported cigarettes. (*Al-Kuwait Al-Yom*, 8 May 1988, No. 1771, p. 15)

Kuw. 88.2

This Decree has been made by the Minister of Public Health in pursuance of, *inter alia*, Decree No. 44 of 1987 on the reduction of the maximum permitted levels of tar and nicotine in cigarettes offered for sale on the Kuwaiti market, and on the modification of the health warning carried on the packaging. Sec. 1 lays down that the Environmental Protection Agency is required, *inter alia*, to ensure that imported cigarettes comply with the requirements. Details are provided of the administrative procedures to be followed in obtaining the certificate of compliance and the marketing licence. It is stated that, if the authorized limits have been exceeded, or if the indications carried on the packaging of the cigarettes do not comply with the requirements, the importer must, within a period of two months, re-export the cigarettes or destroy them under the control of the competent authorities, in particular of the Agency. If the cigarettes are re-exported, the Secretariat for Health Affairs of the Arab Countries of the Gulf Area must be informed so that the cigarettes are not re-exported to a destination in one of the Member States. It is laid down that the importer may request a second analysis if the results of the first analysis do not correspond to the indications carried on the packaging.

---

[a] Resolution No. 981 of 1980 of the Mayor of the Municipality of Kuwait (*Al-Kuwait Al-Youm*, Vol. 26, No. 1299, 4 May 1980, p. 9) provides for the cancellation of all licences for smoking advertisements within the Municipality. — ED.

LEBANON

LEBANON. Decree-Law No. 101 of 16 September 1983 on the warning of citizens of the harmful effects of smoking. (*Al-Jaridah Al-Rasmiyah*, 3 November 1983, No. 45, pp. 517-518) **Leb. 85.3**

Sec. 1 of this Decree-Law imposes a prohibition on the importation, manufacture, or sale of all kinds of cigarettes, cigars, tobacco, pipe tobacco, etc. unless the following legend has been clearly apposed on the packet in a conspicuous and legible manner: "The Minister of Public Health warns you of the harmful effects of smoking". Sec. 2 authorizes advertising for articles and products for smokers provided that the text of the advertising includes the legend mentioned above. Various penal provisions are laid down in Sec. 3. Under Sec. 4, procedures for the implementation of this Decree-Law are to be laid down, as appropriate, by decrees made by the Council of Ministers at the proposal of the Minister of Public Health. Provisions governing the entry into force of this Decree-Law are laid down in Sec. 5 (all the provisions have now come into force).

LUXEMBOURG

LUXEMBOURG. Law of 24 March 1989 restricting the advertising of tobacco and tobacco products and prohibiting smoking in certain places. (*Mémorial: Journal Officiel du Grand-Duché de Luxembourg*, Part A, April 1989, pp. 242-244) **Lux. 89.6**

Sec. 1 of this Law reads as follows:

"**1.** In the interests of public health, the purposes of this Law shall be as follows:

— to prohibit or restrict advertising for tobacco and tobacco products; and

— to prohibit smoking in certain places."

Under Sec. 2, products intended to be smoked, taken as snuff, or chewed are considered to be tobacco products for the purposes of the implementation of this Law, whenever they are made up, even partially, of tobacco.

The remaining substantive provisions are contained in the following Chapters: 1. Provisions concerning promotion and advertising (Secs. 3-8); and 2. Prohibition of smoking in certain places (Sec. 9).

Sec. 5 empowers the Grand Duke to make Regulations for the implementation of this Law.

LUXEMBOURG. Regulations of the Grand Duke of 19 June 1990 for the enforcement of the Law of 24 March 1989 restricting the advertising of tobacco and tobacco products and prohibiting smoking in certain places. (*Memorial: Journal officiel du Grand-Duché de Luxembourg*, 30 June 1990, No. 30, pp. 411-412) **Lux. 90.3**

These Regulations have been made to implement the Law of 24 March 1989 (see *IDHL*, 1989, **40**, 845, **Lux. 89.6**). Among other provisions, it is laid down that each packaging unit of tobacco products must carry the following warning (in French and German): "Smoking is dangerous to your health".

MALTA

MALTA. An Act (No. XLII of 1986) to make provision in respect of the control of tobacco smoking and for matters connected therewith. Dated 12 December 1986. (The Tobacco (Smoking Control) Act, 1986). (8 pp.) **Malta 87.6**

The following are among the principal provisions of this Act, which is to come into force on a date or dates to be appointed by the Minister responsible for Public Health and repeals, *inter alia*, the Tobacco (Control of Advertisement) Act, 1970 (see *IDHL*, 1973, **24**, 183).

Sec. 2 defines various terms, including "cigarette" ("includes cut tobacco rolled up in paper, tobacco leaf, or other material in such form as to be capable of immediate use for smoking"), "public place" ("includes any place to which the public have or are permitted to have access, whether on payment or otherwise"), "smoking requisites", and "tobacco" ("includes cigarettes and smoking mixtures intended as a substitute for tobacco"). Under Sec. 3, nothing in this Act applies to such tobacco or tobacco substitutes as are considered to be medicinal preparations or poisons under the Medical and Kindred Professions Ordinance or "any law substituting that Ordinance".

Under Sec. 4, no person may advertise cigarettes, cigars, or other forms of tobacco, tobacco products, or smoking requisites on television, radio, or other broadcasting media, or in cinemas. Sec. 5 provides for the display of health warnings in cinemas. Secs. 6 (Health warnings and advertisements) and 7 (Exceptions) read as follows:

"**6.** No person shall advertise for sale any of the items mentioned in section 4 of this Act, in any newspaper, magazine or other publication, or promote by distribution of leaflets, by posters, canopies, illuminated signs, or billboards, the sale or supply of such items, unless the advertisements, leaflets, posters, canopies, illuminated signs, or billboards include or contain a health warning acceptable to the Superintendent [of Public Health] indicating that smoking of tobacco is dangerous to health.

7. The provisions of the last preceding section shall not apply to foreign newspapers or magazines imported into Malta and whose main purpose is not that of advertising the said items or any of them or related to the business of any such items."

Sec. 8 provides an interpretation of the term "advertisement". It is indicated that any pricing policy and practice intended to sell the various items referred to in Sec. 4 at a lower price on a long-term basis are not deemed to be advertisements for the purposes of this Act. Similarly, any advertisement which the Minister, after consulting the Committee on Smoking and Health, prescribes as being exempted from "being an advertisement" is not deemed to be an advertisement for the purposes of this Act. Secs. 9 (Health warnings on packages), 10 (Regulations), 11 (Health warning to be displayed in shops), 12 (Tar and nicotine content), 13 (Sales to comply with Act and regulations), 14 (Sale to young persons), 15 (Prohibition of smoking in certain premises and public transport), and 16 (Sale etc., of sweets etc., in cigarette form) read as follows:

"**9.** (1) Every package of cigarettes imported, sold, distributed or supplied, by way of compensation or otherwise, shall contain a health warning on the outside of the package with a clear message in one of the official languages of Malta, and acceptable to the Superintendent, indicating that smoking of tobacco is dangerous to health.

(2) The health warning referred to in subsection (1) of this section shall be printed clearly and be of a reasonable size as to be prominently and easily legible taking into consideration the size and the colour background of the package, to the satisfaction of the Superintendent.

(3) No other wording on any such package or in any medium in outlets where cigarettes, cigars, tobacco or tobacco products are sold shall be used so as to mislead or tend to mislead the public on the concept of the danger and harm which tobacco may cause to health.

(4) The provisions of subsection (1) of this section shall not apply to cigarettes, cigars, tobacco or tobacco products intended for export and which are not sold or distributed for consumption in Malta.

10. The Minister may make regulations for reducing the risks to human health resulting from consumption of tobacco or tobacco products, and in particular and without prejudice to the generality of that power, may make regulations for all or any of the following purposes—

(*a*) to prohibit the advertisement or other promotion of the sale of cigarettes, cigars or other forms of tobacco, tobacco products or smoking requisites, in newspapers, magazines or other publications, other than as stated in section 7 of this Act;

(*b*) to prescribe the contents and format of any health warning required to be shown, affixed or displayed by this Act on any medium or thing whatsoever, as well as the frequency and the times at which any such warning shall be changed or rotated;

(*c*) to extend the provisions of sections 9 and 12 of this Act to other forms of tobacco products;

(*d*) to prescribe that health warnings as are referred to in section 11 of this Act shall be affixed in prominent positions in any public place and inside any vehicle licensed or used for public transport, and that it shall be the duty of the licensee and the driver, as the case may be, to comply with such regulation;

(*e*) to prescribe the maximum permissible tar, nicotine and other content which cigarettes or other forms of tobacco or tobacco products may contain, and the maximum yield of any such substances which may be obtained therefrom;

(*f*) to prescribe the conditions under which the sale or distribution of cigarettes, cigars or other tobacco product shall be prohibited or restricted inside hospitals, clinics and other health institutions;

(*g*) to prohibit or control any advertisement directly or indirectly connected with tobacco or with tobacco smoking;

(*h*) to control the number of cigarettes which may be offered for sale as any one retail packet and to prohibit the sale of single cigarettes:

Provided that the Minister shall not make regulations prohibiting the sale of cigarette packets, containing such number of cigarettes as the cigarette packets as are on sale on the day of the coming into force of this paragraph;

(*i*) to control the size, weight and presentation of cigarettes, cigars and other tobacco products;

(*j*) to prohibit or control smoking in any place;

(*k*) to prescribe any other matter which may be or is required to be prescribed by this Act;

(*l*) to prescribe any other matter which may appear to the Minister necessary or expedient for the better carrying out of the provisions of this Act for securing the health of the public.

11. The licensee of any premises from which cigarettes, cigars, tobacco or tobacco products or smoking requisites are sold, shall ensure that a warning notice acceptable to the Superintendent in respect of language, wording, format, size and presentation, and indicating the dangers to health of smoking, and that such notice be prominently displayed in the premises so as to attract the attention of customers or other persons on the premises and to be easily seen and read by them.

12. (1) No cigarettes may be imported, sold, supplied or distributed by way of compensation or otherwise unless there is printed on the package or on a label affixed thereon, a correct declaration of the content of tar and nicotine in each cigarette.

(2) The provisions of subsection (1) of this section shall not apply to cigarettes, cigars, tobacco or tobacco products intended for export and which are not sold or distributed for consumption in Malta.

13. No person shall sell any cigarettes or other forms of tobacco or tobacco product which do not comply with the provisions of this Act or of any regulation made hereunder.

14. (1) No person shall sell, supply or distribute by way of compensation or otherwise, any cigarettes, cigars, tobacco, tobacco products or smoking requisites to any person who is under the age of sixteen years, or in any manner induce such person to smoke.

(2) No cigarettes, cigars, tobacco or tobacco products may be sold from automatic sales machines except in restaurants and other establishments in respect of which there exists a valid licence to serve alcoholic beverages on the premises, or in other places in which sales from such machines are kept under supervision.

(3) It shall be the responsibility of any person during such time as he is responsible for or has the control of the premises in which any such sales machine is kept to ensure that no person under sixteen years of age shall make use of such machine.

15. (1) No person shall smoke any cigarette, cigar, tobacco or tobacco product on any public transport, in any cinema, theatre, hospital, clinic or other health institution, or in any television studio in any debate, discussion or other programme broadcast locally for public viewing whether live or pre-recorded; nor shall any person smoke any such item in any classroom, corridor, yard or appurtenance of a school, day home or similar premises used by children under sixteen years of age.

For the purposes of this subsection 'school' includes a kindergarten, nursery school or similar premises.

(2) The provisions of the preceding subsection shall not apply—

(*a*) to patients or inmates of a hospital or clinic, in respect of any area in such premises designated by the Superintendent as an area wherein smoking by patients or inmates is permitted; and

(*b*) to persons working in a hospital, clinic, school, day home or similar premises, in respect of any area in such premises approved by the Superintendent as a smoking area.

(3) It shall be the duty of the person in charge of any premises mentioned in subsection (1) of this section and of the driver and conductor of any public transport, to ensure that an appropriate sign or notice is put up in a prominent place or places as the case may require, so as to attract attention that smoking is prohibited, and it shall also be the duty of any such person to ensure that no smoking takes place on the premises or public transport, as the case may be.

16. No person shall import, manufacture, sell, supply or distribute by way of compensation or otherwise any sweets, confectionery or toys in the form of cigarettes, cigars or smoker's pipe."

Under Sec. 17, the provisions of this Act are in addition to and not in derogation of the provisions of any other law prohibiting or restricting the smoking of tobacco for reasons of food hygiene. Various penal matters are dealt with in Secs. 18 and 19. Sec. 20 deals with repeals and savings. Sec. 21 provides for the establishment of a Committee on Smoking and Health and indicates its composition (the Committee is chaired by the Superintendent of Public Health and also includes the Director of Education or his representative, the Secretary of the Ministry of Finance or his representative, the Dean of the Faculty of Medicine at the University of Malta, and five members appointed by the Minister of Heath (including a medical practitioner from the Department of Health engaged in health promotion education, one member involved in the tobacco industry, and one member from among voluntary organizations interested in the reduction of risks to health resulting from smoking)). It is laid down that it is the duty of the Committee to advise the Minister on any measure, including legislation, which may be necessary or expedient to reduce the risk to health arising from the consumption of tobacco or tobacco products and to coordinate and promote activities related to the prevention and control of smoking of such items.

MALTA. The Health Warnings (On Smoking) Regulations, 1987. L.N. 28 of 1987. (2 pp.) **Malta 89.1**

These Regulations have been made by the Minister of Health under powers conferred by Sec. 10 of the Tobacco (Smoking Control) Act, 1986 (see *IDHL*, 1987, **38**, 544, **Malta 87.6**). They provide details of the warnings to appear in cinemas, during broadcasts, in advertisements, on packages, on premises, etc.

The Schedule lists the health warnings that must be used in accordance with the Act, as follows: 1. "Cigarettes can cause lung cancer and heart disease"; 2. "Smoking during pregnancy endangers the health of mother and baby"; 3. "If you stop smoking you improve your health and live longer"; and 4. "The more you smoke the more you risk your health."

MEXICO

MEXICO. The General Law on health. Dated 26 December 1983. (*Diario Oficial*, Part 1, 7 February 1984, pp. 24-80) **Mex. 86.7**

Chapter XI. Tobacco (Secs. 275-277). Under Sec. 275, "tobacco" is interpreted for the purposes of this Law to mean *Nicotiana tabacum* and its substitutes, whether in natural or modified form, in the various presentations used for smoking, chewing, or inhaling. Sec. 276 lays down that labels of packages and containers in which tobacco is sold or supplied must, in addition to the particulars required under Sec. 210, bear the following legend marked in a clear and conspicuous manner: "This product may be harmful to health". Sec. 277 prohibits the sale of tobacco to minors under any circumstances.

308. Advertising for alcoholic beverages and tobacco shall comply with the following requirements:

I. it shall be limited to the provision of information on the characteristics, quality, and techniques of preparation of these products;

II. it shall not present them as conducive to wellbeing or health or associate them with civil or religious celebrations;

III. it shall not associate such products with ideas or images of the enhanced emotional life and sexuality of individuals, or extol social prestige, virility, or femininity;

IV. it shall not associate such products with creative, sports, household, or work activities, or use imperative language that directly induces their consumption;

V. it shall not include in images or sounds the participation of children or adolescents, or be directed towards them; and

VI. in the message, the products in question shall not be ingested or consumed either in reality or apparently."

Sec. 309 deals with the times at which advertising of alcoholic beverages or tobacco may be broadcast by radio or television or shown in cinemas.

MEXICO. Coordination Agreement between the Federal Executive and the Executive of the State of Tabasco, for the purpose of supporting the Smoking Control Programme. Dated 10 November 1986.[a] (*Diario Oficial*, 3 December 1986, No. 22, pp. 14-15) **Mex. 87.4**

Sec. 1 of this Agreement, which was concluded in pursuance of, *inter alia*, certain provisions of the General Law on health of 26 December 1983 (see *IDHL*, 1986, 37, 475, **Mex. 86.7**), lays down that the purpose of the Agreement is to establish the bases for coordination between the Government of the State of Tabasco and the Secretariat for Health in developing the Smoking Control Programme. Under Sec. 2, the State Government is to support the activities of the National Council Against Addictions by assuming the following functions: (1) encouraging revisions of or additions to the legal provisions in force and, where appropriate, proposals for adaptations aimed at improving the implementation of the provisions of the General Law on health in regard to the prevention of smoking and the treatment and rehabilitation of persons suffering from diseases associated with smoking, by assuring the improved compatibility and uniformity of administrative provisions at the Federal level and those provisions applicable at the level of the federative entity; (2) promoting cooperation between the public, social, and private sectors in the implementation of legal and administrative provisions on the subject, at both the Federal and local levels; (3) fostering the integration of joint committees representing the Federal and State authorities and the social and private sectors, with a view to promoting the implementation of the Smoking Control Programme within their respective spheres of jurisdiction; (4) establishing a State centre for information and documentation on smoking; (5) improving, developing, and extending public services that provide care to persons suffering from diseases associated with smoking; (6) stimulating the integration of self-management groups within the community, for the prevention and care of tobacco dependence; (7) fostering the participation of groups against smoking in the implementation of the Programme; (8) strengthening the surveillance of compliance with health control measures relating to the production, marketing, and consumption of the different types of tobacco; (9) implementing smoking control programmes in higher educational institutions; (10) encouraging the authorities responsible for higher educational institutions to develop studies on research methods and techniques on problems related to tobacco consumption through academic programmes in medical and social disciplines; (11) promoting, guiding, and coordinating the conduct of research in this field; (12) developing research programmes oriented towards the study of the production, distribution, and sale of tobacco; (13) undertaking epidemiological studies designed to determine the causal and risk factors and medical and social consequences of smoking; and (14) undertaking studies for the early identification of persons having problems related to smoking.

---

[a] Similar Agreements were concluded on 30 October 1986 between the Federal Executive and the Executive of the State of San Luis Potosí (*Diario Oficial*, 18 November 1986, No. 12, pp. 35-36) and the Executive of the State of Durango (*ibid.*, 25 November 1986, No. 16, pp. 19-21). An Agreement containing corresponding provisions in regard to the Programme for the Control of Alcoholism and the Abuse of Alcoholic Beverages was concluded on 30 October 1986 between the Federal Executive and the State of San Luis Potosí (*ibid.*, 18 November 1986, No. 12, pp. 37-38). Other Coordination Agreements of this type have been concluded between the Federal Executive and certain other States, notably an Agreement with the State of Guanajuato, dated 7 March 1986, concerning the performance of health surveillance and regulatory functions (*ibid.*, 24 November 1986, No. 15, pp. 10-16). — ED.

NETHERLANDS

NETHERLANDS. Decree of 29 April 1981 (Stb. 329) prescribing rules governing cigarettes and cigarette tobacco. (The Cigarette and Cigarette Tobacco Labelling Decree (Commodities Law)). (*Staatsblad van het Koninkrijk der Nederlanden*, 1981, 2 pp.) **Neth. 82.1**

Secs. 1-4 of this Decree read as follows:

"**1.** (1) In the case of cigarettes contained in a packet intended to be supplied or suitable for supply with the cigarettes to a consumer, the following particulars shall appear on the packet:

(*a*) 'Smoking is a threat to health. The Minister of Health and Environmental Protection'; and

(*b*) 1. the nicotine content, indicated by the word 'nicotine', in tenths of a milligram per cigarette; and

2. the tar content, indicated by the word 'tar', in milligrams per cigarette.

(2) The contents referred to in items (*b*) 1 and (*b*) 2 of subsection 1 shall be determined in accordance with a method stipulated by Our Minister of Health and Environmental Protection, Our Minister of Agriculture and Fisheries, and Our Minister for Economic Affairs.

2. The particulars referred to in Section 1 shall be displayed in a clearly legible and indelible manner at least on the largest surface or on one of the largest surfaces of the packet, in the order indicated in Section 1, surrounded by a closed line, in letters or figures measuring not less than 2 mm in height.

3. (1) In the case of cigarette tobacco contained in a packet intended to be supplied or suitable for supply with the cigarette tobacco to a consumer, the following statement shall appear on the packet: 'Smoking is a threat to health. The Minister of Health and Environmental Protection'.

(2) The statement referred to in subsection 1 shall be displayed in a clearly legible and indelible manner at least on the largest surface or on one of the largest surfaces of the packet, surrounded by a closed line, in letters measuring not less than 2 mm in height.

4. In the case of cigarettes or cigarette tobacco contained in a packet intended to be supplied or suitable for supply with the cigarettes or the cigarette tobacco to a consumer, particulars concerning the effect, the nicotine content, or the tar content of the cigarettes or particulars concerning the effect of the cigarette tobacco, other than those stipulated in this Decree, may not be used on the packet."

NETHERLANDS. Decree of 9 December 1986 (Stb. 642) amending the Cigarette and Cigarette Tobacco Labelling Decree (Commodities Law). (*Staatsblad van het Koninkrijk der Nederlanden*, 1986, 4 pp.) **Neth. 88.27**

Secs. 1-3 of the Cigarette and Cigarette Tobacco Labelling Decree (Commodities Law) (Stb. 329) of 29 April 1981 (see *IDHL*, 1982, **33**, 33, **Neth. 82.1**) are amended to read as follows:

"**1.** (1) The following words shall appear on the packaging of cigarettes contained in packaging intended to be supplied or suitable for supply with the cigarettes to a consumer:

(*a*) 'Smoking is harmful to health. It can cause lung cancer or heart problems';

(*b*) 'Crown Decree of 29 April 1981 (Stb. 329)';

(*c*) 1. the nicotine level (designated by the word 'nicotine') in tenths of a milligram per cigarette; and

2. the tar level (designated by the word 'tar') in milligrams per cigarette.

(2) The levels referred to in points 1 and 2 of item (*c*) of subsection 1 shall be determined in accordance with a method to be designated by the Minister of Welfare, Health and Cultural Affairs, the Minister of Agriculture and Fisheries, and the Minister of Economic Affairs.

2. The words referred to in Section 1 shall be displayed in a clearly legible and indelible manner on one of the lateral faces of the packaging, in a colour that clearly contrasts with the background, and in letters or figures measuring at least 3 mm in height with a line thickness of at least 0.3 mm in the case of the words referred to under item (*a*) of subsection 1 and measuring at least 2 mm in height in the case of the words referred to under items (*b*) and (*c*) of subsection 1.

3. (1) The provisions of items (*a*) and (*b*) of Section 1 shall be applicable to hand-rolling tobacco contained in packaging that is intended or suitable for supply with the hand-rolling tobacco to a consumer.

(2) The words referred to in subsection 1 shall be displayed in a clearly legible and indelible manner and in a colour that clearly contrasts with the background on one of the faces of the packaging. The provisions of Section 2 with regard to the letters or figures and their line thickness shall be applicable."

NETHERLANDS. Law of 10 March 1988 (Stb. 342) prescribing measures for the restriction of tobacco use, and in particular for the protection of non-smokers. (The Tobacco Law). (*Staatsblad van het Koninkrijk der Nederlanden*, 6 pp.) **Neth. 89.6**

Parts 1-5 (Secs. 1-11) of this Law read as follows:

"*Part 1*

Definitions

1. In this Law and the provisions laid down in pursuance of it:

(*a*) the term 'tobacco products' means cigars, cigarettes, and cut tobacco, consisting wholly or partially of constituent parts of the plant *Nicotiana*; and

(*b*) the term 'our Minister' means the Minister of Welfare, Public Health and Culture.

Part 2

Labelling and composition

2. (1) In the interests of public health, general administrative regulations shall be issued laying down requirements to be met by tobacco products in respect of the labels that shall be displayed on retail packaging. Where such labels refer to the composition of the product, the regulations may indicate a method of analysis which shall be described in the regulations and form the sole criterion of the acceptability of the labels used in connection with the product.

(2) In the interests of public health, general administrative regulations may be issued laying down requirements to be met by tobacco products in respect of their composition, such as nicotine levels and the quantities of tar and carbon monoxide released during combustion. The regulations may indicate a method of analysis which shall be described in the regulations and form the sole criterion whether the requirements have been met in respect of a product.

3. (1) The commercial supply of tobacco products, or the possession of tobacco products for that purpose, shall be prohibited if the products do not comply with the requirements laid down in pursuance of Section 2.

(2) Subsection 1 shall not be applicable if it can be demonstrated that it is intended to export the product or destroy it or bring it into compliance with the specified requirements.

Part 3

Advertising

4. The Association referred to in subsection 1 of Section 50 of the Broadcasting Law (Stb. 176) of 1967 shall be prohibited from broadcasting advertisements for tobacco products.[a]

5. (1) In the interests of public health, general administrative regulations may be issued laying down requirements to be met by advertisements for tobacco products in or on any establishment that is used wholly or partially for the commercial supply of tobacco products to private individuals. Where such regulations are in force, advertisements that do not comply with the said requirements shall be prohibited.

(2) In the interests of public health, general administrative regulations may likewise be issued laying down requirements to be met by advertisements for tobacco products other than the advertisements referred to in subsection 1. After the entry into force of such regulations, advertisements that do not comply with the requirements shall be prohibited. The prohibition of an advertisement as referred to in the preceding sentence shall become effective only after the body referred to in Section 6 has issued a statement that the advertisement does not comply with the specified requirements. The body shall be notified of all such advertisements for tobacco products. The statement referred to in the third sentence of this subsection shall be issued not later than one month after such notification has been received. The body may extend this period once by a period of one month and shall inform the notifier accordingly in writing before the first one-month period has elapsed.

(3) Any regulations as referred to in subsection 1 or subsection 2 above shall specify the period of time which shall elapse before the prohibitions referred to in those subsections become applicable to advertisements that are already in circulation when the regulations enter into force.

---

[a] The Association has a monopoly on all official broadcasting of advertisements in the Netherlands. — ED.

(4) [*Payment of a charge on notification of an advertisement*]

6. (1) Our Minister shall establish a body responsible for issuing statements as referred to in subsection 2 of Section 5.

(2-4) [*Membership of the body*]

(4) Our Minister shall appoint one member in accordance with a proposal by the National Council on Public Health.

(5)-(7) [*Working procedures*]

7. The requirements referred to in Section 5 may refer to the contents of advertisements, and may lay down prohibitions or other restrictions with regard to the manner and place of advertising.

8. [*Appeals*]

Part 4

Supply to private individuals

9. The commercial supply of tobacco products to private individuals shall be prohibited in health care, social welfare, sports, sociocultural, or educational establishments if such establishments belong to categories indicated in general administrative regulations.

Part 5

Provisions governing the use of tobacco products

10. (1) With regard to establishments, services, and companies administered by the State and public bodies, the competent authority shall take measures to ensure that the facilities provided by the afore-mentioned can be used and activities carried on there without any nuisance arising out of the use of tobacco products.

(2) The measures referred to in subsection 1 shall in any case include the establishment and maintenance of a ban on the use of tobacco products in areas belonging to categories indicated in general administrative regulations issued in consultation with the National Council on Public Health. Such bans may be made subject to limitations in accordance with rules laid down in the said general administrative regulations.

11. (1) General administrative regulations may be issued requiring the measures referred to in subsection 1 of Section 10 to be taken by persons who, in a capacity other than that referred to in Section 10, administer health care, social welfare, sports, sociocultural, or educational establishments belonging to categories indicated in general administrative regulations.

(2) Subsection 2 of Section 10 shall be applicable *mutatis mutandis.*"

Sec. 22 prescribes that the various provisions of this Law are to enter into force on such date or dates as may be specified by Crown decree.

NEW ZEALAND

NEW ZEALAND. The Toxic Substances Regulations 1983, Amendment No. 2. S.R. 1988/51. Dated 21 March 1988. (4 pp.) **NZ 90.6**

The Toxic Substances Regulations 1983 (see *IDHL*, 1984, **35**, 396, **NZ 84.11**), as amended, are further amended, notably by introducing a revised version of Part VIA (Special provisions relating to tobacco products), comprising Secs. 46A-46C. Sec. 46B lays down that: (1) no advertisement for a tobacco product may directly or indirectly state or suggest that the product is suitable for chewing or for any other oral use; and (2) no person may import for sale, sell, pack, or distribute any tobacco product labelled or otherwise described as suitable for chewing or for any other oral use. Sec. 46C imposes a prohibition on sale of tobacco products to persons under 16 years of age.

NEW ZEALAND. An Act (No. 108 of 1990) (a) to reduce the exposure of people who do not themselves smoke to any detrimental effect on their health caused by smoking by others; and (b) to regulate the marketing, advertising, and promotion of tobacco products, whether directly or through the sponsoring of other products, services, or events; and (c) to monitor and regulate the presence of harmful constituents in tobacco products and tobacco smoke; and (d) to establish a Health Sponsorship Council. Dated 28 August 1990. (The Smoke-free Environments Act 1990). (35 pp.) **NZ 90.10**

The following is an outline of some of the principal provisions of this Act.

Sec. 1 (Short title and commencement) indicates the timetable for the entry into force of the Act (Part I is to come into force on the expiry of three months following the date on which the Act receives Royal assent, while Part II is to come into force on 16 December 1990). Sec. 2 (Interpretation) defines a large number of terms, including "smoking accessory", "tobacco product" ("any product manufactured from tobacco and intended for use by smoking, inhalation, or mastication; and includes nasal and oral snuff; but does not include any medicine (being a medicine in respect of which there is in force a consent or provisional consent given under section 20 or section 23 of the Medicines Act 1981 [see *IDHL*, 1982, **33**, 797, **NZ 82.9**] that is sold or supplied wholly or principally for use as an aid in giving up smoking"), "tobacco product advertisement", "to smoke", and "workplace".

Part I. Smoke-free indoor environments (Secs. 4-20)

Sec. 4 lays down that "The purpose of this Part of this Act is to prevent, so far as is reasonably practicable, the detrimental effects of smoking on the health of any person who does not smoke, or who does not wish to smoke, inside any workplace or in certain public enclosed areas". Sec. 5 requires employers to have a written policy on smoking, while Sec. 6 lays down special provisions in respect of certain institutions (hospitals and rest homes; and prisons). The duties of employers are defined in Sec. 7. Under Sec. 8, the operator of an aircraft may not permit any person to smoke on that aircraft while the latter is carrying passengers for hire or reward on any internal flight. No person may smoke while on any such aircraft. The next five Sections are as follows: 9. Smoking restricted in passenger service vehicles; 10. Smoking restricted on ships and trains; 11. Smoking restricted in passenger lounges and waiting rooms; 12. Smoking on licensed premises; and 13. Smoking restricted in restaurants. Under Sec. 14, area health boards are required to ensure that sufficient persons are appointed to enforce the provisions of this Part within its area health district. Sec. 15 deals with complaints relating to workplace smoking policies, and Sec. 16 with complaints to area health boards. Details are given in Sec. 17 of the penalties imposed on persons committing offences in respect of smoking. Other penal matters are dealt with in Secs. 18 and 19. Sec. 20 empowers area health boards to "make bylaws providing greater protection from tobacco smoke than is provided by this Part".

Part II. Tobacco products control (Secs. 21-41)

Sec. 21 (Purpose of this Part) reads as follows:

"**21.** The purpose of this Part of this Act is—

(*a*) To reduce the social approval of tobacco use, particularly among young people, by imposing controls on the marketing, advertising, or promotion of tobacco products and their association through sponsorship with other products and events; and

(*b*) To reduce some of the harmful effects of tobacco products on the health of users by monitoring and regulating the presence of harmful substances in the products and in tobacco smoke."

Promotion and advertising (Secs. 22-29). Sec. 22 (Advertising of tobacco products) reads as follows:

"**22.** (1) Subject to the succeeding provisions of this section and to section 23 of this Act, no person shall publish, or arrange for any other person to publish, any tobacco product advertisement in New Zealand.

(2) Nothing in subsection (1) of this section shall apply to any price list given to retailers of tobacco products if the price list includes the health messages required by or under this Part of this Act.

(3) Nothing in subsection (1) of this section shall apply to any advertisement included in any book, magazine, or newspaper printed outside New Zealand, or in any radio or television transmission originating outside New Zealand, or in any film or video recording made outside New Zealand, unless—

(*a*) The principal purpose of the book, magazine, newspaper, transmission, film, or video recording is the promotion of the use of tobacco products; or

(*b*) The book, magazine, newspaper, film, or video recording is intended for sale, distribution, or exhibition primarily in New Zealand; or

(*c*) In the case of an advertisement in any radio or television transmission, the advertisement is targeted primarily at a New Zealand audience.

(4) Nothing in subsection (1) of this section shall apply to the publication by a tobacco products manufacturer of a tobacco product advertisement in a magazine that is intended for distribution only to employees of the manufacturer.

(5) Nothing in subsection (1) of this section shall apply to—

(*a*) The exhibition, in any museum or art gallery, of any work or artifact:

(*b*) The dissemination, broadcasting, or exhibition of any film, video recording, or sound recording, where—

(i) That film, video recording, or sound recording was made before the 16th day of December 1990; and

(ii) The tobacco product advertisement included in that film, video recording, or sound recording is in the form of a reference to, or a depiction of, a tobacco product trade mark that is only an incidental part of that film, video recording, or sound recording."

The next six Sections are as follows: 23. Exemptions for retailers and vending machines; 24. Use of trade marks, etc., on goods other than tobacco products, or in relation to sponsored events; 25. Organising or promoting activity using trade mark, etc., of tobacco products; 26. Exemptions for participants in certain events; 27. Exemption for craft in emergencies; and 28. Free distribution and rewards prohibited. Under Sec. 29, no person may publish an advertisement for a tobacco product that directly or indirectly states or suggests that the product is suitable for chewing or for any other oral use (other than smoking). Furthermore, no person may import for sale, sell, pack, or distribute any tobacco product labelled or otherwise described as suitable for chewing or for any other oral use (other than smoking).

Sale and labelling (Secs. 30-32). Under Sec. 30, no person may sell any tobacco product to a person who has not attained the age of 16 years. Persons engaging in the retail of tobacco products are required to display clearly for the public a notice to the above effect. Secs. 31 (Limits on harmful constituents) and 32 (Labelling and health messages) read as follows:

"**31.** No manufacturer or importer shall offer for sale or export any tobacco product that—

(*a*) Contains or generates in its smoke a harmful constituent specified for the purposes of this Act in regulations made under this Part of this Act; or

(b) Contains harmful constituents in excess of the limits prescribed by regulations made under this Part of this Act, as determined in accordance with any tests so prescribed.

32. (1) No manufacturer, importer, distributor, or retailer shall sell or offer for sale a tobacco product unless—

(*a*) The package containing the product displays, in accordance with regulations made under this Part of this Act,—

(i) A message relating to the effects of the use of the product on health; and

(ii) A list of the harmful constituents of the product; and

(iii) In the case of a tobacco product intended for smoking, a list of the harmful constituents, and their respective quantities, present in the smoke; and

(*b*) A leaflet containing information relating to the effets of the use of the product on health is placed inside the package with the product, if and as required by regulations made under this Part of this Act.

(2) In subsection (1) of this section the term "harmful constituent" means any substance declared by regulations made under this Part of this Act to be a harmful constituent for the purposes of that subsection.

(3) Every person who offers for sale, by way of an automatic vending machine, any tobacco product shall, in accordance with regulations made under this Act, display on the vending machine such health message as is required by or under this Act."

Testing, reports, and returns (Secs. 33-35). This rubric comprises the following Sections: 33. Annual testing for constituents; 34. Director-General [of Health] may require further testing; and 35. Offences in respect of tobacco products.

Offences (Secs. 36-38). Details are given in Sec. 36 of the penalties imposed on persons guilty of offences in respect of tobacco products. It is laid down in Sec. 37 that the Director-General is responsible for enforcing the provisions of this Part.

Miscellaneous provisions (Secs. 39-40). Sec. 39 empowers the Governor-General to make regulations, by Order in Council, for the implementation of this Part. Details are given of the matters that may be covered by such regulations. A number of transitional provisions are laid down in Sec. 40. Sec. 41 provides for a number of consequential amendments, repeals, and revocations, in respect to the Toxic Substances Act 1979 (see *ibid.*, 1980, **31**, 855), the Toxic Substances Amendment Act 1986 (see *ibid.*, 1989, **40**, 440, **NZ 89.19**), the Toxic Substances Regulations 1983 (see *ibid.*, 1984, **35**, 396, **NZ 84.11**), and the Toxic Substances Regulations 1983, Amendment No. 2 (see *ibid.*, 1990, **41**, 313, **NZ 90.6**).

Part III. Health Sponsorship Council (Secs. 42-65)

Sec. 42 (Meaning of "sponsorship") reads as follows:

"**42.** (1) In this Part of this Act, 'sponsorship' means, in broad terms, the provision of assistance by the Council to any person or organisation and, in return, the promotion by that person or organisation of health and healthy lifestyles in a manner agreed by the Council.

(2) Without limiting the generality of the term, such assistance by the Council may take the form of—

(*a*) Money, whether by way of grant or otherwise; or

(*b*) Goods and services; or

(*c*) Trophies, prizes, awards, and scholarships.

(3) Also, without limiting the generality of the term, such promotion by the person or organisation receiving assistance may take the form of—

(*a*) Publicising messages relating to health and healthy lifestyles; or

(*b*) Publicising messages relating to ill-health and unhealthy lifestyles; or

(*c*) Promoting the aims and objectives of the Council."

Sec. 43 provides for the establishment of a council known as the Health Sponsorship Council. Sec. 44 (Principal functions of Council) reads as follows:

"**44.** (1) The principal functions of the Council shall be—

(*a*) To promote health and to encourage healthy lifestyles, whether through the provision of sponsorship or otherwise; and

(*b*) To make sponsorship available to any person or organisation in accordance with section 56 of this Act.

(2) For the purposes of its principal functions, the Council may provide sponsorship to—

(*a*) Any person or organisation involved in sports participation, artistic endeavour, cultural pursuits, or recreational activities; or

(*b*) Any person or organisation involved in arranging any sporting, artistic, or recreational activity; or (*c*) Any person or organisation in accordance with section 56 of this Act."

Various provisions relating to the Council (membership, meetings, staff, appointment of advisory and technical committees, co-opting of specialist advice, powers, etc.) are laid down in Secs. 45-62. Sec. 63 requires the Council to prepare an annual report as soon as practicable after the end of each financial year.

NEW ZEALAND. 1990, No. 108

An Act

(a) To reduce the exposure of people who do not themselves smoke to any detrimental effect on their health caused by smoking by others; and

(b) To regulate the marketing, advertising, and promotion of tobacco products, whether directly or through the sponsoring of other products, services, or events; and

(c) To monitor and regulate the presence of harmful constituents in tobacco products and tobacco smoke; and

(d) To establish a Health Sponsorship Council

28 August 1990

BE IT ENACTED by the Parliament of New Zealand as follows:

1. Short Title and commencement–

(1) This Act may be cited as the Smoke-free Environments Act 1990.

(2) Part I of this Act shall come into force on the expiry of 3 months after the date on which this Act receives the Royal assent.

(3) Part II of this Act shall come into force on the 16th day of December 1990.

(4) Except as provided in subsections (2) and (3) of this section, this Act shall come into force on the day after the date on which it receives the Royal assent.

2. Interpretation – In this Act, unless the context otherwise requires,–

"Aircraft" has the same meaning as in section 2 of the Civil Aviation Act 1964:

"Area health board" means an area health board established under the Area Health Boards Act 1983:

"Company name" includes any corporate name, firm name, or business name, whether or not it is registered or registrable under the Companies Act 1955 or any other enactment:

"Council" means the Health Sponsorship Council established by section 43 of this Act:

"Craft" means–

(a) An aircraft:

(b) A ship (as defined in section 2(1) of the Shipping and Seamen Act 1952):

"Director" means the Director appointed under section 49 of this Act:

"Director-General" means the Director-General of Health:

"Distributor" means a person engaged in the business of selling tobacco products otherwise than at retail only:

"Employee" means any person of any age employed under a contract of service by an employer to do any work for hire or reward:

"Employer" means a person who employs any employee:

"Hospital" means–

(a) A hospital or an institution, within the meaning of the Hospitals Act 1957, under the control of an area health board; and

(b) A private hospital licensed under Part V of the Hospitals Act 1957;

"Internal flight" means a flight–

(a) Between any 2 or more places in New Zealand; or

(b) That commences from any place in New Zealand and is intended to terminate at that same place;

"Licensed premises" means any premises, or any part of any premises, on which liquor may be sold pursuant to any on-licence, off-licence, or special licence under the Sale of Liquor Act 1989;

"Manufacturer" includes any company with which a manufacturer is associated within the meaning of section 8 of the Income Tax Act 1976;

"Minister" means the Minister of Health:

"New Zealand resident" means–

(a) A New Zealand citizen;

(b) A permanent resident of New Zealand within the meaning of section 38 of the Electoral Act 1956;

(c) A company incorporated in New Zealand;

"Office" means a place in which any person is employed, directly or indirectly, to do any clerical work in connection with any business carried on by the occupier of that place;

"Organised activity" means any cultural, educational, sporting, or recreational activity or event;

"Package" means any pack, carton, wrapping, or other container in which tobacco products are customarily sold at retail;

"Passenger service vehicle" and "small passenger service vehicle" have the same meaning as in section 2 of the Transport Services Licensing Act 1989;

"Permitted smoking area" means any room or area in a workplace that is designated by an employer in accordance with Part I of this Act as a place where persons may smoke;

"Prison" means any penal institution within the meaning of the Penal Institutions Act 1954;

"Publish" means–

(a) Insert in any newspaper or other periodical publication printed, published, or distributed in New Zealand; or

(b) Send to any person, by post or otherwise; or

(c) Deliver to any person or leave upon premises in the occupation of any person; or
(d) Broadcast within the meaning of the Broadcasting Act 1989; or
(e) Include in any film or video recording; or
(f) Include in any disk for use with a computer; or
(g) Disseminate by means of any other electronic medium; or
(h) Distribute by any means; or
(i) Bring to the notice of the public in New Zealand in any other manner;

"Restaurant" means any premises, or any part of any premises, where the principal business is the selling of meals or refreshments to the general public for consumption on the premises, whether or not liquor is or may be sold on those premises or that part of those premises; and includes any room or area on a ship or train where meals or refreshments are provided for passengers to consume;

"Rest home" means a home for aged persons licensed in accordance with regulations made under section 120A of the Health Act 1956;

"Retailer" means a person engaged in any business that includes the sale of tobacco products at retail;

"Smoking accessory" means any article or substance that is used in conjunction with smoking, including cigarette papers, pipe cleaners, cigarette lighters, lighter fuel, and ashtrays; and includes the packaging, carton, wrapping, or other container in which smoking accessories are customarily sold at retail;

"Tobacco product" means any product manufactured from tobacco and intended for use by smoking, inhalation, or mastication; and includes nasal and oral snuff; but does not include any medicine (being a medicine in respect of which there is in force a consent or provisional consent given under section 20 or section 23 of the Medicines Act 1981) that is sold or supplied wholly or principally for use as an aid in giving up smoking;

"Tobacco product advertisement" means any words, whether written, printed, or spoken, including on film, video recording, or other medium broadcast or telecast, and any pictorial representation, design, or device, used to encourage the use or notify the availability or promote the sale of any tobacco product or to promote smoking behaviour; and includes–

(a) Any trade circular, any label, and any advertisement in any trade journal; and
(b) Any depiction, in a film, video recording, telecast, or other visual medium, of a tobacco product or a tobacco product trade mark, where in return for that depiction any money is paid, or any valuable thing is given, whether to the maker or producer of that film, video recording, telecast, or visual medium or to any other person; and
(c) The use in any advertisement or promotion to the public of a tobacco products manufacturer's company name where that name or any part of that name is used as, or is included in, a tobacco product trade mark;–

and "advertise" has a corresponding meaning;

"To smoke" means to smoke, hold, or otherwise have control over an ignited tobacco product, weed, or plant; and "smoked" and "smoking" have corresponding meanings;

"Trade mark" includes any trade mark whether or not it is registered or registrable as such under the Trade Marks Act 1953; and also includes–

(a) Any brand name;

(b) Any company name, where that name is used for advertising or promotional purposes;

(c) Any name, word, or mark that so resembles any trade mark that it is likely to be taken as, or confused with, that trade mark;

"Workplace" means any indoor or enclosed area that is occupied by an employer and that employees usually frequent during the course of their employment; and includes any aircraft, ship, train, cafeteria, corridor, lift, lobby, stairwell, toilet, and washroom; and also includes any enclosed common areas and employer provided vehicles normally used by employees; but does not include any place of residence occupied by the employer.

3. Act binds the Crown– This Act shall bind the Crown.

PART I
SMOKE-FREE INDOOR ENVIRONMENTS

4. Purpose of this Part– The purpose of this Part of this Act is to prevent, so far as is reasonably practicable, the detrimental effects of smoking on the health of any person who does not smoke, or who does not wish to smoke, inside any workplace or in certain public enclosed areas.

5. Employers to have written policy on smoking–

(1) Every employer shall, within 3 months after the commencement of this Part of this Act, prepare a written policy on smoking for every workplace of that employer.

(2) In preparing the written policy, the employer shall consult with the employees affected, or with a representative of the employees nominated by them for the purposes of this Part of this Act.

(3) Every written policy prepared for the purposes of subsection (1) of this section shall be based on the principle that employees who do not smoke, or who do not wish to smoke in their workplace, shall, so far as is reasonably practicable, be protected from tobacco smoke in the workplace.

(4) Every written policy on smoking shall include, at the minimum, the following requirements:

(a) That smoking shall not be permitted–

(i) In lifts, or in office areas where more than 1 person works in a common air space; or

(ii) In at least half of the total area of any cafeteria or lunchroom at the workplace or, where there is more than 1 session of any tea break or lunch break in the cafeteria or lunchroom and employees can freely choose which session to attend, during the first such session; or

(iii) In any part of the workplace to which the public normally have access;

(b) The procedure for an employee or employees in any workplace that is not an office to request that the employer will not permit smoking within 2 metres of the usual work area of that employee or those employees;

(c) The procedure for making complaints under this Part of this Act.

(5) The employer shall ensure that the written policy on smoking prepared for the purposes of subsection (1) of this section is reviewed in consultation with the employees or a representative of the employees at intervals of not more than 1 year.

(6) Nothing in this section shall prevent an employer from agreeing that smoking may be permitted in each enclosed area occupied exclusively by employees each of whom, in writing,–

(a) Requests that smoking be permitted there; or

(b) States that he or she does not object to that area being designated as a permitted smoking area.

6. Special provisions for certain institutions–

(1) In respect of any hospital or rest home, the written policy on smoking required by section 5 of this Act shall also include a requirement that any patient or resident who is so incapacitated as to be unable to move readily or to be moved readily may be permitted to smoke in an area that is not a permitted smoking area, but the employer shall take all such steps as may be practicable in such a case to ensure that other persons in the vicinity of the incapacitated person will not be affected adversely by the smoke.

(2) In respect of any prison, the superintendent shall, within 3 months after the commencement of this Part of this Act, prepare a written policy on smoking in respect of the inmates, and the following provisions shall apply:

(a) The policy shall be drawn up in such a way as to be consistent with the written policy on smoking required by section 5 of this Act;

(b) The policy shall be based on the principle that inmates who do not smoke, or who do not wish to smoke, in the prison shall, except where it is impracticable, be protected from tobacco smoke in the prison;

(c) Any inmate who requests that he or she be secured in a cell in which smoking will not be permitted while he or she is there shall, unless it is impracticable, be placed in such a cell;

(d) Subject to paragraphs (a) and (b) of this subsection, the superintendent may designate any enclosed area used in common by inmates as an area in which smoking is permitted.

7. Duties of employer– For every workplace occupied by any employee, the employer shall–

(a) Ensure that there are prominent notices indicating the workplace areas where smoking is not permitted, and identifying and locating any permitted smoking areas; and
(b) Display prominently in the workplace copies of the written policy on smoking for the workplace; and
(c) Supply on request a copy of the written policy on smoking to any employee, prospective employee, or representative of any employee; and
(d) Implement the written policy on smoking for the workplace.

8. Smoking prohibition on aircraft–

(1) The operator of an aircraft shall not permit any person to smoke on that aircraft while the aircraft is carrying passengers for hire or reward on any internal flight.
(2) No person shall smoke while on any aircraft that is carrying passengers for hire or reward on any internal flight.

9. Smoking restricted in passenger service vehicles–

(1) Subject to subsection (3) of this section, the operator of a passenger service vehicle shall not permit any person to smoke in that vehicle while it is carrying passengers.
(2) Subject to subsection (3) of this section, no person shall smoke in any passenger service vehicle while it is carrying passengers.
(3) Nothing in this section shall apply to any small passenger service vehicle where the driver and every passenger in the vehicle agree that smoking shall be permitted.

10. Smoking restricted on ships and trains–

(1) The operator of any passenger ship that is registered in New Zealand, or of any passenger train, shall not permit any person to smoke in any enclosed area in the ship or train that is normally used by passengers, except in a permitted smoking area.
(2) No person on any passenger ship that is registered in New Zealand, or on any passenger train, shall smoke in any enclosed area on the ship or train that is normally used by passengers, except in a permitted smoking area.
(3) Subject to the succeeding provisions of this section, the operator of any passenger ship that is registered in New Zealand, or of any passenger train, may, after consultation with a representative of the employees working on the ship or train, designate not more than one-half of the areas designed for accommodating passengers as permitted smoking areas.
(4) No enclosed corridor, gangway, accessway, or thoroughfare that is used by passengers may be included in any permitted smoking area.

(5) Where, on any passenger ship that is registered in New Zealand, or on any passenger train, any room or area is available for the consumption of liquor, the operator shall comply with the provisions of section 12 of this Act.

11. Smoking restricted in passenger lounges and waitingrooms–

(1) The owner or occupier of any booking area or passenger queuing area shall not permit any person to smoke in that area if the area is located within an enclosed travel terminal.

(2) Where any passenger waitingroom or passenger lounge is located within an enclosed travel terminal, the owner or occupier of that waitingroom or lounge shall not permit any person to smoke in any part of that waitingroom or lounge, except in a permitted smoking area.

(3) No person shall smoke in any booking area or passenger queuing area that is located within an enclosed travel terminal.

(4) Where any passenger waitingroom or passenger lounge is located within an enclosed travel terminal, no person shall smoke in that passenger waitingroom or passenger lounge, except in a permitted smoking area.

(5) The owner or occupier of any passenger lounge or passenger waitingroom may designate not more than half of its area as a permitted smoking area.

12. Smoking on licensed premises–

(1) Notwithstanding anything in section 5 of this Act, but subject to subsection (2) of this section and to section 13 of this Act, where, in any licensed premises, any room or enclosed area is set aside primarily for the consumption of liquor by patrons, the license may permit smoking in that room or area.

(2) Where, in any such room or enclosed area, seating is set aside for the consumption of meals by patrons, the license shall ensure that–
  (a) At least half of that seating is designated for persons who do not wish to smoke, and shall prominently display signs accordingly; and
  (b) Such designated seating, so far as is reasonably practicable, is separate from the seating where smoking is permitted; and
  (c) No person smokes in seating designated for persons who do not wish to smoke.

(3) No person shall smoke in any licensed premises in seating designated for persons who do not wish to smoke.

13. Smoking restricted in restaurants–

(1) Where, in any restaurant, there is only 1 room or enclosed area set aside for the consumption of food by patrons, the restaurateur shall ensure that–
  (a) At least half of the seating in that room or area is designated for persons who do not wish to smoke, and shall prominently display signs accordingly; and
  (b) Such designated seating, so far as is reasonably practicable, is

separate from the seating where smoking is permitted; and

(c) No person smokes in seating designated for persons who do not wish to smoke.

(2) Where, in any restaurant, there is more than 1 room or enclosed area set aside for the consumption of food by patrons, the restaurateur shall–

(a) Designate at least 1 such room or area for patrons who do not wish to smoke and prominently display signs accordingly; and

(b) Ensure that at least half of the seating in that restaurant is designated for persons who do not wish to smoke; and

(c) Ensure that no person smokes in that area so designated.

(3) No person shall smoke in any restaurant in seating designated for persons who do not wish to smoke.

(4) Where, in any premises or any part of any premises, or on any ship or train, more than 1 room or enclosed area is used as a restaurant, and 1 or more of those rooms or enclosed areas, or any combination of them, is treated as a separate restaurant by reason that it caters for a different category of patron, or offers a different type of meal or refreshment or a different type of service, the provisions of this section shall apply, in respect of each such room or enclosed area or, as the case may be, each such combination of them so treated, as if it were a separate restaurant.

14. Area health boards to enforce this Part–

(1) Every area health board shall ensure that sufficient persons are appointed to enforce the provisions of this Part of this Act within its area health district.

(2) Appointed people may be identified by name, or as the incumbent from time to time of one or more nominated positions within the area health board staffing establishment, and, if the board so resolves, may include any person appointed under the Factories and Commercial Premises Act 1981 as an Inspector of Factories, or any person appointed under the Construction Act 1959 as a Construction Safety Inspector, or the incumbent of any nominated position within the staffing establishment of a local authority under the Local Government Act 1974.

(3) Every person appointed under this section shall be given an instrument of appointment identifying the holder as a person appointed under this section, and may be required to produce it to any person of whom investigation or inquiry is being made under this Part of this Act.

15. Complaints relating to workplace smoking policies–

(1) Where any person believes on reasonable grounds that any person has contravened any provision of this Part of this Act in so far as it relates to any workplace, the person may complain to the employer of that workplace, or to the area health board for the district in which the workplace is situated, specifying the particulars of the complaint.

(2) Where an employer receives a complaint under subsection (1) of this

section, or a complaint is referred to an employer under section 16 (2) (a) of this Act, the employer shall, within 20 working days after receipt of the complaint, investigate the complaint, and, if it appears that a contravention has occurred, shall try to resolve the complaint.

(3) Where the contravention is on the part of the employer, the employer shall settle the cause of the complaint, or give an assurance that satisfies the complainant that there will be no repetition of the cause of the complaint.

(4) Where the contravention is on the part of an employee, the employer shall seek to obtain from the employee an assurance that satisfies the employer that there will be no repetition of the cause of the complaint.

(5) The representative of the employees in the workplace shall be entitled to be present at any meeting called by the employer for the purpose of resolving the complaint and avoiding future cause for complaint.

(6) Where the employer is unable to resolve the complaint by agreement, the employer shall refer the complaint in writing to the area health board for the district in which the workplace is situated.

16. Complaints to area health board–

(1) Any person may make a complaint to an area health board concerning a contravention by any person of any provision of this Part of this Act.

(2) When an area health board receives any complaint alleging contravention of this Part of this Act, the following provisions shall apply:

(a) Where–

(i) The contravention allegedly occurred in any workplace; and

(ii) The person who is the subject of the complaint is the employer for that workplace, or an employee of that employer; and

(iii) The complaint was not referred to the board by the employer under subsection (6) of section 15 of this Act–

the complaint shall be forwarded by the area health board to the employer to be dealt with under that section:

(b) In all other cases, the matter shall be dealt with as though it were a complaint to which subsection (3) of this section applied.

(3) On receipt by an area health board of a complaint under this Part of this Act, a person appointed under section 14 of this Act may make further inquiries by way of investigation in respect of the complaint.

(4) The person who investigates the complaint may take no further action if the complaint is trivial, frivolous, vexatious, or not made in good faith, or if, during the investigations, the person receives a satisfactory assurance that there will be no repetition of the cause for the complaint; and in any such case the person who made the complaint shall be advised of the reasons why no further action is being taken.

(5) The person investigating the complaint may, on investigation, try to settle the cause of the complaint and obtain a satisfactory assurance against repetition of the cause of the complaint.

(6) Where no such settlement and assurance can be obtained, or if the cause of

complaint is in breach of a previously given assurance, a complaint may be laid under the Summary Proceedings Act 1957 in respect of the relevant offence.

17. Offences in respect of smoking–

(1) Every employer who, without reasonable excuse, fails to prepare a written policy on smoking as required by section 5 (1) of this Act, or to review that policy as required by section 5 (5) of this Act, commits an offence and is liable,–

(a) In the case of a body corporate, to a fine not exceeding $4,000; or

(b) In the case of an individual, to a fine not exceeding $400.

(2) Every employer who fails, without reasonable excuse, to comply with any of the requirements of section 7 of this Act commits an offence and is liable,–

(a) In the case of a body corporate, to a fine not exceeding $4,000; or

(b) In the case of an individual, to a fine not exceeding $400.

(3) The operator of any aircraft who, without reasonable excuse, permits any person to smoke in contravention of section 8 (1) of this Act commits an offence and is liable,–

(a) In the case of a body corporate, to a fine not exceeding $4,000; or

(b) In the case of an individual, to a fine not exceeding $400.

(4) The operator of any passenger service vehicle who, without reasonable excuse, permits any person to smoke in contravention of section 9 (1) of this Act commits an offence and is liable,–

(a) In the case of a body corporate, to a fine not exceeding $4,000; or

(b) In the case of an individual, to a fine not exceeding $400.

(5) The operator of any passenger ship or train who, without reasonable excuse, permits any person to smoke in contravention of section 10 (1) of this Act commits an offence and is liable,–

(a) In the case of a body corporate, to a fine not exceeding $4,000; or

(b) In the case of an individual, to a fine not exceeding $400.

(6) Every owner or occupier of any enclosed travel terminal booking area, passenger queuing area, passenger waitingroom, or passenger lounge who, without reasonable excuse, permits any person to smoke in contravention of section 11 of this Act commits an offence and is liable,–

(a) In the case of a body corporate, to a fine not exceeding $4,000; or

(b) In the case of an individual, to a fine not exceeding $400.

(7) Every licensee who, without reasonable excuse, fails to comply with any of the requirements of section 12 (2) of this Act commits an offence and is liable,–

(a) In the case of a body corporate, to a fine not exceeding $4,000; or

(b) In the case of an individual, to a fine not exceeding $400.

(8) Every restaurateur who, without reasonable excuse, fails to comply with any of the requirements of subsection (1) or subsection (2) of section 13 of this Act commits an offence and is liable,–

(a) In the case of a body corporate, to a fine not exceeding $4,000; or
(b) In the case of an individual, to a fine not exceeding $400.

(9) Every person who smokes in contravention of section 8 (2) of this Act commits an offence and is liable to a fine not exceeding $400.

18. Prosecution of offences–

(1) No prosecution for an offence against any provision of this Part of this Act shall be commenced except on the information of a person appointed pursuant to section 14 of this Act.

(2) Notwithstanding anything in section 14 of the Summary Proceedings Act 1957, any information in respect of any offence against any provision of this Part of this Act may be laid at any time within 1 year after the time when the matter of the information arose.

19. Protection of persons acting under authority of Act–No person appointed under section 14 of this Act who does any act in pursuance or intended pursuance of any of the functions, duties, or powers conferred by or under this Act shall be under any civil or criminal liability in respect of the act, whether on the grounds of want of jurisdiction, or mistake of law or fact, or on any other ground unless he or she has acted in bad faith or without reasonable care.

20. Saving of powers to make bylaws–Nothing in this Part of this Act shall limit or affect the powers of an area health board under section 64 (1) (a) of the Health Act 1956, or of a local authority under section 684 (8) of the Local Government Act 1974, to make bylaws providing greater protection from tobacco smoke than is provided by this Part of this Act.

PART II
TOBACCO PRODUCTS CONTROL

21. Purpose of this Part–The purpose of this Part of this Act is–

(a) To reduce the social approval of tobacco use, particularly among young people, by imposing controls on the marketing, advertising, or promotion of tobacco products and their association through sponsorship with other products and events; and

(b) To reduce some of the harmful effects of tobacco products on the health of users by monitoring and regulating the presence of harmful substances in the products and in tobacco smoke.

Promotion and Advertising

22. Advertising of tobacco products–

(1) Subject to the succeeding provisions of this section and to section 23 of this Act, no person shall publish, or arrange for any other person to publish, any tobacco product advertisement in New Zealand.

(2) Nothing in subsection (1) of this section shall apply to any price list given to retailers of tobacco products if the price list includes the health messages required by or under this Part of this Act.

(3) Nothing in subsection (1) of this section shall apply to any advertisement included in any book, magazine, or newspaper printed outside New Zealand, or in any radio or television transmission originating outside New Zealand, or in any film or video recording madc outside New Zealand, unless–

(a) The principal purpose of the book, magazine, newspaper, transmission, film, or video recording is the promotion of the use of tobacco products; or

(b) The book, magazine,newspaper, film, or video recording is intended for sale, distribution, or exhibition primarily in New Zealand; or

(c) In the case of an advertisement in any radio or television transmission, the advertisement is targeted primarily at a New Zealand audience.

(4) Nothing in subsection (1) of this section shall apply to the publication by a tobacco products manufacturer of a tobacco product advertisement in a magazine that is intended for distribution only to employees of the manufacturer.

(5) Nothing in subsection (1) of this section shall apply to–

(a) The exhibition, in any museum or art gallery, of any work or artifact;

(b) The dissemination, broadcasting, or exhibition of any film, video recording, or sound recording, where–

(i) That film, video recording, or sound recording was made before the 16th day of December 1990; and

(ii) The tobacco product advertisement included in that film, video recording, or sound recording is in the form of a reference to, or a depiction of, a tobacco product trade mark that is only an incidental part of that film, video recording, or sound recording.

23. Exemptions for retailers and vending machines–

(1) Notwithstanding anything in section 22 of this Act, a retailer of tobacco products may do all or any of the following things:

(a) Expose any tobacco product for sale inside the retailer's place of business so long as no such product is visible from outside that place:

(b) Display, in accordance with regulations made under this Part of this Act, inside the retailer's place of business, any notice identifying the tobacco products that are available for purchase in that place and indicating their price;

(c) Display, in accordance with regulations made under this Part of this Act, at the retailer's place of business (not being a temporary or mobile place of business), at any time before the 1st day of January 1995, any sign that indicates that any tobacco product is offered for sale, so long as that sign–

(i) Was erected at that place of business before the 16th day of December 1990; and

(ii) Has not, since that date, been altered in any way (whether by way of repair, or repainting, or otherwise);

(d) Display the retailer's name or trade name on the exterior of the retailer's place of business, in accordance with regulations made under this Part of this Act, even though the name contains any word or expression signifying that any tobacco product is available in that place for purchase, so long as the name does not include the trade mark of a tobacco product or the company name of a tobacco products manufacturer.

(2) Any person who offers for sale, by way of an automatic vending machine, any tobacco product may, in accordance with regulations made under this Part of this Act, identify or depict that tobacco product, and its price, on the exterior of the vending machine.

24. Use of trade marks, etc., on goods other than tobacco products, or in relation to sponsored events–

(1) No person shall use, otherwise than in a private capacity, a tobacco product trade mark–

(a) On any article other than a tobacco product or a package or container in which a tobacco product is sold or shipped; or

(b) For the purpose of advertising or identifying to the public–

(i) Any article other than a tobacco product; or

(ii) Any service, activity, or event; or

(iii) Any scholarship, fellowship, or other educational benefit,–

even though that person would be, but for this Act, entitled to use the trade mark on that article or for that purpose.

(2) Where a trade mark includes the company name, or part of the company name, of a manufacturer, importer, or distributor in New Zealand of any tobacco product, no person shall, otherwise than in a private capacity, use that company name for the purpose of advertising or identifying to the public–

(a) Any article other than a tobacco product; or

(b) Any service, activity, or event; or

(c) Any scholarship, fellowship, or other educational benefit,–

even though that person would be, but for this Act, entitled to use that trade mark or company name for that purpose.

(3) No person shall distribute, sell, or offer or expose for sale any article, other than a tobacco product or a package or container in which a tobacco product is sold or shipped, that bears a trade mark of a tobacco product that is sold in New Zealand.

(4) Nothing in subsections (1) to (3) of this section shall apply to a trade mark or company name that, during the year ending with the 31st day of March 1990, was applied to tobacco products and other articles sold at retail in

New Zealand if the estimated retail value of those other articles sold during that year exceeded one-quarter of the estimated retail value of those tobacco products sold during that year.

(5) Nothing in subsections (1) to (3) of this section shall apply to the use, by any person (other than a manufacturer, an importer, a distributor, or a retailer of any tobacco products, or a person acting on behalf of any such manufacturer, importer, distributor, or retailer), of a trade mark or company name for any purpose (other than for application to, or for use in connection with, tobacco products or smoking accessories) if the trade mark or company name–

- (a) Was in use in New Zealand for that purpose before the 17th day of May 1990; or
- (b) Was in use for that purpose at any time before that trade mark or company name was first used, in New Zealand, for application to, or in connection with, any tobacco product or smoking accessory.

25. Organising or promoting activity using trade mark, etc., of tobacco products–No manufacturer, importer, distributor, or retailer of tobacco products shall–

- (a) Organise or promote any organised activity that is to take place, in whole or in part, in New Zealand; or
- (b) Make any financial contribution towards any organised activity that is to take place, or is taking place, or has taken place, in whole or in part, in New Zealand; or
- (c) Make any financial contribution to any person in respect of–
  - (i) The organisation or promotion, by that person, of; or
  - (ii) The participation, by the person, in–

  any organised activity that is to take place, or is taking place, or has taken place, in whole or in part, in New Zealand–

where that organised activity involves the use, in the name of that activity, or on any article other than a tobacco product, of a tobacco product trade mark, or of a company name or any part of a company name included in that tobacco product trade mark.

26. Exemptions for participants in certain events–

(1) Nothing in section 22 or section 24 or section 25 of this Act shall apply to the display, on any craft, of any tobacco product trade mark or the company name of any tobacco products manufacturer, where–

- (a) That craft is participating in an international race; and
- (b) The tobacco products manufacturer who manufactures that tobacco product, or whose company name is so displayed, is sponsoring, in whole or in part, the participation of that craft in that race; and
- (c) New Zealand is a port of call for that race.

(2) Notwithstanding anything in section 22 or section 24 or section 25 of this Act, the Minister may, by notice in writing, grant an exemption from any

of the provisions of those sections in respect of the promotion of any international craft race where New Zealand is a port of call for that race.

(3) Notwithstanding anything in section 22 or section 24 or section 25 of this Act, where–

(a) The Minister is satisfied that any competition is of international significance; and

(b) Any part of that competition is to take place in New Zealand,–

the Minister may, by notice in writing, grant an exemption from any of those sections in respect of any participant in that competition (not being a participant who is a New Zealand resident) for the purpose of allowing that participant to fulfil any obligation imposed on that participant to acknowledge any sponsor (being an obligation incurred before that participant submitted that person's entry for that competition).

(4) The Minister may grant an exemption under subsection (2) or subsection (3) of this section either unconditionally or subject to such conditions as the Minister thinks fit.

(5) The Minister may from time to time, by notice in writing to the person to whom any exemption is granted under subsection (2) or subsection (3) of this section, amend or revoke that exemption.

27. Exemption for craft in emergencies–Where any craft on which is displayed any tobacco product trade mark or the company name of any tobacco products manufacturer is compelled, for reasons of health or safety, or for the preservation of life or property, to enter New Zealand, nothing in section 22 or section 24 or section 25 of this Act shall apply to the display, on that craft, of that tobacco product trade mark or that company name for as long as that craft is in New Zealand for any of those reasons.

28. Free distribution and rewards prohibited–

(1) No manufacturer, distributor, importer, or retailer of tobacco products shall–

(a) Distribute any tobacco product; or

(b) Supply any tobacco product to any person for subsequent distribution; or

(c) In the case of a retailer, supply any tobacco product to any person for the purpose of that retailer's business,–

free of charge, or at a reduced charge other than a normal trade discount.

(2) No person shall offer any gift or cash rebate, or the right to participate in any contest, lottery, or game, to the purchaser of a tobacco product in consideration for the purchase of that product, or to any person in consideration for the provision of evidence of such a purchase.

29. Tobacco product not to be advertised or labelled as suitable for chewing, etc.–

(1) No person shall publish an advertisement for a tobacco product that

directly or indirectly states or suggests that the product is suitable for chewing or for any other oral use (other than smoking).

(2) No person shall import for sale, sell, pack, or distribute any tobacco product labelled or otherwise described as suitable for chewing, or for any other oral use (other than smoking).

Sale and Labelling

30. Prohibition of sales of tobacco products to persons under 16–

(1) No person shall sell any tobacco product to a person who has not attained the age of 16 years.

(2) It shall be a defence to a charge under subsection (1) of this section to prove that the person who sold the tobacco product believed on reasonable grounds that the person to whom it was sold was of or over the age of 16 years.

(3) Except as permitted by regulations made under this Part of this Act, no person shall permit any tobacco product to be sold by way of an automatic vending machine from any place to which a person who has not attained the age of 16 years may lawfully have access.

(4) Subsection (3) of this section shall not apply to–

(a) Any premises in respect of which a club licence is in force under the Sale of Liquor Act 1989; or

(b) Any premises in respect of which an on-licence is in force under that Act; or

(c) Any canteen, cafetaria, or similar facility provided by an employer for the provision of refreshments to that person's employees during working hours.

(5) Every person who sells by retail any tobacco product shall display clearly for the public a notice to the effect that the sale of any tobacco product to persons who have not attained the age of 16 years is prohibited.

31. Limits on harmful constituents–No manufacturer or importer shall offer for sale or export any tobacco product that–

(a) Contains or generates in its smoke a harmful constituent specified for the purposes of this Act in regulations made under this Part of this Act; or

(b) Contains harmful constituents in excess of the limits prescribed by regulations made under this Part of this Act, as determined in accordance with any tests so prescribed.

32. Labelling and health messages–

(1) No manufacturer, distributor, importer, or retailer shall sell or offer for sale a tobacco product unless–

(a) The package containing the product displays, in accordance with regulations made under this Part of this Act,–

(i) A message relating to the effects of the use of the product on health; and

(ii) A list of the harmful constituents of the product; and

(iii) In the case of a tobacco product intended for smoking, a list of the harmful constituents, and their respective quantities, present in the smoke; and

(b) A leaflet containing information relating to the effects of the use of the product on health is placed inside the package with the product, if and as required by regulations made under this Part of this Act.

(2) In subsection (1) of this section the term "harmful constituent" means any substance declared by regulations made under this Part of this Act to be a harmful constituent for the purposes of that subsection.

(3) Every person who offers for sale, by way of an automatic vending machine, any tobacco product shall, in accordance with regulations made under this Act, display on the vending machine such health meassage as is required by or under this Act.

Testing, Reports, and Returns

33. Annual testing for constituents–

(1) This section applies to each class of tobacco products that may be prescribed for the purposes of this section by regulations made under this Part of this Act.

(2) Every manufacturer and every importer of any class of tobacco product to which this section applies shall in each year conduct, in accordance with regulations made under this Part of this Act, a test for the constituents of each brand of that class of product sold by the manufacturer or importer, and the respective quantities of those constituents.

34. Director-General may require further testing–

(1) Subject to subsection (3) of this section, in addition to the annual test required by subsection (2) of section 33 of this Act, the Director-General may, by notice in writing to the manufacturer or importer of any class of tobacco product to which that section applies, require a further test to be carried out for the constituents of any brand of that class of product sold by the manufacturer or importer and the respective quantities of those constituents.

(2) Any such additional test shall be carried out in a laboratory nominated by the Director-General, but at the expense in all respects of the manufacturer or importer.

(3) The Director-General shall not, in any year, require tests under this section in respect of more than 10 percent of the brands of tobacco products sold by any particular manufacturer or importer.

35. Returns and reports–

(1) Every manufacturer and every importer of any class of tobacco product shall, not later than the 31st day of January in each year, file with the

Director-General, in the prescribed form and manner,–

(a) A return showing–

(i) The weight of tobacco and of all additives used in the manufacture of each such product sold by the manufacturer or importer during the previous year; and

(ii) The quantity of each brand, and of each brand variant, of each such product sold by the manufacturer or importer during the previous year; and

(iii) The recommended price of each brand, and each brand variant, of each such product sold by the manufacturer or importer during the previous year; and

(b) A report of the results of all tests that, during the previous year, have been conducted by that manufacturer or importer for the purposes of section 33 or section 34 of this Act.

(2) Where any report is received by the Director-General under subsection (1) (b) of this section, the Director-General may publish or make publicly available the report or such parts of the report as he or she thinks fit.

Offences

36. Offences in respect of tobacco products–

(1) Every person who, without reasonable excuse, publishes any advertisement for a tobacco product in contravention of section 22 of this Act commits an offence and is liable,–

(a) In the case of a manufacturer, an importer, or a distributor, to a fine not exceeding $50,000; or

(b) In any other case, to a fine not exceeding $10,000.

(2) Every person who, without reasonable excuse, uses any trade mark or company name in contravention of subsection (1) or subsection (2) of section 24 of this Act, or who distributes, sells, or offers or exposes for sale any article in contravention of subsection (3) of that section commits an offence and is liable,–

(a) In the case of a manufacturer, an importer, or a distributor, to a fine not exceeding $50,000; or

(b) In any other case, to a fine not exceeding $10,000.

(3) Every manufacturer, importer, distributor, or retailer of tobacco products who, in contravention of section 25 of this Act, organises or promotes any organised activity, or makes any financial contribution towards any organised activity, or makes any financial contribution to any other person in respect of the organisation or promotion, by that other person, of, or the participation, by that other person, in, any organised activity, commits an offence and is liable,–

(a) In the case of a manufacturer, an importer, or a distributor, to a fine not exceeding $50,000; or

(b) In any other case, to a fine not exceeding $10,000.

(4) Every manufacturer, distributor, importer, or retailer of tobacco products

who distributes or supplies any tobacco product in contravention of section 28 (1) of this Act commits an offence and is liable to a fine not exceeding $50,000.

(5) Every person who offers any gift, cash rebate, or right of participation in contravention of section 28 (2) of this Act, or who publishes any advertisement in contravention of section 29 (1) of this Act, or who imports, sells, packs, or distributes any tobacco product in contravention of section 29 (2) of this Act, commits an offence and is liable,–

(a) In the case of a manufacturer, an importer, or a distributor, to a fine not exceeding $50,000; or

(b) In any other case, to a fine not exceeding $10,000.

(6) Every person who sells any tobacco product in contravention of section 30 (1) of this Act, or who permits any tobacco product to be sold in contravention of section 30 (3) of this Act, commits an offence and is liable to a fine not exceeding $2,000.

(7) Every retailer of tobacco products who fails, without reasonable excuse, to display the notice required by section 30 (5) of this Act commits an offence and is liable to a fine not exceeding $2,000.

(8) Every manufacturer or importer who offers for sale or export any tobacco product without conducting reasonable tests to establish whether or not it contains or generates in its smoke–

(a) Any harmful constituent prohibited by regulations made under this Part of this Act for the purposes of section 31 (a) of this Act; or

(b) Any harmful constituent in excess of the level permitted by regulations made under this Part of this Act for the purposes of section 31 (b) of this Act,–

commits an offence and is liable to a fine not exceeding $10,000.

(9) Every manufacturer, importer, distributor, or retailer of tobacco products who sells or offers for sale any tobacco product knowing that it contravenes section 32 (1) of this Act commits an offence and is liable,–

(a) In the case of a manufacturer, an importer, or a distributor, to a fine not exceeding $10,000; or

(b) In any other case, to a fine not exceeding $4,000.

(10) Every person who offers for sale, by way of an automatic vending machine, any tobacco product and who, in contravention of section 32 (3) of this Act, fails, without reasonable excuse, to display on that vending machine such health message as is required by or under this Act commits an offence and is liable to a fine not exceeding $4,000.

(11) Every manufacturer or importer of tobacco products who fails,without reasonable excuse,–

(a) To conduct any test required by section 33 (2) of this Act; or

(b) To conduct any further test required under section 34 of this Act; or

(c) To submit any return required by section 35 (1) (a) of this Act; or

(d) To submit any report required by section 35 (1) (b) of this Act,–

commits an offence and is liable to a fine not exceeding $10,000.

37. Enforcement–

(1) It shall be the duty of the Director-General to enforce the provisions of this Part of this Act.

(2) No prosecution for an offence against any provision of this Part of this Act shall be commenced except on the information of the Director-General or of some other person authorised for that purpose by the Director-General.

(3) Notwithstanding anything in section 14 of the Summary Proceedings Act 1957, any information in respect of any offence against any provision of this Part of this Act may be laid at any time within 1 year after the time when the matter of the information arose.

38. Principals and agents–For the purpose of this Part of this Act, every person shall be deemed to advertise a tobacco product, whether he or she does so on his or her own account or as the agent or employee of any other person.

Miscellaneous Provisions

39. Regulations–The Governor-General may from time to time, by Order in Council, make regulations for all or any of the following purposes:

(a) Prescribing forms, certificates, leaflets, signs, particulars, and notifications, and the persons by whom and the persons to whom any such forms, certificates, leaflets, signs, particulars, and notifications are to be supplied;

(b) Prescribing records and registers for the purposes of this Part of this Act; prescribing the manner in which and the period during which any such records and registers are to be kept; and prescribing the persons to whom, and the conditions on which, any such records and registers may be available for searching, inspections, and copying;

(c) Prescribing the form and manner in which tobacco products may be identified and depicted on the exterior of vending machines;

(d) Prescribing the form and manner in which a retailer of tobacco products may advertise tobacco products at that person's place of business;

(e) Prescribing the form, size, and content of information and messages to be displayed with, on, or in packages of, tobacco products or on automatic vending machines that dispense tobacco products; and prescribing the circumstances and manner in which the information and messages are to be so displayed;

(f) Prescribing the class or classes of tobacco products to which section 33 of this Act is to apply, and regulating the tests that are to be conducted under that section;

(g) Specifying harmful substances and other constituents of tobacco products for the purpose of section 33 of this Act;

(h) Prescribing the method of determining the constituents of tobacco products and the smoke produced from their combustion;

(i) Prescribing the form and manner in which returns and reports are to be filed under section 35 of this Act;

(j) Providing for such other matters as are contemplated by or necessary for giving full effect to the provisions of this Part of this Act or its due administration.

40. Transitional provisions–

(1) Nothing in section 24 (3) of this Act shall apply in respect of the distribution or sale before the 1st day of January 1996 of any article that was–

(a) Manufactured before the 17th day of May 1990; or

(b) Ordered before the 17th day of May 1990 from the manufacturer or distributor otherwise than by the placing of a standing order that required confirmation, or that was subject to cancellation, after that date.

(2) Notwithstanding anything in section 22 or section 24 or section 25 of this Act, where it is so required by a contract entered into before the 17th day of May 1990, the name of any manufacturer or importer of tobacco products or the trade mark of any tobacco product may be used until the close of the 30th day of June 1993, otherwise than in association with a tobacco product, in a representation to the public–

(a) That promotes or is associated with an organised activity; or

(b) That acknowledges financial or other contributions made by the manufacturer or importer of the tobacco product toward any such activity

(3) The first reports required by section 35 (1) (b) of this Act shall be submitted to the Director-General–

(a) By the 31st day of January 1991, in the case of cigarettes; or

(b) By the 31st day of January 1992, in the case of cigarette tobacco; or

(c) By the date specified by the Director-General by notice in writing to the manufacturer or importer, in the case of any other tobacco product.

41. Amendment, repeals, and revocations–

(1) Section 2 (1) of the Toxic Substances Act 1979 is hereby amended by repealing paragraph (c) of the definition of the term "toxic substance" (as substituted by section 2 of the Toxic Substances Amendment Act 1986).

(2) Section 2 (3) of the Toxic Substances Act 1979 is hereby repealed.

(3) Part VIII of the Toxic Substances Act 1979 (comprising sections 72 to 74) is hereby repealed.

(4) Section 2 of the Toxic Substances Amendment Act 1986 is hereby repealed.

(5) Part VIA of the Toxic Substances Regulations 1983 (comprising regulations 46A to 46C) (as substituted by regulation 3 of the Toxic Substances Regulations 1983, Amendment No. 2) is hereby revoked.

(6) Regulation 3 of the Toxic Substances Regulations 1983, Amendment No. 2 is hereby revoked.

PART III
HEALTH SPONSORSHIP COUNCIL

42. Meaning of "sponsorship"–

(1) In this Part of this Act, "sponsorship" means, in broad terms, the provision of assistance by the Council to any person or organisation and, in return, the promotion by that person or organisation of health and healthy lifestyles in a manner agreed by the Council.

(2) Without limiting the generality of the term, such assistance by the Council may take the form of–
   (a) Money, whether by way of grant or otherwise; or
   (b) Goods and services; or
   (c) Trophies, prizes, awards, and scholarships.

(3) Also, without limiting the generality of the term, such promotion by the person or organisation receiving assistance may take the form of–
   (a) Publicising messages relating to health and healthy lifestyles; or
   (b) Publicising messages relating to ill-health and unhealthy lifestyles; or
   (c) Promoting the aims and objectives of the Council.

43. Council established–

(1) There is hereby established a council, to be known as the Health Sponsorship Council.

(2) The Council shall be a body corporate with perpetual succession and a common seal, and shall be capable of suing and being sued and of doing and suffering all that bodies corporate may do and suffer.

44. Principal functions of Council–

(1) The principal functions of the Council shall be–
   (a) To promote health and to encourage healthy lifestyles, whether through the provision of sponsorhip or otherwise; and
   (b) To make sponsorhip available to any person or organisation in accordance with section 56 of this Act.

(2) For the purposes of its principal functions, the Council may provide sponsorship to–
   (a) Any person or organisation involved in sports participation, artistic endeavour, cultural pursuits, or recreational activities; or
   (b) Any person or organisation involved in arranging any sporting, artistic, or recreational activity; or
   (c) Any person or organisation in accordance with section 56 of this Act.

45. Membership of Council–

(1) The Council shall have such number of members, being not fewer than 3 nor more than 6, as the Minister may from time to time determine.

(2) Each member shall be appointed by the Minister.

(3) One member of the Council shall be appointed as Chairperson of the

Council.

(4) The powers of the Council shall not be affected by any vacancy in its membership.

46. Term of office of members of Council–

(1) Subject to the succeeding provisions of this section, every member of the Council shall hold office for such term, not exceeding 3 years, as the Minister shall specify in the instrument of appointment of that member, but may from time to time be reappointed.

(2) Any member of the Council may resign at any time by notice in writing to the Minister.

(3) Any member of the Council may be removed from office at any time by the Minister by notice in writing to the member.

(4) Every member of the Council whose term of office expires shall nevertheless continue in office until that member's successor comes into office.

47. Meetings of Council–

(1) The first meeting of the Council shall be held on a day to be fixed by the Minister.

(2) Subsequent meetings of the Council shall be held at such times and places as the Council or the chairperson from time to time decides.

(3) At all meetings of the Council, the quorum necessary for the transaction of business shall be 3 members.

(4) The Council shall keep, in the custody of the Director, a minute book in which shall be recorded all resolutions and decisions of the Council.

(5) The entries in the minute book relating to a meeting of the Council shall be signed by the person who presided at that meeting, one other member, and the Director.

(6) Subject to the provisions of this Part of this Act, the Council may regulate its procedure in such manner as it thinks fit.

48. Conflict of interest–

(1) If any member has any interest in any contract under consideration by the Council, or is a member of, or is affiliated to, or is otherwise interested in, any organisation with whom the Council is considering entering into any contract, the member shall declare that interest at the first meeting of the Council at which or after which the member first becomes aware of the matter.

(2) In such a case, the member shall take no further part in the discussion or deliberations of the Council on that matter and shall, if the person presiding at the time so requests, withdraw from the room while the matter is being discussed or determined.

49. Council to appoint Director–

(1) The Council shall appoint and employ a suitably qualified person to be the

Director of the Council.

(2) The Director shall be the principal administrative officer of the Council, and shall be responsible to the Council for–

(a) The performance of other members of the staff of the Council; and

(b) The keeping of proper accounts and records; and

(c) The annual preparation of the budget, the strategic plan, and the annual plan required by section 58 of this Act; and

(d) Such other matters as may be required of the Director from time to time by the Council.

50. Other staff–

(1) The Council may from time to time engage such other persons as may be required to enable the Council to carry out its functions under this Act.

(2) The Council may pay to any such persons such remuneration by way of fees, salary, wages, or allowances, and such travelling allowances and expenses, as may from time to time be fixed, either generally or in respect of any particular person or persons, by the Council.

51. Council may appoint advisory and technical committees–

(1) The Council may from time to time appoint advisory, technical, and other committees to advise it on such matters as it may refer to them.

(2) Any person may be appointed to be a member of any such committee even though that person is not a member of the Council.

(3) Every such committee shall in all matters be subject to the control of the Council, and shall carry out all directions, general or special, of the Council in relation to the Council or its affairs.

(4) Subject to the provisions of this Act, every committee appointed under this section may regulate its procedure within the limits of the authority conferred on it by the Council.

52. Council may co-opt specialist advice–

(1) The Council, and any advisory, technical, or other committee appointed by the Council, may from time to time invite any person, or any officer employed in a Government department, or a representative of any organisation, who, in its opinion, possesses expert knowledge or is otherwise able to assist it in connection with the exercise of its functions, to attend any of its meetings or to advise it on any matter with which it is concerned.

(2) Any person attending a meeting under this section may, if invited, take part in any discussion at the meeting, but shall not have any voting rights.

53. Remuneration and allowances for members of Council and committees–

(1) The Council is hereby declared to be a statutory Board within the meaning of the Fees and Travelling Allowances Act 1951.

(2) There shall be paid to the members of the Council, and to every member of any committee appointed by the Council, remuneration by way of fees, salary, or allowances, and travelling allowances and expenses, in accordance with the Fees and Travelling Allowances Act 1951, and the provisions of that Act shall apply as if in the case of any such committee, that committee were a statutory Board within the meaning of that Act.

54. Salaries, etc., to be paid out of funds of Council–All fees, salaries, allowances, and other expenditure payable or incurred under or in the administration of this Part of this Act shall be payable out of the funds of the Council.

55. Powers of Council–

(1) Subject to the succeeding provisions of this Part of this Act, the Council shall have all such powers as may be reasonably necessary to enable it to carry out its functions.

(2) The Council may from time to time delegate to the Director power to execute contracts on behalf of the Council, either in a particular case or a particular class of case, or within such limits as the Council may specify.

56. Council to provide alternative sponsorship–

(1) This section applies to any person or organisation that–

(a) During the year ending with the 17th day of May 1990, received, from any manufacturer, importer, or distributor of any tobacco product, any financial or other assistance in respect of the organisation or promotion of, or participation in, any organised activity; and

(b) When that assistance was provided, had a reasonable expectation of receiving future financial or other assistance from that manufacturer, importer, or distributor, being assistance the provision of which would be an offence against any provision of Part II of this Act; and

(c) Is unable to obtain assistance from some other source as an alternative to the future assistance referred to in paragraph (b) of this subsection.

(2) Every person or organisation that applies to the Council for the provision of sponsorship and that satisfies the Council that he or she or it is a person to whom or an organisation to which this section applies,–

(a) Shall be entitled to have made available to that person or organisation, by the Council, not less than the amount of sponsorship that the Council is satisfied is equivalent to the amount or value of the future financial or other assistance referred to in subsection (1) (b) of this section which that person or organisation reasonably expected to receive, and which that person or organisation is unable to obtain from some other source, during the period of 2 years immediately following–

(i) The date on which that person or organisation ceases to receive the financial or other assistance referred to in subsection (1) (a) of this section; or

(ii) The 30th day of June 1993,–

whichever occurs first; and

(b) Shall, unless the Council considers that there is good reason not to do so, be entitled to have made available to that person or organisation, by the Council, not less than the amount of sponsorship that the Council is satisfied is equivalent to the amount or value of the future financial or other assistance referred to in subsection (1) (b) of this section which that person or organisation reasonably expected to receive, and which that person or organisation is unable to obtain from some other source, during the period of 1 year immediately following the period of 2 years referred to in paragraph (a) of this subsection.

57. Minister may give Council directions–

(1) The Minister may from time to time give to the Council a written direction relating to the performance of the Council's functions or the exercise of its powers, either generally or specifically, and the Council shall comply with the terms of the direction.

(2) Every such direction shall be included in the Council's annual report for the year in which it is received.

58. Council to submit annual budget and plans for Minister's approval–

(1) Not later than 1 month before the start of each financial year, the Council shall prepare and submit to the Minister for the Minister's approval, in respect of that year,–

(a) A budget of planned income and expenditure, including balance sheets and a statement of cash flows; and

(b) A strategic plan of the intended health directions and programmes to be published through sponsorship over the next 5 years, but subject to annual review; and

(c) An annual plan setting out the specific activities and priorities planned by the Council for the year.

(2) The Council shall not commit any of its funds to any form of sponsorship until its first budget and annual plan have been approved by the Minister.

59. Funds of Council–

(1) The funds of the Council shall consist of–

(a) Money from time to time appropriated by Parliament for the purposes of the Council; and

(b) Any interest earned on any such money pending its application by the Council; and

(c) Any proceeds of sale received by the Council on the sale of any of its assets; and

(d) Any donations, grants, or bequests received by the Council for its purposes.

(2) The funds of the Council shall be held in such bank account as the Council may from time to time determine, of which the Council shall give written notice to the Minister and to the Secretary to the Treasury.

(3) The Council may keep any of its funds not immediately required for its purposes in an interest-bearing account, but shall not have any other powers of investment.

(4) The funds of the Council shall be expended–

(a) In accordance with sponsorship arrangements designed to promote the principal functions of the Council; and

(b) For the purposes specified in section 54 of this Act.

60. Further provisions relating to funds–

(1) Any funds received by the Council in one year and not expended by the Council in that year shall, without further appropriation by Parliament, be available to, and may be expended by, the Council, in any subsequent year.

(2) Subject to subsection (3) of this section, the Council shall not commit itself to expend any money by way of sponsorship unless it has the money in hand at the time.

(3) The Council may in any year commit itself to expend by way of sponsorship in the next succeeding year in aggregate up to 25 percent of the amount of the money appropriated by Parliament for the purposes of the Council for the current year.

61. Liability of Council and members–

(1) The liability of the Council shall be limited to the aggregate value of its assets, including all money standing to its credit at a bank, and all money to which it is entitled by way of repayment of any loan.

(2) No member of the Council or of any committee appointed by the Council shall be liable for anything done or omitted to be done by the Council or the committee unless the member has acted in bad faith.

62. Accounts–

(1) The Council shall keep proper books of account, on a normal accrual basis in accordance with accepted accounting principles, in which shall be kept full, true, and complete accounts of the affairs and transactions of the Council.

(2) As soon as practicable after the end of each financial year the Council shall prepare a proper statement of accounts for that year and a balance sheet as at the end of that year, and shall submit the accounts of the Council to the Audit Office for audit.

(3) For the purpose of the audit of the accounts, the funds of the Council shall be deemed to be public money within the meaning of the Public Finance Act 1989; and the Audit Office shall have the same duties and powers in

respect of the funds, and of every person dealing with them, as it has in respect of public money and accounts and of persons dealing with them.

63. Annual reports–

(1) As soon as practicable after the end of each financial year, the Council shall prepare a report for that year.

(2) The Council shall include in the report–

(a) A statement of its activities during the year in performance of its principal functions, a summary of the sponsorship arrangements entered into, and an assessment of their effectiveness; and

(b) The manner in which the Council has attempted to achieve, or work towards achieving, the goals set out in its current annual plan and strategic plan; and

(c) The terms of any direction given to the Council during the year by the Minister under section 57 of this Act; and

(d) The manner in which the Council has complied with any such direction (whether given in that year or in any previous year); and

(e) A copy of its audited accounts for the year.

(3) The Minister shall table a copy of the report in the House of Representatives within 16 sitting days after receiving it.

(4) The requirements of this section are in addition to any requirement to report imposed on the Council by any of sections 41 to 43 of the Public Finance Act 1989.

64. Ombudsmen Act 1975 amended–Part II of the First Schedule to the Ombudsmen Act 1975 is hereby amended by inserting, in its appropriate alphabetical order, the following item:

"The Health Sponsorship Council."

65. Films Act 1983 amended–Part II of the Schedule to the Films Act 1983 is hereby amended by inserting, in its appropriate alphabetical order, the following item:

"The Health Sponsorship Council."

This Act is administered in the Department of Health.

NIGERIA

NIGERIA. The Tobacco Smoking (Control) Decree 1990. Decree No. 20. Dated 25 June 1990. (3 pp.) **Nig. 90.13**

Secs. 1-3 of this Decree, which is to come into operation on a date to be published in the *Gazette*, read as follows:

"**1.** Notwithstanding anything contained in the Constitution of the Federal Republic of Nigeria 1979, as amended, or in any other enactment or law, no person shall, as from the commencement of this Decree, engage in or continue to engage in tobacco smoking in the places specified in Schedule 1 to this Decree.

2. (1) In pursuance of this Decree, no person shall advertise tobacco products to the general public in a bid to encourage tobacco smoking through any of the means specified in Schedule 2 to this Decree unless the advertisement contains a warning that tobacco smoking is dangerous to health.

(2) Pursuant to subsection (1) of this Section, no tobacco industry, firm or association of individuals or any other body corporate shall sponsor or promote any of their products at any sports event sponsored or promoted by them.

3. (1) Except as provided by this Decree, no package containing tobacco products meant for smoking shall be sold in Nigeria, unless the following rotating warnings are inscribed on the package, that is—

(*a*) 'The Federal Ministry of Health warns that tobacco smoking is dangerous to health'; and

(*b*) 'Smokers are liable to die young'.

(2) Pursuant to subsection (1) of this Section, it shall be unlawful for any person to sell any tobacco product in Nigeria unless the amount of the tar and nicotine contents of each unit of the product is stated on the package."

Secs. 4-6 deal with penal and other legal matters. Sec. 7 defines "tobacco" to include manufactured and unmanufactured tobacco of every description which is processed and used for smoking (in pipes, cigars, and cigarettes).

Schedule 1 lists the following: (*a*) cinema, theatre, or stadium; (*b*) offices; (*c*) public transportation; (*d*) lifts; (*e*) medical establishments; (*f*) schools; and (*g*) nursery institutions.

Schedule 2 lists the following: (*a*) newspapers; (*b*) magazines; (*c*) radio; (*d*) television; (*e*) cinema; (*f*) billboards; and (*g*) handbills.

NORWAY

NORWAY. Regulations No. 830 of 25 March 1983 on the labelling of packets of cigarettes, packets of smoking tobacco, and packets of cigarette paper. (*Norsk Lovtidend*, Section I, 4 May 1983, No. 9, pp. 305-307) **Norw. 84.12**

These Regulations have been made by the Ministry of Social Affairs in pursuance of certain provisions of Law No. 14 of 9 March 1973 on restrictive measures in trade in tobacco products, etc. (see *IDHL*, 1975, **26**, 571) and revoke the Regulations of 25 October 1974 on the same subject (see *ibid.*, 572). The following are among the principal provisions.

Chapter I. General provisions (Secs. 1-6). Sec. 1 provides that products subject to compulsory labelling may not be imported into or sold or supplied in Norway unless their packaging is labelled in accordance with these Regulations. Under Sec. 2, the requirements concerning labelling apply to cigarettes, smoking tobacco, and cigarette paper. Sec. 3 prohibits any person manufacturing or selling tobacco products (cigarettes, cigars, smoking tobacco, chewing tobacco, snuff, cigarette paper, cigarette-rolling equipment, and pipes) from providing his own information, by means of symbols or words on the packaging, concerning the effects of tobacco on health. Sec. 4 prescribes that products to which the labelling requirement applies are to carry a symbol approved by the Ministry of Social Affairs and a warning, in Norwegian, pointing out the danger to health entailed by the use of cigarettes. The content and wording of the warning are to be approved by the Directorate of Health Services. Cigarette packets must also bear a statement of composition in accordance with these provisions. Under Sec. 5, the statement is to be printed directly on individual packets or to take the form of a label appended to the packet in such a way that it is difficult to remove. The external packaging must also be labelled if this is required under the special provisions laid down in Chapter II. Sec. 6 provides that the symbol and printed warning are to be located in a prominent part of the cigarette packet and framed with a continuous line. The symbol, text, and frame must stand out clearly against the background, which is to be of a single colour. The statement of composition is to be situated apart from the symbol and warning.

Chapter II. Special provisions (Secs. 7-9). Sec. 7 specifies the dimensions and positioning of the symbol, warning, and statement of composition that must appear on cigarette packets in accordance with the provisions of Annexes A and B.[a] Sec. 8 provides that packets and tins of smoking tobacco are to display the symbol and warning prescribed for cigarette packets. Under Sec. 9, packets of cigarette paper must display the following warning: "Warning by the Directorate of Health Services: daily cigarette smoking is dangerous to health".

Chapter III. Sanctions, exemptions, etc. (Secs. 10-13). Under Sec. 11, the Ministry of Social Affairs may, in exceptional circumstances, grant exemptions from the provisions of these Regulations. All applicants for an exemption in respect of a particular kind of packaging must submit a new proposal for labelling for the approval of the Ministry of Social Affairs, which will in general be given only after consultation with the National Council on Smoking and Health [*Statens tobakkskaderåd*].

NORWAY. Law No. 24 of 6 May 1988 amending Law No. 14 of 9 March 1973 on restrictive measures in trade in tobacco products, etc. (*Norsk Lovtidend*, Part I, 26 May 1988, No. 8, pp. 287-288)

Norw. 88.9

Law No. 14 of 9 March 1973 (see *IDHL*, 1975, **26**, 571) is henceforth designated as the "Law on protection against tobacco-induced injury". A new Sec. 6 reading as follows is introduced (the existing Secs. 6-10 are renumbered as Secs. 7-11):

"**6.** The air shall be smoke-free in premises and means of transport to which the public has access, as well as in meeting rooms and work premises in which two or more persons are present. This measure shall not apply to restaurants, hotels, and other catering and lodging premises.

In the event that several premises have the same purpose within a single establishment, smoking may be permitted in not more than half of them. In premises or vehicles, smoking and no-smoking areas may only be demarcated if the smoke cannot spread into the no-smoking area. The no-smoking premises and areas shall not be smaller or of a lower standard than the smoking premises and areas.

The owner of premises or vehicles, or any other person in charge thereof, shall be responsible for ensuring that these provisions, or rules issued for their implementation, are complied with. In the event of any doubt as to the status of particular premises, a notice shall clearly indicate that smoking is prohibited.

If a person, in spite of a warning notice displayed by the owner or operator of premises or a vehicle, or his representative, contravenes the provisions laid down in this Section, or provisions issued for its implementation, he may be expelled from the said premises or vehicle.

The Directorate of Health and Social Affairs may, in certain special cases, grant an exemption from the rules laid down in this Section or provisions issued for its implementation, and define the conditions under which this exemption may be granted. Exemptions applicable to work premises shall be determined by the Labour Inspectorate.

The Directorate of Health and Social Affairs shall be responsible for carrying out surveillance to ensure that the provisions laid down in this Section and the rules issued for its implementation are complied with. In the case of work premises, surveillance shall be the responsibility of the Labour Inspectorate."

It is laid down that the above provisions are applicable without prejudice to those laid down by Law No. 66 of 19 November 1982 on health surveys in communes (see *ibid.*, 1983, **34**, 483, **Norw. 83.23**) and Law No. 4 of 4 February 1977 on the protection of workers and the working environment (see *ibid.*, 1979, **30**, 109). The Crown may issue further rules on the enforcement and implementation of these provisions, grant exemptions from the said provisions, and lay down regulations on requirements for smoke-free air in restaurants, hotels, and other catering and lodging premises.

NORWAY. Regulations No. 563 of 8 July 1988 on protection against tobacco-induced injury. (*Norsk Lovtidend*, Part I, 29 July 1988, No. 13, pp. 634-656)

Norw. 88.13

These Regulations have been made by the Ministry of Social Affairs in pursuance of certain provisions of Law No. 14 of 9 March 1973, as amended by Law No. 24 of 6 May 1988 (see *supra*). The following are the principal provisions.

Sec. 1 (New food-consumption premises and canteens at places of work) lays down that the construction of new premises or significant alterations must be such that the requirements laid down in the second paragraph of Sec. 6 of the said Law are complied with. Sec. 2 (Exceptional provisions applicable to existing food-consumption premises and canteens at places of work) lays down that, if there are technical or financial difficulties in the way of a total separation between the smoking and no-smoking zones, the arrangements adopted are to be defensible from a health point of view. In addition to the considerations set out in Sec. 2, Sec. 3 (Exemptions) lays down that exemptions may be envisaged, accompanied in appropriate cases by a timetable for the introduction of the necessary alterations, if it would be unreasonable to comply with the provisions of Sec. 6 of the Law. Sec. 5 lays down the respective functions of the Health and Social Affairs Board and the Directorate of Labour Inspection.

Sec. 6 (Ships, including vessels and installations in the petroleum sector) states that, without prejudice to the provisions of Sec. 2 applicable to rooms for common use, smoking is to be prohibited in the corridors, toilets, and similar common areas, and in not less than one-third of the cabins on such vessels and installations. Sec. 9 (Catering and lodging premises) reads as follows:

"Restaurants, hotels, and other catering and lodging premises shall gradually introduce no-smoking environments, in particular in reception areas, corridors, and similar common areas. In the case of new constructions and alterations, regard shall be had for this factor in drawing up plans. Within five years of the entry into force of the Law, not less than one-third of the tables, seating accommodation, and rooms shall be no-smoking. The said common areas shall likewise be no-smoking."

NORWAY. Regulations No. 925 of 4 September 1989 amending the Regulations concerning exceptions to the ban on advertising contained in Section 2 of the Law on protection against tobacco-induced injury.[a] (*Norsk Lovtidend*, Part I, 12 October 1989, No. 18, pp. 825-826) **Norw. 90.2**

The principal Regulations were issued on 25 October 1974 in pursuance of Law No. 14 of 9 March 1973 (see *IDHL*, 1975, **26**, 571). As amended by Law No. 24 of 6 May 1988 (see *ibid.*, 1988, **39**, 862, **Norw. 88.9**) that Law is now known as the "Law on the protection against tobacco-induced injury". Sec. 1 of the principal Regulations now reads as follows:

"**1.** Insofar as the cases fall within the scope of the ban on advertising referred to in the first and second paragraphs of Section 2 of Law No. 14 of 9 March 1973... and the regulation issued by the Ministry of Social Affairs in pursuance of Section 8 (cf. the second paragraph of Section 7) of the Law, the following exceptions shall apply:

1. advertising in foreign publications imported into Norway unless the main purpose of the publication or of its importation is to advertise tobacco products in Norway;
2. information to retailers, etc., referring entirely to the product itself, and having a neutral typographical design consisting of black letters on a white background and no illustrations;

[a] This summary is based on an English translation prepared in Norway and kindly made available to WHO by the National Council on Tobacco and Health, Oslo. — ED.

3. information given in a publication concerning the marketing of a new, specifically defined product that is substantially less injurious to health than previous products of a corresponding nature;

4. announcements or other information in a publication concerning the opening up of a new retail outlet, stating the outlet's name, location, and opening hours as well as the range of goods, restricted to the following designations: cigarettes, cigars, smoking tobacco, chewing tobacco, snuff, cigarette paper, cigarette rollers, and pipes. No colour other than black, and printing as normally employed in the publication in question, must be used.

The above also applies to any change of ownership of the outlet.

5. indirect publicity of minor importance in programmes of the Norwegian Radio and Television Broadcasting Network and in films;

6. signboards of ordinary size and design (not electric light advertisements), whose sole function is to provide information, e.g. 'Tobacco', in connection with tobacconists' retail outlets; and

7. the display of tobacco products on the premises of the retail outlet, insofar as such displays are appropriate for effective sales."

NORWAY. Regulations No. 1044 of 13 October 1989 on the prohibition of new products containing tobacco and nicotine.[a] (*Norsk Lovtidend*, Part I, 31 October 1989, No. 19, pp. 913-915) **Norw. 90.3**

The following are among the principal provisions of these Regulations, which have been made by the Ministry of Social Affairs in pursuance of item e of Sec. 4 and Sec. 15 of Law No. 79 of 11 June 1976 on product control (see *IDHL*, 1977, **28**, 653).

Sec. 1 (Objective) states that the objective of these Regulations is to limit damage to health resulting from the use of products containing tobacco and nicotine. Sec. 2 (Prohibition) prohibits the importation, sale, and supply of new forms of products containing tobacco and nicotine. This applies to products containing tobacco and nicotine intended for use in other ways than are usual in Norway, other than products traditionally marketed in Norway (cigarettes, cigars, cigarillos, smoking tobacco, chewing tobacco, and snuff). Sec. 4 (Relationship to other laws) lays down that products containing tobacco and nicotine used for the purposes of giving up smoking are classified as medicaments requiring a prescription and are to be sold in pharmacies, in accordance with the provisions of Law No. 5 of 20 June 1964 on medicaments, etc. (see *ibid.*, 1965, **16**, 154). Sec. 5 (Supervisory authority) specifies that the Ministry of Social Affairs has overall responsibility for the enforcement of these Regulations, while the Directorate of Health is responsible for ensuring compliance with the provisions laid down in them.

Sec. 6 (Duty to provide information) lays down that the authorities mentioned in Sec. 5 may require producers, importers, or dealers to provide samples of the product in question or to carry out at their own expense, the investigations necessary to assess the characteristics and effects of the product. These authorities may themselves carry out such investigations, and if appropriate, require the manufacturer or importer to bear the costs. Sec. 7 (Access to premises, etc.) defines certain powers of the said authorities. Sec. 8 (Exemptions) reads as follows:

[a] Account has been taken of amendments introduced by Regulations No. 1325 of 22 November 1989 (*Norsk Lovtidend*, Part I, 26 January 1990, No. 25, p. 1274). — ED.

"**8.** The Directorate of Health may grant an exemption from the prohibition laid down in Section 2 if the manufacturer or importer is able to establish that a new product, or the method of using it, is significantly less harmful to health than products already on the market.

The manufacturer or importer of a product shall be entitled to apply for an exemption. The exemption shall be submitted to the Directorate. The application shall incorporate the information necessary to assess the characteristics and effects of the product.

The exemption may be granted subject to conditions if it is found that they are necessary to prevent or limit possible damage to health.

The Directorate may revoke an exemption if:

(*a*) new information on, or assessments of, the product, its method of use, or its effects indicate that such a revocation is desirable; or

(*b*) the party obtaining the exemption fails to comply with the conditions laid down."

Other Sections deal with appeals (Sec. 9), fines for non-compliance (Sec. 10), confidentiality (Sec. 11), and criminal liability (Sec. 12). Sec. 14 lays down that the Ministry of Social Affairs is empowered to supplement or amend these Regulations.

PAKISTAN

PAKISTAN. An Ordinance (No. LXXIII of 1979) to provide for printing of a health warning on pockets of cigarettes. Dated 31 December 1979. (The Cigarettes (Printing of Warning) Ordinance, 1979).[a] (*The Gazette of Pakistan, Extraordinary*, Part I, 31 December 1979, 2 pp.) **Pak. 84.1**

Sec. 3 of this Ordinance (which applies only to cigarettes manufactured for consumption in Pakistan) states that cigarette packets are to bear, in English und Urdu, the following legend: "WARNING: Smoking is injurious to health". Other Sections deal with penalties for offences under the Ordinance. Sec. 8 empowers the Federal Government to make rules for the implementation of this Ordinance.

PAKISTAN. The Cigarettes (Printing of Warning) Rules, 1982. S.R.O. 441 (I)/82. Dated 5 May 1982. (*The Gazette of Pakistan, Extraordinary*, Part II, 5 May 1982, pp. 605-606) **Pak. 84.2**

These Rules have been made under powers conferred by Sec. 8 of the Cigarettes (Printing of Warning) Ordinance, 1979 (see *supra*). Rule 2 contains details of the dimensions, etc., of the health warning to be carried by cigarette packets.

[a] Account has been taken of amendments introduced by Ordinance No. XL of 1980 (*The Gazette of Pakistan, Extraordinary*, Part I, 21 July 1980, 1 p.). — ED.

PAPUA NEW GUINEA

PAPUA NEW GUINEA. The Tobacco Products (Health Control) Act 1987. Act No. 30 of 1987. Dated 25 November 1987. (13 pp.)

PNG 88.1

The following are among the principal provisions of this Act.

Part I. Preliminary (Secs. 1-4). Sec. 2 (Interpretation) defines various terms, including "advertisement", "cigarettes" ("cigarettes that contain cut or sliced tobacco"), "package", "sell", and "tobacco product" ("tobacco product declared under Section 3"). Sec. 3 empowers the Minister, by notice in the *National Gazette*, to declare goods, items, substances, articles, or products to be tobacco products for the purposes of this Act (the term "Act" is defined to include any Regulations made thereunder). Sec. 4 empowers the Minister to make exemptions from all or certain of the provisions of this Act.

Part II. Restriction on importation, manufacture, etc. of tobacco products (Secs. 5-13). Under Sec. 5, the Minister is empowered to fix a day to be the "appointed day" for the purposes of this Act.[a] Sec. 6 lays down that a person may not, on or after the appointed day, manufacture, sell, distribute, advertise, or import tobacco products. Secs. 7 (Importation, manufacture and sale of tobacco products), 8 (Advertising of tobacco products), 9 (Sale of tobacco products to persons under 18 years of age), and 10 (Restriction on use of tobacco products in declared places) read as follows:

"**7.** (1) Subject to this section, it is prohibited—

(*a*) to import into Papua New Guinea, tobacco products; and

(*b*) to manufacture, sell or distribute tobacco products,

which are not marked with a declaration stating the level of harmful substances contained in or released by the tobacco products, and in addition—

(*c*) in the case of cigarettes, to sell cigarettes unless they are in package and each package, whether an inner or outer package, in which they are enclosed, is marked in the prescribed manner with the prescribed health warning; and

(*d*) in all cases, to sell tobacco products, unless they are marked with such symbol and such text pointing out the risk to health inherent in the consumption of tobacco products, as may be required by the Minister or as prescribed.

Penalty: .....

(2) The Regulations shall prescribe the conditions relating to the content, weight, filters and packaging of tobacco products.

[a] WHO has been informed that this Act came into force in April 1988. However, tobacco manufacturers and dealers are exempted from compliance with Part II until April 1989. — ED.

8. (1) The advertisement of—

(*a*) tobacco products; and

(*b*) tobacco products included in the advertisement of other goods or services,

is prohibited.

(2) The Regulations may prescribe further matters for the purposes of this section.

9. A person shall not sell or hand over—

(*a*) tobacco products to a person who is or apparently is under the age of 18 years; or

(*b*) imitations of tobacco products which may encourage or induce the use of, or consumption by, a person who is or apparently is under the age of 18 years.

Penalty: .....

10. (1) The Minister may, by notice in the National Gazette, declare a place, including a part or section of a public transport vehicle, to be a place to which this section applies.

(2) A declaration under Subsection (1) shall specify—

(*a*) any limitation on the use of tobacco products; and

(*b*) the extent of the limitation (which may extend to prohibition),

in the declared place, and may specify any conditions subject to which the limitation is to operate.

(3) A person who uses tobacco products in a place declared under Subsection (1) otherwise than in compliance with the limitations specified in the declaration, is guilty of an offence.

Penalty: .....".

Sec. 12 is entitled "Offences by corporation". Sec. 13 empowers the Head of State, acting on advice, to make regulations for the implementation of this Act.

PARAGUAY

PARAGUAY. Law No. 836/80 promulgating the Health Code. Dated 15 December 1980. (36 pp.) **Par. 81.1**

Sec. 202 prescribes that tobacco advertisements must not encourage consumption of tobacco but may only refer to its quality and origin. The use of figures or characters representing children or adolescents is prohibited in such advertising, as is its association[a] with sports, work, study, or the home. Sec. 203 empowers the Ministry, when it considers this necessary, to order containers of tobacco products to display a clear and visible warning that such products may be harmful to health.

PERU

PERU. Law No. 23482 of 20 October 1982 on the selective consumption tax on cigarettes made from blond tobacco. (3 pp.) **Peru 87.1**

Under Sec. 1 of this Law, the tax referred to in the title is increased by 9%. Sec. 2 prescribes that the revenues from the tax increase are to be earmarked for the completion of the construction and equipping of the new hospital for neoplastic diseases under construction by the Peruvian Cancer Foundation. Sec. 4 lays down that, on completion of the hospital, the revenue from the tax is to be earmarked as a priority for the construction and equipping of centres for the detection of neoplastic diseases in various localities throughout the country, and/or for the acquisition of new equipment in the hospital referred to in Sec. 2, and for grants for research on neoplastic diseases in faculties of medicine in universities and other research centres.

PORTUGAL

PORTUGAL. Law No. 22/82 of 17 August 1982 on the control of smoking. (*Diário da República*, Part I, 17 August 1982, No. 189, p. 2408) **Port. 85.7**

This Law, which sets out the general principles for the control of smoking, contains the following Sections: 1. Definition of tobacco; 2. Prohibition of advertising; 3. Prohibition of smoking [in certain places]; 4. Warning and [nicotine, etc.] content; 5. Maximum content [of nicotine, etc.]; 6. Statistics; 7. Implementing regulations; 8. Penalties for contraventions; and 9. Entry into force.

PORTUGAL. Decree-Law No. 226/83 of 27 May 1983 for the implementation of Law No. 22/82 of 17 August 1982 on the control of smoking, and establishing the Smoking Control Council (CPT). (*Diário da República*, Part I, 27 May 1983, No. 122, pp. 1940-1945) **Port. 85.10**

This Decree-Law has been made for the implementation of Sec. 7 of Law No. 22/82 of 17 August 1982 (see *supra*) and repeals Orders No. 212/78 of 18 April 1978 (see *IDHL*, 1979, **30**, 638) and No. 375/78 of 11 July 1978 (see *ibid.*, 639). The following are among its main provisions.

Sec. 1 (Definitions) defines, *inter alia*, the term "tobacco" to include cigarettes, cigarillos, and cigars as well as tobacco for pipes and cigarettes. Sec. 2 imposes a prohibition on smoking on the premises of health care units, in teaching establishments, and on premises intended for persons aged under 16 years, cinemas, theatres, etc., and on enclosed premises for sports. Nevertheless, zones may be expressly reserved for smokers on the above-mentioned premises, provided that they are isolated from the transit areas for patients, persons aged less than 16 years, pregnant or breast-feeding women, and participants in sport. Sec. 3 (Prohibition on smoking in public transport) reads as follows:

"**3.** (1) Smoking is prohibited on vehicles assigned to public transport on urban, suburban, or inter-urban routes, or on hired or tourist vehicles on journeys not exceeding one hour by road, rail, or river.

(2) On inter-urban routes and in hired or tourist vehicles, passengers occupying the back three rows of seats may smoke if the duration of the journey exceeds one hour. The area reserved for smokers may be extended to one-third of the total seats provided that the vehicle is fitted with effective equipment for removing smoke.

(3) Compartments or carriages may be reserved for smokers in public transport by rail if the duration of the journey exceeds one hour; nevertheless, the smoking area may not exceed half the total of the places available in each class or make it possible, through the absence of appropriate equipment, for smoke to spread into the non-smoking areas.

(4) On vessels intended for river transport, smoking may be authorized only in uncovered areas, if the duration of the journey exceeds one hour; the foregoing is without prejudice to restrictions laid down in rules issued by transport undertakings or port authorities.

(5) Pending the publication of specific rules, smokers on air and sea transport remain subject to the existing regulations."

Sec. 4 lays down the specifications for notices prohibiting smoking while Secs. 6 and 7 prohibit advertising for tobacco in the national advertising media and by the apposition of the name, brand, or symbol of a tobacco product to consumer goods which are not directly connected with the use of tobacco. Sec. 8 specifies in particular that the packaging of all cigarettes intended for inland consumption are to carry the following information, which is to be clearly visible: a warning of the harmful effects of tobacco, an indication of the nicotine and tar content, and an indication of the category of such content. Details are given of the specifications for such information. Sec. 9 prescribes that statistics are to be compiled concerning the implementation of this Decree-Law, to enable the Smoking Prevention Council (CPT) to propose any amendments required by developments in tobacco consumption, while Sec. 10 specifies the penalties for contraventions of prohibitions on smoking.

Sec. 13 provides for the establishment of the Smoking Prevention Council (CPT). Under Sec. 14, the functions of the CPT are, *inter alia*, as follows: to draw up guiding principles concerning the prevention of smoking; to propose a coordinated action programme, subject to appraisal and revision, for the progressive reduction of the harmful effects of tobacco on the population, giving priority to the protection of nonsmokers; to give its opinion on legislation, action programmes, and expenditure related to smoking prevention measures; to promote studies and research on the prevention of smoking in order to identify, *inter alia*, substances which must be excluded from tobacco; to ensure that this Decree-Law is duly enforced; to promote the exchange, with other national or international organizations, of knowledge, experiences, and techniques concerning the prevention of smoking; and to draw up an annual report on the general situation in this sector, and on the activities of the CPT. Sec. 15 prescribes that the working procedures and the composition of the CPT are to be specified by joint order of the competent ministers. Secs. 16 and 17 contain transitional and financial provisions, respectively. Models of the "no smokers" and "smokers" signs are annexed.

PORTUGAL (MACAO). Law No. 3/83/M of 11 June 1983 on the prevention and control of smoking. (*Boletim oficial de Macau*, 11 June 1983, No. 24, pp. 1218-1220) **Port. (Mac) 85.1**

Sec. 1 (Definition of tobacco) of this Law defines the term "tobacco" to include cigarettes, cigarillos, and cigars, as well as tobacco for pipes and cigarettes. Sec. 2 (Prohibitions concerning advertising) lays down in particular that any advertising for tobacco must include the warning notices provided for in subsection 1 of Sec. 4 of the Law. Subsection 1 of Sec. 3 (Prohibitions concerning smoking) prohibits smoking particularly in health care units and in premises intended for minors. Under the terms of subsection 2, prohibitions on smoking must be clearly and conspicuously indicated. Subsection 4 lays down that, in double-decker public transport vehicles, the upper deck may be reserved for smokers. Sec. 4 (Warning notices and contents) reads as follows:

"4. (1) The packaging of cigarettes intended for consumers and the packaging of other tobacco-containing products shall set out, clearly, conspicuously, and legibly, the following information:

(*a*) warning notices alerting the consumer to the harmful effects of tobacco and discouraging its use;

(*b*) the contents of nicotine and of condensate or tar, expressed in milligrams per cigarette or according to a classification as low, medium, or high corresponding to these contents.

(2) The information referred to in the preceding subsection shall be in Portuguese and in Chinese and shall occupy a surface area not less than 10% of the total surface area of the packaging.

(3) In the case of packaging of tobacco originating in countries where tobacco control measures have been adopted, warning notices conforming to the regulations in force in the country of origin and aimed at local consumers shall be regarded as sufficient, while the burden of proving the regulations relied upon shall rest with the importers, suppliers, and vendors."

Sec. 5 (Restrictions on advertising for sales purposes) contains provisions relating to the location and dimensions of advertising notices. Sec. 6 deals with the confiscation of articles, products, packaging, and advertising notices associated with tobacco, while Sec. 7 lays down the penalties for breaches of this Law. Under the terms of Sec. 11 (Information on the harmful effects of smoking), the Directorate of Health Services is responsible for periodically disseminating reports and information at its disposal on the harmful effects of smoking and for encouraging campaigns and measures against smoking, particularly in establishments intended for adolescents.

SAUDI ARABIA

SAUDI ARABIA. Circular prohibiting smoking in ministerial offices, government agencies, and public institutions. Dated 18 October 1983.[a] (1 p.) **Sau. 86.1**

This Circular has been issued by the King in his capacity as Head of the Cabinet. It lays down that smoking is prohibited in all the above-mentioned offices, etc. and that "No smoking" signs are to be posted therein. The strict implementation of these measures is to be closely monitored.

[a] This summary is based on an English translation made available by the WHO Regional Office for the Eastern Mediterranean, Alexandria, Egypt. — ED.

SENEGAL

SENEGAL. Law No. 81-58 of 9 November 1981 prohibiting advertising for tobacco and smoking in certain public places. (*Journal officiel de la République du Sénégal*, 14 November 1981, No. 4865, pp. 1013-1015) **Sen. 83.5**

This Law contains provisions that are largely similar, *mutatis mutandis*, to those contained in the French Law No. 76-616 of 9 July 1976 concerning measures to combat smoking (see *IDHL*, 1976, **27**, 732). The following are the principal differences.

The Senegalese text does not require psychological and prophylactic health information to be provided in educational establishments or in the Armed Forces (cf. Sec. 6 of the French text).

There are no provisions in the Senegalese text limiting the area allocated in the press for advertising of tobacco or tobacco products (cf. Sec. 8 of the French text).

Under the provisions of Sec. 8 of the Senegalese text, the warning that must appear on the packages of tobacco or tobacco products is "Misuse is dangerous to your health [*Abus dangereux pour votre santé*]".

Sec. 10 of the French text contains a prohibition on sponsorship of sporting events; the Senegalese text (Sec. 9) extends this to include cultural events, and does not exempt sporting events restricted to motor vehicles. The specific prohibition regarding sponsorship of events intended for children or minors contained in Sec. 11 of the French text is not included in the Senegalese text.

Sec. 13 of the Senegalese text prohibits smoking in places intended for communal use in which smoking may endanger health. Decrees are to be issued identifying such places, places in which no-smoking areas must be provided, and places and institutions in which health information must be provided.

SENEGAL. Ministerial Order No. 8236 M.S.P.-D.PH. of 30 July 1982 prescribing the substances that must be indicated on the packaging units of tobacco or tobacco products and the conditions for determining the presence of such substances. (*Journal officiel de la République du Sénégal*, 23 October 1982, No. 4915, pp. 686-692) **Sen. 83.12**

Sec. 1 of this Order, which has been made in pursuance of Law No. 81-58 of 9 November 1981 (see *supra*), prescribes that the presence of nicotine and tar must be indicated on the packaging of tobacco and tobacco products (in the case of cigarettes, the mean levels of these substances per cigarette must also be indicated). This requirement does not apply to cigars, cigarillos, or pipe tobacco.

Various Annexes to the Order indicate methods for determining tar and nicotine levels in tobacco smoke, sampling procedures, etc.

SENEGAL. Law No. 85-23 of 25 February 1985 amending Law No. 81-58 of 9 November 1981 prohibiting the advertising of tobacco and smoking in certain public places. (*Journal officiel de la République du Sénégal*, 9 March 1985, No. 5053, pp. 143-144) **Sen. 86.4**

This Law repeals Secs. 4 and 9 of Law No. 81-58 of 9 November 1981 (see *IDHL*, 1983, **34**, 90, **Sen. 83.5**), and amends certain other provisions, including Secs. 2, 7, and 13, which now read as follows:

"**2.** Tobacco and tobacco products may not be promoted or advertised through television broadcasts."

"**7.** Where the promotion or advertising of tobacco or tobacco products is authorized, it may be effected only under conditions specified by decree.

The packaging of tobacco or tobacco products may not carry legends or representations other than the name of the product, its composition, the name and address of the manufacturer, and, as appropriate, the name and address of the distributor."

"**13.** Smoking shall be prohibited in the public places designated by decision of the administrative authorities.

That prohibition shall take the form of a 'No smoking' notice affixed to the walls of public places for collective use or where smoking may have harmful consequences on health.

Persons in breach of this Section shall be liable to imprisonment for a period between one day and one month and to a fine between 1000 and 20 000 Francs [CFA], or to only one of these penalties.

The procedures laid down by Articles 512 and 516 of the Code of Criminal Procedure concerning fines payable by instalment and fines payable as a lump sum shall be applicable."

SENEGAL. Decree No. 85-1375 of 28 December 1985 specifying the conditions governing the promotion or advertising of tobacco or tobacco products. (*Journal officiel de la République du Sénégal*, 25 January 1986, No. 5102, pp. 45-46) **Sen. 86.5**

Secs. 1-4 of this Decree read as follows:

"**1.** Advertising announcements or messages for tobacco or tobacco products may not, irrespective of their form, employ the voice of or depict a person under 21 years of age.

2. Posters and articles advertising tobacco or tobacco derivatives may only be placed in localities and networks officially approved by the administrative authority and assigned, at the request of the authority, to approved advertising agencies.

3. Films advertising tobacco or tobacco products may not be projected during programmes for young persons.

4. The Minister of the Interior, the Minister for Culture, and the Minister of Information, Telecommunications and Relations with the Assemblies shall be responsible, within their respective spheres of jurisdiction, for the implementation of this Decree, which shall be published in the *Journal officiel*."

SINGAPORE

SINGAPORE. The Smoking (Prohibition in Certain Places) Notification 1988. No. S 171. Dated 15 June 1988. (*Republic of Singapore Government Gazette, Subsidiary Legislation Supplement*, 24 June 1988, No. 29, pp. 444-446) **Sing. 90.5**

This Notification has been made by the Permanent Secretary of the Ministry of the Environment in pursuance of Sec. 3 of the Smoking (Prohibition in Certain Places) Act (see *IDHL*, 1973, **24**, 217). It lays down that smoking is not to be permitted in the following places: hospitals, maternity homes, medical clinics, and nursing homes (in each case as defined); indoor areas of certain food establishments (as specified); and indoor roller-skating rinks and roller discothèques.

SINGAPORE. The Consumer Protection (Labelling of Tobacco Product Containers) Regulations 1989. No. S 9. Dated 11 January 1989. (*Republic of Singapore Government Gazette, Subsidiary Legislation Supplement*, 13 January 1989, No. 2, pp. 10-12) **Sing. 90.10**

These Regulations have been made by the Permanent Secretary of the Ministry of Trade and Industry under powers conferred by Secs. 11 and 32 of the Consumer Protection (Trade Descriptions and Safety Requirements) Act, and repeal the Consumer Protection (Warning Against Danger of Smoking) Regulations 1980 (see *IDHL*, 1981, **32**, 460, **Sing. 81.16**). Reg. 3 lays down, among other provisions, that any one of the following warnings (in English) is to be clearly and conspicuously printed or otherwise marked in a prominent position on every container of tobacco products sold or offered for sale in Singapore: (*a*) Health Warning — Smoking causes heart disease; (*b*) Health Warning — Smoking causes cancer; (*c*) Health Warning — Smoking damages your lungs; or (*d*) Health Warning — Smoking harms those around us. Each of these warnings is to be displayed with equal frequency on the container of each type of any brand of tobacco products in a 12-month period.

Reg. 4 lays down that, in the case of cigarettes, "there shall also be printed or otherwise marked on each container of cigarettes the nicotine level expressed in tenths of a milligram per cigarette and the tar content expressed in milligrams per cigarette".

Reg. 5 deals with the furnishing of statements, etc., in respect of tobacco products, to the Director.

SINGAPORE. GOVERNMENT GAZETTE SUBSIDIARY LEGISLATION SUPPLEMENT. Friday, January 13, 1989

THE CONSUMER PROTECTION (TRADE DESCRIPTIONS AND SAFETY REQUIREMENTS) ACT. (CHAPTER 53).

THE CONSUMER PROTECTION (LABELLING OF TOBACCO PRODUCT CONTAINERS) REGULATIONS 1989.

In exercise of the powers conferred by sections 11 and 32 of the Consumer Protection (Trade Descriptions and Safety Requirements) Act, the Minister for Trade and Industry hereby makes the following Regulations:

1. These Regulations may be cited as the Consumer Protection (Labelling of Tobacco Product Containers) Regulations 1989 and shall come into operation on 2nd October 1989.

2. In these Regulations, unless the context otherwise requires – "tobacco products" means –
   (*a*)cigarettes;
   (*b*)cigars; and
   (*c*)any product manufactured wholly or partly from tobacco and which is capable of being smoked;
   "container" includes a box, tin or packet but does not include any outer wrapper or cellophane or other transparent material;
   "warning" means any of the warnings specified in regulation 3 (1).

3.–(1) There shall be clearly and conspicuously printed or otherwise marked in a prominent position on every container of tobacco products sold or offered for sale in Singapore any one of the following warnings in the English language, namely:
(*a*)Health Warning – Smoking causes heart disease;
(*b*)Health Warning – Smoking causes cancer;
(*c*)Health Warning – Smoking damages your lungs;
(*d*)Health Warning – Smoking harms those around us.

(2) Each of the warnings specified in paragraph (1) shall be displayed with equal frequency on the container of each type of any brand of tobacco products in a 12 month period.

(3) Where the container is a packet, each warning shall be displayed on the largest external surface of the packet and where the container is not a packet, the warning shall be displayed on the largest external surface of the container.

(4) No warning specified in paragraph (1) may be displayed on the underside of the container of tobacco products.

(5) The warning shall be enclosed in a boxed area which shall be white in colour and shall not be less than 20% of the total area of the surface of the container on which the warning is displayed.

(6) The warning shall be in block letters of not less than 3 mm in height and shall be printed or otherwise marked in black.

(7) Nothing else may appear in the boxed area of a container other than any of the warnings referred to in paragraph (1).

(8) If the warning appears on a label, the label shall be securely affixed to the container.

(9) Where the warning is printed on a label, the label shall not be affixed to the container of tobacco products in such a manner that the label may be damaged when the container is opened.

4.–(1) In the case of cigarettes, there shall also be printed or otherwise marked on each container of cigarettes the nicotine level expressed in tenths of a milligram per cigarette and the tar content expressed in milligrams per cigarette.

(2) The nicotine and tar content of the cigarettes shown on each container of cigarettes shall be in block letters of not less than 8 points in a colour most conspicuous against the colour of the background of the container.

(3) The nicotine and tar content of the cigarettes in each container of cigarettes shall not be printed or otherwise marked on the same side of the packet which displays any of the warnings specified in rule 3 (1).

5.–(1) Every manufacturer, importer and distributor of tobacco products shall–

(*a*) annually cause to be sent to the Director a statement stating the amount of tobacco products manufactured in, imported into or distributed by him or it in Singapore; and

(*b*) keep or cause to be kept records showing the batch numbers of the warning labels used in respect of every batch of tobacco products manufactured in, imported into or sold by him or it in Singapore.

(2) The records referred to in paragraph (1) shall be kept at the registered office of the manufacturer, importer or distributor, as the case may be, and shall at all times be open to inspection by the Director.

6. Any person who contravenes or fails to comply with any of the provisions of regulation 3, 4, or 5 shall be guilty of an offence and shall be liable on conviction to a fine not exceeding $2,000 or to imprisonment for a term not exceeding one year or to both.

7. The Consumer Protection (Warning Against Danger of Smoking) Regulations 1980 are revoked.

Made this 4th day of January 1989.

LAM CHUAN LEONG,
Permanent Secretary,
Ministry of Trade and Industry,
Singapore.

SPAIN

SPAIN. Crown Decree No. 1259 of 4 April 1979 on the designation of cigarette products as "low-nicotine" and "low-tar". (*Boletín Oficial del Estado, Gaceta de Madrid*, 31 May 1979, No. 130, Serial No. 13529, p. 12028) **Sp. 81.1**

Under the provisions of Sec. 2 of this Crown Decree, the expression "low nicotine" may be used in connexion with the marketing and advertising of cigarettes only if the nicotine yield of one cigarette of the brand concerned is less than 1 mg (as measured in accordance with the International Standard ISO 3400), while the expression "low tar" may be so used only if the tar yield of one cigarette is less than 16 mg (as measured in accordance with International Standard ISO 3308); the expression "low nicotine and tar" may be used only if both of the above conditions are satisfied. Sec. 3 prescribes that samples of all cigarette products must be submitted prior to marketing to the competent Government authority [Delegación del Gobierno en "Tabacalera S.A."] in order to ensure compliance with the above provisions, and Sec. 4 prohibits the use of the above expressions (or similar ones which might mislead the consumer) in advertisements for cigarette products which do not comply; the expressions may be printed on the cigarette packages or on labels which are firmly attached to them. Sec. 5 requires the Government authority to take periodic samples of cigarettes and to order the withdrawal from the market of products which fail to comply with the provisions of this Decree.

SPAIN. Order of 23 May 1980 approving the technological standards necessary in order to perform the chemical analysis of cigarette products as referred to in Crown Decree No. 1259 of 4 April 1979. (*Boletín Oficial del Estado, Gaceta de Madrid*, 10 June 1980, No. 139, Serial No. 11758, pp. 12714-12716) **Sp. 81.23**

Sec. 1 of this Order, which has been made in pursuance of Crown Decree No. 1259 of 4 April 1979 (see *supra*), prescribes that low-tar and low-nicotine cigarette products may not be marketed or advertised without the prior authorization of the competent Government authority [Delegación del Gobierno en "Tabacalera S.A."]. Sec. 2 requires manufacturers wishing to market or advertise such products to submit samples to the authority for analysis of their tar and nicotine levels. Under the provisions of Sec. 4, the authority may license the advertising and marketing of the products concerned under any of the designations "low nicotine", "low tar", or "low nicotine and tar", provided that the mean levels of those substances do not exceed the limits specified in Sec. 2 of the Crown Decree. The expressions referred to may be printed on the packets or on labels firmly attached to them; no other expressions which may mislead the consumer may be used. Sec. 5 requires the authority to periodically take samples of cigarettes for purposes of analysis in order to ensure that they comply with the provisions of the preceding Sections (provision is made for withdrawal from the market of any brand of tobacco products which fails to comply). Sec. 7 prescribes that licences to market and advertise existing brands of low-nicotine and low-tar cigarettes are to be issued on the basis of the analyses prescribed in this Order, and that products which fail to meet the requirements laid down above may not be marketed or advertised.

A technological standard for the mechanical smoking of cigarettes and the determination of nicotine and tar levels in cigarette smoke is appended to the Order.

SPAIN. Crown Decree No. 709/1982 of 5 March 1982 regulating the advertising and use of tobacco. (*Boletín Oficial del Estado, Gaceta de Madrid*, 15 April 1982, No. 90, Serial No. 8958, p. 9585) **Sp. 85.36**

Sec. 1 of this Decree lays down that, as soon as advertising commitments in effect at the time of its entry into force have terminated, and in any case within two years following that date, public communications media that are directly responsible to the State Administration and other agencies under public law are to cease advertising intended to promote the use of tobacco. These provisions do not apply to purely informational advertising concerning the introduction of new products which, on account of their low tar or nicotine levels or other characteristics, entail a lesser health hazard. In the case of such products, advertising of the characteristics concerned is to be permitted for a period of two years following their initial introduction. Sec. 2 prescribes that a warning regarding the hazards of the use of tobacco, in the form of the legend "The General Directorate of Public Health warns that the use of tobacco is harmful to your health", is to appear, in Spanish and with details of its origin, on the outside of packages of tobacco that constitute a sales unit intended for the domestic market. Sec. 3 prohibits the sale of tobacco to persons under 16 years of age. Under Sec. 4, new tobacco products intended for the domestic market and that contain more than 24 mg of tar and 1.8 mg of nicotine per cigarette, as determined in accordance with the provisions of the relevant legal texts, may not be introduced. Restrictions on smoking in various categories of public transport vehicles are laid down in Sec. 5. Sec. 6 reads as follows:

"**6.** Smoking areas shall be established in indoor public establishments and large commercial premises provided that this is compatible with their dimensions, characteristics, and purposes for which they are intended, and that smoking is not prohibited therein. A Commission comprising representatives of the Ministry of Finance, the Ministry of Health and Consumer Affairs, and the Ministry of Economic Affairs and Trade shall be set up for this purpose."

Sec. 7 lays down that, in the special case of health and educational establishments, the areas in which smoking is permitted (which must always be duly signposted) are to be determined in each case by the management of the establishment or centre concerned. Under Sec. 8, failure to comply with the provisions of this Decree is to be punishable in accordance with the regulations applicable to each matter governed by the Decree.

A number of transitional provisions are laid down.

SPAIN. Crown Decree No. 192/1988 of 4 March 1988 laying down restrictions on the sale of tobacco, for the protection of the health of the population. (*Boletín Oficial del Estado*, 9 March 1988, No. 59, pp. 7499-7501) **Sp. 88.9**

This Decree has been made in pursuance of General Law No. 26/1984 of 19 July 1984 for the protection of consumers and users (see *IDHL*, 1986, **37**, 73, **Sp. 86.43**) and subsection 2 of Sec. 25 of the General Law on health (No. 14/1986) of 25 April 1986 (see *ibid.*, 1987, **38**, 1, **Sp. 87.18**) and repeals all prior contrary provisions, including Secs. 2 and 5-7 of Crown Decree No. 709/1982 of 5 March 1982 on the advertising and use of tobacco (see *ibid.*, 1985, **36**, 403, **Sp. 85.36**), as amended by Crown Decree No. 2072/1983 of 28 July 1983 (see *ibid.*, footnote).

Sec. 1 declares tobacco to be harmful to health for the purposes of subsection 2 of Sec. 25 of the General Law on health and that consequently, where there is a conflict of rights, the right of non-smokers to health is to prevail over the right of smokers to consume tobacco in all places or circumstances in which the right of the former to health may be adversely affected. Secs. 2-3 read as follows:

"**2.** The exterior of packets of tobacco products intended for the national market and consisting solely of units for sale, shall display a warning of the risks of tobacco consumption in the form of any of the legends set out in the Annex to this Decree.

This warning shall be displayed, as a minimum, in the official national Spanish language, and be printed on the original materials, which may not be printed over, with clearly legible and indelible printed letters no smaller than 3 mm. It shall occupy at least 5% of the outer surface and be so positioned that it is not destroyed by the usual mode of opening the packet, and may never be on the bottom of the packet.

3. (1) All packets of tobacco products shall display the nicotine and tar contents, in a clearly visible form on a surface other than that carrying the legend referred to in the preceding Section.

Such information shall appear:

(*a*) on new products launched on the national market — from the time they are first placed on the market;

(*b*) on products already marketed — not more than two months from the entry into force of this Decree; and

(*c*) on products which, in accordance with the transitional provisions of this Decree, are required to reduce their present content in nicotine and tar and incorporate information on the reduced levels — at the time of launching the modified products.

(2) The health administration shall require from manufacturers or importers information on the content of technical additives or residues of technical adjuvants and products derived from combustion for tobacco products where there is evidence that they constitute an additional risk to health."

Sec. 4 prohibits the sale of tobacco products in health establishments, educational establishments, and establishments primarily intended for the care of children and adolescents. Tobacco products may be sold from automatic vending machines only on enclosed premises and the machine is to display a non-removable health warning not less than 20 cm^2 in area. Sec. 5 lays down that persons less than 16 years of age may not be sold or supplied with tobacco products, or imitations of such products, or products conducive to the smoking habit which are harmful to health, while notices of this prohibition are to be displayed at sales outlets. The prohibition applies to vending machines, and is to be enforced by the person in charge of the establishment where the machine is situated. Secs. 6-8 read as follows:

"**6.** (1) Smoking shall be absolutely prohibited on all urban and long-distance vehicles and means of collective transport admitting standing passengers. Funicular cars and cabins shall be considered equivalent to such vehicles.

(2) In such means of transport admitting only seated passengers, a zone consisting of not more than 50% of the seats shall be set aside, at the rear, for smokers.

International transport vehicles shall comply with international standards and recommendations and, as a minimum, with the restrictions applicable in national transport.

(3) Smoking shall be prohibited on school transport vehicles and on all vehicles intended, wholly or in part, for the transport of persons less than 16 years of age or persons suffering from a disease.

(4) In rail and sea transport, the allocation of places for smokers may be by entire carriages, cabins, or compartments, including cabins and bunks used by more than one person; such places for smokers may nevertheless not exceed 50% of the total accommodation.

(5) In pursuance of this Decree, and under their powers, the local authorities may prohibit smoking in taxis whose home base is in their area while such taxis are carrying a fare. If no prohibition has been laid down, the rights of the non-smoker, whether driver or fare, are to take precedence.

(6) Transport undertakings shall be responsible for strict compliance with these provisions. They shall in addition provide leaflets for noting complaints for their customers, indicating the restrictions on smoking, any zones reserved for smokers, and any penalties for failure to comply with this requirement. The prohibition on smoking outside the reserved zone shall be printed on travel tickets.

7. (1) Smoking shall not be permitted in:

(*a*) places where there is an increased risk to the health of workers through the combination of the harm caused by tobacco with the adverse effects of an industrial contaminant; and

(*b*) any occupational area where pregnant women work.

(2) Subject to the exceptions set out in Section 8 of this Decree, smoking shall not be permitted in:

(*a*) welfare centres for persons less than 16 years of age;

(*b*) the health centres, services, and establishments defined in Crown Decree No. 2177 of 1 September 1978 on the registration, classification, and inspection of health centres, services, and establishments [see *ibid.*, 1980, **31**, 730];

(*c*) teaching centres;

(*d*) areas of the premises of the public administration to which the public has direct access;

(*e*) premises for the production, processing, preparation, or sale of food, other than premises intended primarily for consumption of food, and subject always to the prohibition of smoking applicable to food handlers in accordance with Crown Decree No. 2505/1983 [of 4 August 1983] approving the Regulations applicable to food handlers [see *ibid.*, 1986, **37**, 69, **Sp. 86.20**];

(*f*) halls for use by the general public, reading rooms, and exhibition halls;

(*g*) enclosed commercial premises where persons frequently assemble;

(*h*) theatres, cinemas, and other halls for public entertainment or sports events, being enclosed premises specified in Crown Decree No. 2816/1982 of 27 August 1982 approving police regulations concerning public entertainment and recreational activities; and

(*i*) lifts.

(3) The cooperation of occupational health and safety committees and works committees shall be required in the establishment and surveillance of these rules.

8. (1) Clearly distinguished smoking areas shall be established on the premises of theatres and other enclosed premises for public entertainment or sports events, waiting-rooms in the public transport system, and any other premises on which smoking is prohibited. Where it is impossible to delimit separate areas for smokers, the prohibition on smoking shall apply throughout the premises and be made known through appropriate notices to members of the public.

(2) On enclosed commercial premises where considerable numbers of people are present, smoking areas shall be delimited with special clarity in order to avoid infringements of the rules in lightly supervised areas and the resultant hazards.

(3) In health centres and establishments, the person in charge shall determine and delimit the particular areas where smoking is permitted, which shall in all cases be separated for users of the services, visitors, and staff.

(4) In teaching centres, smoking shall be permitted only in areas expressly reserved for the purpose by the person in charge of the centre and may not extend in any case to places where teaching staff and students meet if the latter are less than 16 years of age."

Under Sec. 9, the management or proprietors of the means of transport, premises, and establishments mentioned in Secs. 6-8 are responsible for ensuring strict compliance with these rules, while Sec. 10 empowers the Ministry of Health and Consumer Affairs, acting on the proposal of the Interterritorial Council for the National Health System, to suggest a general logo and standard models of the no-smoking notices and admonitory notices and to promote campaigns to heighten public awareness. Sec. 11 deals with penal matters.

The third of the Additional Provisions specifies that this Decree applies to tobacco seized by the authorities, chewing tobacco, and other products similar to tobacco, used as such, and intended for smoking. The first of the Transitional Provisions lays down that cigarettes sold on the national market after 31 December 1992 are to have a tar content not exceeding 15 mg and a nicotine content not exceeding 1.3 mg. Cigarettes classified as "low nicotine and tar" (including "light" and "mild" cigarettes, and any similar designations subsequently adopted) are to have, six months after the entry into force of this Decree, a tar content not exceeding 13 mg and a nicotine content not exceeding 0.9 mg, and after 31 December 1992, a tar content not exceeding 10 mg and a nicotine content not exceeding 0.8 mg. New cigarette products introduced onto the market are to have a tar content not exceeding 15 mg and a nicotine content not exceeding 1.3 mg; in the case of low nicotine and tar cigarettes the levels are 10 mg for tar and 0.8 mg for nicotine. The first of the Final Provisions empowers the Minister of Health and Consumer Affairs to lay down provisions for the implementation of this Decree.

The Annex (Warning legends on the risks of tobacco consumption) sets out the text of the warning to be carried, namely "The health authorities give warning that", followed immediately by one of the following legends: "Smoking seriously harms your health"; "Smoking causes cancer"; "Smoking causes heart diseases"; or "Smoking during pregnancy harms the future child".

SPAIN. Order of 8 June 1988 for the implementation of Crown Decree No. 192/1988 laying down restrictions on the sale of tobacco, for the protection of the health of the population. (*Boletín Oficial del Ministerio de Sanidad y Consumo*, April-June 1988, No. 22, pp. 678-679) **Sp. 89.24**

This Order has been made by the Minister of Health and Consumer Affairs in pursuance of the first of the Final Provisions of Crown Decree No. 192/1988 of 4 March 1988 (see *IDHL*, 1988, **39**, 653, **Sp. 88.9**). Sec. 1 lays down that the symbols, signs, and similar warnings used to delimit smoking areas or specified prohibitions referred to in Secs. 6, 7, 8, and 9 of the said Crown Decree are to be sufficiently visible and intelligible, with regard to both design and format, that they are unambiguous, while Sec. 2 provides details concerning the leaflets for noting complaints referred to in Secs. 6 and 9 of the Crown Decree. Under Sec. 3, the requirement to state the nicotine and tar contents laid down in Sec. 3 of the Crown Decree applies solely to packets of cigarettes marketed in Spain.

SPAIN (CATALONIA). Law No. 20 of 25 July 1985 on prevention and care in regard to potentially dependence-producing substances.[a] (*Diari Oficial de la Generalitat de Catalunya*, 7 August 1985, No. 572, pp. 2650-2656) **Sp. (Cat) 86.1**

Title V. Measures to control the promotion of tobacco, and other measures (Secs. 24-30)

Chapter I. Restrictive measures (Secs. 24-28). Sec. 24 prohibits the sale of tobacco in health centres, educational centres, and sports centres under the jurisdiction of the Public Administration as well as, in general, to persons under 16 years of age. Sec. 25 imposes a ban on tobacco advertising corresponding to that laid down in Sec. 19 in respect of certain alcoholic beverages. Secs. 26 and 27 prohibit smoking in public transport vehicles and in health centres, establishments intended for persons under 16 years of age, educational establishments, offices of the Public Administration open to the public, theatres, cinemas, and similar premises, as well as on premises in which foods are handled.

Chapter II. Other measures (Secs. 29-30). Under Sec. 29, the Department of Health and Social Security is made responsible for periodically analysing the nicotine, tar, and carbon monoxide content of cigarettes, and for publishing the results of these analyses.

SPAIN (VALENCIA). Order of 20 June 1988 of the Council on Health and Consumer Affairs approving the Programme on the Reduction of Tobacco Consumption. (*Boletín Oficial del Ministerio de Sanidad y Consumo*, April-June 1988, No. 22, pp. 899-900) **Sp. (Val) 89.6**

This Order has been made having regard to, *inter alia*, the Action Plan on Tobacco for the period 1987-1991 of the WHO Regional Committee for Europe, certain proposals put forward by WHO in 1988, and Crown Decree No. 192/1988 of 4 March 1988 laying down restrictions on the sale of tobacco, for the protection of the health of the population (see *IDHL*, 1988, **39**, 653, **Sp. 88.9**). Sec. 1 approves the Programme referred to in the title, which is stated in Sec. 2 to include activities intended to reduce the numbers of adolescents taking up smoking, increase the number of persons giving up smoking, and restrict public places for consuming tobacco, upholding areas free from tobacco smoke for the benefit of nonsmokers. Sec. 3 reads as follows:

---

[a] This Law appears in Spanish in the *Diari Oficial*. — ED.

"**3.** The development and implementation of the Programme shall comprise the following activities:

1. the conduct of studies aimed at compiling information on the incidence and prevalence of smoking, the reasons for taking up the smoking habit, and the attitudes of the public towards the different measures to be taken. The purpose of these studies shall be to enable an assessment to be made of the results of the activities carried out within the Programme;

2. *Educational activities*

These activities shall be carried out principally at two levels, viz.:

(*a*) the school environment — activities aimed at adolescents, with the objective of preventing them from taking up the habit and, in addition, stressing the exemplar role of wholesome habits on the part of teachers; and

(*b*) the health environment — activities aimed at reducing the number of smokers among health professionals, and trying to stop tobacco consumption during the provision of health care as well as supporting users of the health service in giving up tobacco;

3. *Information activities*

These activities are intended to gain the attention of the public and to promote understanding of the magnitude of the adverse effects of smoking on health, both in smokers and in nonsmokers. The purpose of these activities shall be to create an environment in which educational activities can make headway.

In this connection, handouts (brochures, leaflets, etc.) shall be prepared that emphasize the advantages of a tobacco-free life and of a healthy environment and provide information on the hazards of smoking to [active] smokers and to passive smokers;

4. *Activities to support passive smokers aimed at protecting the health of nonsmokers and aimed at reducing tobacco consumption*

(*a*) activities that support and amplify the measures referred to in Crown Decree No. 192/88 of 4 March 1988...; and

(*b*) activities that support initiatives and/or activities of the local authorities and citizens' associations concerning the protection of nonsmokers; and

5. activities that support the abandonment of the smoking habit, by the adoption of relevant measures to assist smokers who wish to give up smoking."

Sec. 4 deals with community participation, while Sec. 5 establishes a Technical Commission. The membership of the Commission comprises members of citizens' groups, scientific associations, and institutions interested in reducing tobacco consumption. Details are given of the functions of the Commission.

SUDAN

SUDAN. The Regulation of Cigarette Smoking Act, 1982. Dated 12 April 1983.[a] (3 pp.) **Sud. 83.1**

Sec. 2 of this Act defines "cigarettes" to mean cigars and cigarettes made from all types of tobacco; pipe tobacco and all accessories used for tobacco smoking are included. The term "enclosed public places" is defined to include public vehicles, indoor cinemas, and any other enclosed places frequented by members of the public.

Sec. 3 prescribes that all manufacturers and importers of cigarettes must ensure that the following statement appears on every packet of cigarettes, whether produced locally or imported: "Smoking is harmful to health". The competent court may authorize the seizure of any packet of cigarettes that does not bear the above statement.

Sec. 4 prohibits advertising for cigarettes in the press, on radio or television, on hoardings, in cinema or theatre productions, by oral publicity, or by any other means; this ban applies to advertising originating in Sudan or prepared for publication within the country.

Sec. 5 prohibits smoking in enclosed public places, while Sec. 6 empowers the police to arrest, without a warrant from a judge, any person contravening Sec. 5. Sec. 7 indicates the penalties imposed for contraventions of Secs. 3-5.

Sec. 8 empowers the Minister of Health to issue regulations for the implementation of this Act.

SUDAN. Regulations No. 16 of 1983 on the control of smoking. (1 p.) **Sud. 86.1**

The following are among the principal provisions of these Regulations, which have been made by the Minister of Health in pursuance of Sec. 8 of the Control of Smoking Act, 1983 (see *IDHL*, 1983, **34**, 769, **Sud. 83.1**). Sec. 2 (Form of warning "Smoking is harmful to health" on cigarette packets) reads as follows:

"**2.** (1) The warning 'Smoking is harmful to health' shall be printed in Arabic on the left side of each cigarette packet covering an area not less than two-thirds of that side.

(2) The warning 'Smoking is harmful to health' shall be written in a different colour from that of the cigarette packet and within a rectangle or square of the same colour as that of the text of the warning."

Sec. 3 prohibits the distribution and use of any form of poster, picture, or publication for the advertising of cigarettes, while Sec. 4 prohibits the holding of a lighted cigarette on any enclosed public premises. Under Sec. 5, the management of such premises is to display in a prominent place a clear warning sign "No smoking" in Arabic and English.

Sec. 6 indicates the penalties imposed for breaches of the Regulations.

---

[a] This summary is based on an English translation prepared in Sudan. According to information available to WHO, the Act came into force on 6 August 1983. — ED.

SWEDEN

SWEDEN. Order No. 11 of 22 February 1982 of the National Board of Health and Welfare amending Order No. 32 of 1976 of the National Board of Health and Welfare concerning the warning notices and declaration of contents to be displayed on tobacco products. (*Socialstyrelsens författningssamling, 1982*, 12 May 1982, 4 pp.)

Swed. 82.57

This Order introduces various amendments to the Order referred to in the title (see *IDHL*, 1976, **27**, 869), as last amended by Order No. 17 of 26 February 1981 (see *ibid.*, 1981, **32**, 460, **Swed. 81.30**), and reproduces the text of the Order and Annex B in their entirety, as amended.

Under the amended provisions of Sec. 5, the mean values for the levels of harmful substances in cigarette smoke, together with the year to which they are applicable, must now be displayed on cigarette packages. The amended provisions of Sec. 7 raise to 15% the permitted discrepancy between the declared levels of harmful products and the actual levels found in the packaged product.

SWEDEN. General Recommendations (AFS 1983: 10) concerning smoking restrictions. Issued by the National Board of Occupational Safety and Health and the National Board of Health and Welfare on 25 April 1983.[a] (Arbetarskyddsstyrelsen, Stockholm, 1984, 15 pp.)

Swed. 88.1

The preamble to these Recommendations reads as follows:

"The National Board of Occupational Safety and Health and the National Board of Health and Welfare hereby jointly present general recommendations concerning the restriction of smoking on communal promises.

These recommendations refer to working premises and personnel facilities as well as public premises and other indoor spaces to which the general public have access. They include examples of measures which can be taken to limit the harmful effects of tobacco. Other measures producing similar results may of course be considered. The purpose of these recommendations is to reduce smoking, but an attempt has also been made to provide for the interests of smokers.

The aim of these general recommendations is for nobody to be unwillingly exposed to discomfort or health hazards from smoking on communal premises which both smokers and non-smokers are entitled or required to frequent. The recommendations advocate an attitude whereby a smokeless environment is regarded as normal. The essential principle is that a smoker's desire to smoke should be overridden by other people's desire for a smokeless environment.

The responsibilities of the National Board of Occupational Safety and Health and the National Board of Health and Welfare overlap to some extent, and these

[a] The original Swedish text of these Recommendations was unavailable. — ED.

recommendations are therefore to be regarded as a 'co-production' by both authorities."

The text comprises the following rubrics: General background; Hazards of smoking; Contents of tobacco smoke: Smoking and the occupational environment; Passive smoking; Ventilation; Some important groups and environments; Present opportunities of achieving a smokeless occupational environment; Practical application; Information and training; Further reading; and Organizations producing information on the harmful effects of tobacco.

SWEDEN. Order No. 10 of 10 April 1986 of the National Board of Health and Welfare amending Order No. 32 of 1976 of the National Board of Health and Welfare concerning the warning notices and declarations of contents to be displayed on tobacco products. (*Socialstyrelsens författningssamling, 1986*, 13 June 1986, 4 pp.)

Swed. 88.5

This Order introduces, *inter alia*, further modifications to Annexes A and D to Order of 31 May 1976 (see *IDHL*, 1976, **27**, 869), as amended by Order No. 11 of 22 February 1982 (see *ibid.*, 1982, **33**, 738, **Swed. 82.57**).

The 13 alternative warnings to be displayed on cigarette packets are now the following: "Do not exposure your colleagues to tobacco smoke. It is harmful and irritating. National Board of Health and Welfare"; "Tobacco smoke contains many carcinogens. The smoke in passive smoking, which affects those in the vicinity of the smoker, contains the highest level of carcinogens. National Board of Health and Welfare"; "Tobacco smoking lowers resistance to infections, including those of the respiratory tract. National Board of Health and Welfare"; "Do not smoke when children are present. Smoke irritates their respiratory tract. National Board of Health and Welfare"; "If you are pregnant or breast-feeding, do not smoke; both you and your child may be harmed. National Board of Health and Welfare"; "In 1983, 779 persons died in traffic accidents and at least 8000 from tobacco smoking. National Board of Health and Welfare"; "Lung cancer among women will soon be commoner than breast cancer. Smoking is the cause. National Board of Health and Welfare"; "Almost all persons suffering from arteriosclerosis affecting the blood vessels of the legs and having difficulty in walking are smokers. National Board of Health and Welfare"; "It is practically only smokers who have a heart attack before they are 50. National Board of Health and Welfare"; "Smoking heightens the risk of inflammation of the gums. This can lead to loss of teeth. National Board of Health and Welfare"; "If one person smokes, everyone smokes. Most tobacco smoke enters the air breathed by everyone. Your smoking may harm others. National Board of Health and Welfare"; and "The combination of smoking and contraceptive pills heightens the risk of a heart attack for women over 30. National Board of Health and Welfare".

Annex D (Warning texts on packaging containing tobacco products other than cigarettes) now contains the following warnings: "Tobacco smoking is harmful to health even if you smoke a pipe or roll your own cigarettes. National Board of Health and Welfare"; "Tobacco smoking is harmful to health even if you smoke cigars and cigarillos. National Board of Health and Welfare"; and "Snuff and chewing tobacco contain nicotine. That is why snuff is just as addictive as smoking tobacco. The mucous membranes and gums may be harmed. National Board of Health and Welfare".

SWEDEN. Order No. 6 of 5 February 1988 of the National Board of Health and Welfare amending Order No. 32 of 1976 of the National Board of Health and Welfare concerning the warning notice and declaration of contents to be displayed on tobacco products. (*Socialstyrelsens författningssamling, 1988*, 16 May 1988, 3 pp.)

Swed. 89.5

This Order introduces various amendments to Order No. 32 of 31 May 1976 (see *IDHL*, 1976, **27**, 869), as last amended by Order No. 10 of 10 April 1986 (see *ibid.*, 1988, **39**, 89, **Swed. 88.5**). Sec. 7, as amended, states that the actual values obtained in verifications of cigarettes in packets chosen at random may not exceed the stated values by more than 15%. Nevertheless, variations of 1.5 mg/cigarette for smoke condensates and carbon monoxide, and 0.15 mg/cigarette for nicotine, are permissible.

UNION OF SOVIET SOCIALIST REPUBLICS

UNION OF SOVIET SOCIALIST REPUBLICS. Resolution No. 706 of 12 June 1980 of the Central Committee of the Communist Party of the Soviet Union and the USSR Council of Ministers on measures to intensify the campaign against smoking. (*Socialističeskaja Zakonnost'*, December 1980, No. 12, pp. 63-64) **USSR 81.1**

1. The Central Committees of the Communist Parties of the Union Republics, the *kraj, oblast*, municipal, and *rajon* committees of the Party, the Councils of Ministers of the Union and Autonomous Republics, the executive committees of the *kraj, oblast*, municipal, and *rajon* councils of people's deputies, and the ministries and agencies of the USSR, in collaboration whith the trade union, Young Communist League, and other social organizations, shall carry out systematic activities to inform the broad masses of the population of the harmful effects of smoking upon human health, with a view to progressively eradicating this habit and, in particular, shall:

— ensure that measures are implemented in undertakings, establishments, and organizations to restrict, and subsequently to prohibit, smoking in official and work premises, provision being made for the designation of special smoking areas, and strengthen the obligation upon economic and other leaders to implement such measures;

— strengthen activities in workers' collectives, educational establishments, and dwelling places with a view to turning public opinion against smoking, making wide use of mass communication media and visual propaganda facilities for such purposes.

2. The USSR Ministry of Health shall:

— take the necessary measures to enhance the effectiveness of public propaganda designed to disseminate health information on the harmful effects of smoking and to supply medical establishments with the necessary literature, and systematically organize seminars and consultations for medical workers on matters relating to smoking control;

— extend scientific research into more effective means and methods of controlling smoking, and improve the rendering of medical assistance in outpatient policlinics to persons wishing to stop smoking.

3. The USSR Ministry of Education, the USSR Ministry of Higher and Secondary Specialized Education, and the USSR State Committee on Vocational Technical Training shall strengthen health education and organizational activities in educational establishments to prevent smoking by teachers and students, and acknowledge the need to prohibit smoking in schools providing general education. There shall be close cooperation between educational establishments, families, and the general public in carrying out the above activities in connexion with children and adolescents.

4. The USSR Ministry of Culture, the USSR State Committee for Cinematography, the USSR State Committee for Television and Radio, and the USSR State Committee for Publishing, Printing, and Bookselling shall ensure, when determining the programmes of places of entertainment and the planning of topics by film studios and publishing houses, the presentation of productions and television and radio broadcasts aimed at smoking control, and shall also increase the quantity and improve the quality of literature and visual propaganda on this subject.

5. The Councils of Ministers of the Union Republics, the USSR Ministry of Trade, the Central Cooperative Union, and ministries possessing a commercial network shall:

— prohibit the establishment of kiosks and shops selling tobacco products in the vicinity of schools providing general education or vocational/technical, higher, and intermediate special educational establishments, and also take measures to progressively restrict and eventually abolish the sale of such products in commercial undertakings operating on such premises;

— ensure strict compliance with commercial regulations prohibiting the sale of tobacco to persons under 16 years of age.

6. The USSR Ministry of Food Industry shall:

— examine how to cut back the production of non-filter cigarettes and convert to the production primarily of filter cigarettes;

— during the period 1980-1983, introduce, in collaboration with the Ministry of Pulp and Paper Industry and the Ministry of Chemical Industry, and master the production of new filters for tobacco products that ensure maximum retention of nicotine, carbon monoxide, and other harmful substances;

— during 1980, complete the preparation of equipment for printing on the packaging of tobacco products a statement, adopted in consultation with the USSR Ministry of Health, warning of the health hazards of smoking, and eliminate all advertising material from the packaging of tobacco products;

— by 1 January 1982, master the production of reconstituted tobacco, ensuring a significant reduction in the levels of harmful substances contained in it.

7. The USSR State Planning Committee and the USSR Ministry of Food Industry shall examine, in consultation with the USSR Ministry of

Health and the USSR Ministry of Trade, how to increase production and extend the assortment of chewing gum.

8. The USSR Ministry of Agriculture and the V. I. Lenin All-Union Academy of Agriculture Sciences shall accelerate the activities laid down by Resolution No. 390 of 28 May 1976 of the USSR Council of Ministers on measures to increase the quality of tobacco, designed to create new high-yielding varieties of tobacco with reduced levels of nicotine that are necessary for the production of an improved range of tobacco products, with a view to establishing such varieties of tobacco in production during the period 1983-1985.

9. It is considered advisable to establish, under the auspices of the USSR Ministry of Health, an Inter-Agency Council on the Dissemination of Information Concerning the Hazards of Smoking, responsible for drawing up and implementing the relevant measures and coordinating the activities of ministries and agencies in this field, as well as publicizing and disseminating experience on smoking control.

The Ministry of Health of the USSR shall approve the composition and statutes of the Council.

10. The USSR Ministry of Health, acting in collaboration with the All-Union Central Council of Trade Unions and the Central Council of the All-Union Leninist Young Communist League, shall draw up, in consultation with the ministries and agencies concerned, and approve the plan of basic measures for the dissemination of health information on the hazards of smoking.

UNITED KINGDOM

UNITED KINGDOM. An Act (Chapter 34) to amend the Children and Young Persons Act 1933, and the Children and Young Persons (Scotland) Act 1937, to make it an offence to sell any tobacco product to persons under the age of sixteen; and for connected purposes. Dated 8 July 1986. (The Protection of Children (Tobacco) Act 1986). (3 pp.) **UK 86.45**

This Act amends Sec. 7 of the Children and Young Persons Act 1933 (Sale of tobacco &c. to persons under sixteen) to read as follows:[a]

"7. (1) Any person who sells to a person apparently under the age of sixteen years any tobacco or cigarette papers, whether for his own use or not, shall be liable, on summary conviction, in the case of a first offence to a fine not exceeding two pounds, in the case of a second offence to a fine not exceeding five pounds, and in the case of a third or subsequent offence to a fine not exceeding ten pounds.

(2) If on complaint to a court of summary jurisdiction it is proved to the satisfaction of the court that any automatic machine for the sale of tobacco kept on any premises is being extensively used by persons apparently under the age of sixteen years, the court shall order the owner of the machine, or the person on whose premises the machine is kept, to take such precautions to prevent the machine being so used as may be specified in the order or, if necessary, to remove the machine, within such time as may be specified in the order, and if any person against whom such an order has been made fails to comply therewith, he shall be liable, on summary conviction, to a fine not exceeding five pounds, and to a further fine not exceeding one pound for each day during which the offence continues.

(3) It shall be the duty of a constable and of a park-keeper being in uniform to seize any tobacco or cigarette papers in the possession of any person apparently under the age of sixteen years whom he finds smoking in any street or public place, and any tobacco or cigarette papers so seized shall be disposed of, if seized by a constable, in such manner as the police authority may direct, and if seized by a park-keeper, in such manner as the authority or person by whom he was appointed may direct.

(4) Nothing in this section shall make it an offence to sell tobacco or cigarette papers to, or shall authorise the seizure of tobacco or cigarette papers in the possession of, any person who is at the time employed by a manufacturer of or dealer in tobacco, either wholesale or retail, for the purposes of his business, or is a boy messenger in uniform in the employment of a messenger company and employed as such at the time.

(5) For the purposes of this section the expression 'tobacco' includes cigarettes, any product containing tobacco and intended for oral or nasal use and smoking mixtures intended as a substitute for tobacco, and the expression 'cigarettes' includes cut

[a] The sums referred to in the penal provisions listed here have been altered on a number of occasions, evidently by the Magistrates' Courts Act 1980 and the Criminal Penalties etc (Increase) Order 1984 and, according to the Department of Health and Social Security in London, failure to observe the law could lead to prosecution and a fine of up to £400. — ED.

tobacco rolled up in paper, tobacco leaf, or other material in such form as to be capable of immediate use for smoking."

A number of amendments, certain corresponding to those reported above, are made to Sec. 18 of the Children and Young Persons (Scotland) Act 1937.

UNITED KINGDOM. Circular LAC(86)14 of October 1986 of the Department of Health and Social Security on the Protection of Children (Tobacco) Act 1986. (4 pp.) **UK 86.47**

This Circular describes the content and implications of the Act referred to in the title (see *supra*), which came into force on 8 October 1986. The Explanatory Memorandum is reproducted below:

"1. The Act amends section 7 of the Children and Young Persons Act 1933 concerned with the sale of tobacco to persons under the age of sixteen.

2. Under section 7(1) of the Children and Young Persons Act 1933 it was not illegal to sell tobacco (in forms other than cigarettes) to anyone under sixteen if the seller had reasonable grounds for believing that it was for someone else's use. Section 1(1)(*a*) of the 1986 Act removes this defence, making it an offence to sell any tobacco to a person apparently under the age of sixteen, irrespective of the intended user.

3. Section 1(1)(*b*) of the 1986 Act amends section 7(2) of the Children and Young Persons Act 1933 to impose a mandatory obligation on the court to order the owner of a tobacco vending machine, or the person on whose premises the machine is kept, to take precautions to prevent the machine being used extensively by persons apparently under the age of sixteen years or to remove the machine.

4. Section 1(1)(*c*) of the 1986 Act extends the definition of tobacco in section 7 of the Children and Young Persons Act 1933 to include any product containing tobacco and intended for oral or nasal use."

UNITED KINGDOM. The Oral Snuff (Safety) Regulations 1989. S.I. 1989/2347. Dated 13 December 1989. (2 pp.) **UK 90.16**

Reg. 2 of these Regulations lays down that no person may supply, offer to supply, agree to supply, expose for supply, or possess for supply any oral snuff (defined in Reg. 1 to mean "goods which consist wholly or mainly of tobacco in fine cut, ground or particulate form or in any combination of those forms and which are for oral use other than smoking").

UNITED STATES OF AMERICA

UNITED STATES OF AMERICA. Smoking aboard aircraft. Part 252 of Title 14 (Aeronautics and Space) of the United States Code of Federal Regulations. Dated 19 May 1983.[a] (*Federal Register*, Vol. 48, No. 108, 3 June 1983, pp. 24866-24868) **USA 84.11**

The first sentence of the summary of this text reads as follows:

"The [Civil Aeronautics Board] affirms and provides further explanation for its earlier decision not to ban smoking on short flights and not to include vague language in its smoking rule prohibiting unreasonable burdens on nonsmokers from breathing tobacco smoke."

UNITED STATES OF AMERICA. Smoking aboard aircraft. Part 252 of Title 14 (Aeronautics and Space) of the United States Code of Federal Regulations. Dated 1 June 1984. (*Federal Register*, Vol. 49, No. 120, 20 June 1984, pp. 25407-25420) **USA 84.87**

The summary of this text reads as follows:

"The [Civil Aeronautics Board (CAB)] adopts new rules to ban smoking on small aircraft and to ban cigar and pipe smoking on all flights. The CAB also retains current rules requiring fully functioning ventilation systems and discouraging airlines from sandwiching nonsmokers between two smoking sections, and rejects proposals to ban smoking on short flights or to require special provisions for passengers especially sensitive to smoke."

UNITED STATES OF AMERICA. An Act (Public Law 98-474) to establish a national program to increase the availability of information on the health consequences of smoking, to amend the Federal Cigarette Labeling and Advertising Act to change the label requirements for cigarettes, and for other purposes. Dated 12 October 1984. (The Comprehensive Smoking Education Act). (*U.S. Code Congressional and Administrative News*, December 1984, No. 10, pp. 2200-2205) **USA 85.30**

Sec. 2 of this Act prescribes that its purpose is "to provide a new strategy for making Americans more aware of any adverse health effects of smoking, to assure the timely and widespread dissemination of research findings and to enable in-

---

[a] The requirement that airlines must ensure that if a no-smoking section is placed between two smoking sections, nonsmokers are not unreasonably burdened was reinstated by a text dated 27 July 1983 (*Federal Register*, Vol. 48, No. 154, 9 August 1983, pp. 36093-36094). — ED.

dividuals to make informed decisions about smoking". Subsection (*a*) of Sec. 3 reads as follows:

"(*a*) The Secretary of Health and Human Services (hereinafter in this section referred to as the 'Secretary') shall establish and carry out a program to inform the public of any dangers to human health presented by cigarette smoking. In carrying out such program, the Secretary shall—

(1) conduct and support research on the effect of cigarette smoking on human health and develop materials for informing the public of such effect;

(2) coordinate all research and educational programs and other activities within the Department of Health and Human Services (hereinafter in this section referred to as the 'Department') which relate to the effect of cigarette smoking on human health and coordinate, through the Interagency Committee on Smoking and Health (established under subsection (*b*)), such activities with similar activities of other Federal agencies and of private agencies;

(3) establish and maintain a liaison with appropriate private entities, other Federal agencies, and State and local public agencies respecting activities relating to the effect of cigarette smoking on human health;

(4) collect, analyze, and disseminate (through publications, bibliographies, and otherwise) information, studies, and other data relating to the effect of cigarette smoking on human health, and develop standards, criteria, and methodologies for improved information programs related to smoking and health;

(5) compile and make available information on State and local laws relating to the use and consumption of cigarettes; and

(6) undertake any other additional information and research activities which the Secretary determines necessary and appropriate to carry out this section."

Subsection (*b*) provides for the establishment of an Interagency Committee on Smoking and Health. Details are given of its composition. Under subsection (*c*), the Secretary is to transmit a report to Congress not later than 1 January 1985, and biennially thereafter. This report is to contain: (1) an overview and assessment of Federal activities undertaken to inform the public of the health consequences of smoking and the extent of public knowledge of such consequences; (2) a description of the Secretary's and Committee's activities under subsection (*a*); (3) information regarding the activities of the private sector taken in response to the effects of smoking on health; and (4) such recommendations as the Secretary may consider appropriate. Sec. 4 amends Sec. 4 of the Federal Cigarette Labeling and Advertising Act, as amended by the Public Health Cigarette Smoking Act of 1969 (see *IDHL*, 1971, **22**, 998), to read substantially as follows:

"**Sec. 4.** (*a*) (1) It shall be unlawful for any person to manufacture, package, or import for sale or distribution within the United States any cigarettes the package of which fails to bear, in accordance with the requirements of this section, one of the following labels:

SURGEON GENERAL'S WARNING: Smoking Causes Lung Cancer, Heart Disease, Emphysema, And May Complicate Pregnancy.

SURGEON GENERAL'S WARNING: Quitting Smoking Now Greatly Reduces Serious Risks to Your Health.

SURGEON GENERAL'S WARNING: Smoking By Pregnant Women May Result in Fetal Injury, Premature Birth, And Low Birth Weight.

SURGEON GENERAL'S WARNING: Cigarette Smoke Contains Carbon Monoxide.

(2) It shall be unlawful for any manufacturer or importer of cigarettes to advertise or cause to be advertised (other than through the use of outdoor billboards) within the United States any cigarette unless the advertising bears, in accordance with the requirements of this section, one of the following labels:

> SURGEON GENERAL'S WARNING: Smoking Causes Lung Cancer, Heart Disease, Emphysema, And May Complicate Pregnancy.
>
> SURGEON GENERAL'S WARNING: Quitting Smoking Now Greatly Reduces Serious Risks to Your Health.
>
> SURGEON GENERAL'S WARNING: Smoking By Pregnant Women May Result in Fetal Injury, Premature Birth, And Low Birth Weight.
>
> SURGEON GENERAL'S WARNING: Cigarette Smoke Contains Carbon Monoxide.

(3) It shall be unlawful for any manufacturer or importer of cigarettes to advertise or cause to be advertised within the United States through the use of outdoor billboards any cigarette unless the advertising bears, in accordance with the requirements of this section, one of the following labels:

> SURGEON GENERAL'S WARNING: Smoking Causes Lung Cancer, Heart Disease, And Emphysema.
>
> SURGEON GENERAL'S WARNING: Quitting Smoking Now Greatly Reduces Serious Health Risks.
>
> SURGEON GENERAL'S WARNING: Pregnant Women Who Smoke Risk Fetal Injury And Premature Birth.
>
> SURGEON GENERAL'S WARNING: Cigarette Smoke Contains Carbon Monoxide.

(*b*) [*Provisions concerning the location and format of label statements*]

(*c*) The label statements specified in paragraphs (1), (2), and (3) of subsection (*a*) shall be rotated by each manufacturer or importer of cigarettes quarterly in alternating sequence on packages of each brand of cigarettes manufactured by the manufacturer or importer and in the advertisements for each such brand of cigarettes in accordance with a plan submitted by the manufacturer or importer and approved by the Federal Trade Commission. The Federal Trade Commission shall approve a plan submitted by a manufacturer or importer of cigarettes which will provide the rotation required by this subsection and which assures that all of the labels required by paragraphs (1), (2) and (3) will be displayed by the manufacturer or importer at the same time.

(*d*) Subsection (*a*) does not apply to a distributor or a retailer of cigarettes who does not manufacture, package, or import cigarettes for sale or distribution within the United States."

The principal Act is amended by redesignating Secs. 7-12 as Secs. 8-13 respectively, and by inserting after Sec. 5 a new Sec. 7 (Cigarette ingredients), reading substantially as follows:

"**Sec. 7.** (*a*) Each person who manufactures, packages, or imports cigarettes shall annually provide the Secretary with a list of the ingredients added to tobacco in the manufacture of cigarettes which does not identify the company which uses the ingredients or the brand of cigarettes which contain the ingredients. A person or group of persons required to provide a list by this subsection may designate an individual or entity to provide the list required by this subsection.

(*b*) (1) At such times as the Secretary considers appropriate, the Secretary shall transmit to the Congress a report, based on the information provided under subsection (*a*), respecting—

(A) a summary of research activities and proposed research activities on the health effects of ingredients added to tobacco in the manufacture of cigarettes and the findings of such research;

(B) information pertaining to any such ingredient which in the judgement of the Secretary poses a health risk to cigarette smokers; and

(C) any other information which the Secretary determines to be in the public interest.

(2) [*Provisions concerning the confidentiality of information*]"

It is laid down that the above-mentioned Section is to take effect upon the expiration of a one-year period beginning on the date of enactment of the present Act.

UNITED STATES OF AMERICA. An Act (Public Law 99-252) to provide for public education concerning the health consequences of using smokeless tobacco products. Dated 27 February 1986. (The Comprehensive Smokeless Tobacco Health Education Act of 1986). (6 pp.)

USA 87.1

Sec. 2 (Public education) reads as follows:

"(*a*) DEVELOPMENT. — (1) The Secretary of Health and Human Services shall establish and carry out a program to inform the public of any dangers to human health resulting from the use of smokeless tobacco products. In carrying out such program the Secretary shall—

(A) develop educational programs and materials and public service announcements respecting the dangers to human health from the use of smokeless tobacco;

(B) make such programs, materials, and announcements available to States, local governments, school systems, the media, and such other entities as the Secretary determines appropriate to further the purposes of this Act;

(C) conduct and support research on the effect of smokeless tobacco on human health; and

(D) collect, analyze, and disseminate information and studies on smokeless tobacco and health.

(2) In developing programs, materials, and announcements under paragraph (1) the Secretary shall consult with the Secretary of Education, medical and public health entities, consumer groups, representatives of manufacturers of smokeless tobacco products, and other appropriate entities.

(*b*) ASSISTANCE. — The Secretary of Health and Human Services may provide technical assistance and may make grants to States—

(1) to assist in the development of educational programs and materials and public service announcements respecting the dangers to human health from the use of smokeless tobacco,

(2) to assist in the distribution of such programs, materials, and announcements throughout the States, and

(3) to establish 18 as the minimum age for the purchase of smokeless tobacco."

Subsection (*a*) (General rule) of Sec. 3 (Smokeless tobacco warning) lays down that it is unlawful for any person to manufacture, package, or import for sale or distribution within the United States any smokeless tobacco product unless the product package bears, in accordance with the requirements of this Act, one of the following labels: "WARNING: THIS PRODUCT MAY CAUSE MOUTH CANCER"; "WARNING: THIS PRODUCT MAY CAUSE GUM DISEASE AND TOOTH LOSS"; and "WARNING: THIS PRODUCT IS NOT A SAFE ALTERNATIVE TO CIGARETTES".

It is unlawful for any manufacturer, packager, or importer of smokeless tobacco products to advertise or cause to be advertised (other than through the use of outdoor billboard advertising) within the United States any such product unless the advertising bears (in accordance with the requirements of this Act) one of the above-mentioned labels. Subsection (*b*) (Label format) prescribes that the Federal Trade Commission (FTC) is to issue regulations regarding the method of apposition of the above-mentioned label statements on smokeless tobacco packages and in advertising. Subsections (*c*)-(*f*) read as follows:

"(*c*) LABEL DISPLAY. — The Federal Trade Commission shall issue regulations requiring each label statement required by subsection (*a*) to—

(1) in the case of a smokeless tobacco product package, be randomly displayed by each manufacturer, packager, or importer of a smokeless tobacco product in each 12-month period in as equal a number of times as is possible on each brand of the product and be randomly distributed in all parts of the United States in which such product is marketed, and

(2) in the case of any advertisement of a smokeless tobacco product, be rotated every 4 months by each manufacturer, packager, or importer of a smokeless tobacco product in an alternating sequence in the advertisement for each brand of the product.

(*d*) PLAN. — (1) Each manufacturer, packager, or importer of a smokeless tobacco product shall submit a plan to the Federal Trade Commission which specifies the method such manufacturer, packager, or importer will use to rotate, display, and distribute the statements required by subsection (*a*) in accordance with the requirements of subsections (*b*) and (*c*).

(2) The Federal Trade Commission shall approve a plan submitted by a manufacturer, packager, or importer of a smokeless tobacco product under paragraph (1) if such plan provides for the rotation, display, and distribution on smokeless tobacco product packages and advertisements of the statements required by subsection (*a*) in a manner which complies with this section and the regulations promulgated pursuant to this section.

(*e*) APPLICATION. — This section does not apply to a distributor or a retailer of any smokeless tobacco product which does not manufacture, package, or import smokeless tobacco products for sale or distribution within the United States.

(*f*) TELEVISION AND RADIO ADVERTISING. — Effective 6 months after the date of the enactment of this Act, it shall be unlawful to advertise smokeless tobacco on any medium of electronic communications subject to the jurisdiction of the Federal Communications Commission."

Subsection (*a*) (In general) of Sec. 4 (Ingredient reporting) prescribes that each person who manufactures, packages, or imports smokeless tobacco products is to annually provide the Secretary with: (A) a list of the ingredients added to tobacco in the manufacture of smokeless tobacco products which does not identify the company which uses the ingredients or the brand of smokeless tobacco which contains the ingredients; and (B) a specification of the quantity of nicotine contained in each such product. Subsection (*b*) (1) reads as follows:

"(*b*) REPORT. — (1) At such times as the Secretary considers appropriate, the Secretary shall transmit to the Congress a report, based on the information provided under subsection (*a*), respecting—

(A) a summary of research activities and proposed research activities on the health effects of ingredients added to tobacco in the manufacture of smokeless tobacco products and the findings of such research;

(B) information pertaining to any such ingredient which in the judgment of the Secretary poses a health risk to users of smokeless tobacco; and

(C) any other information which the Secretary determines to be in the public interest."

Other provisions in this Section deal with the confidentiality of information. Sec. 5 (Enforcement, regulations, and construction) includes provisions dealing with the modalities for the issuance of regulations by the FTC under Sec. 3. The three subsections of Sec. 7 (Preemption) read as follows:

"(*a*) FEDERAL ACTION. — No statement relating to the use of smokeless tobacco products and health, other than the statements required by section 3, shall be required by any Federal agency to appear on any package or in any advertisement (unless the advertisement is an outdoor billboard advertisement) of a smokeless tobacco product.

(*b*) STATE AND LOCAL ACTION. — No statement relating to the use of smokeless tobacco products and health, other than the statements required by section 3, shall be required by any State or local statute or regulation to be included on any package or in any advertisement (unless the advertisement is an outdoor billboard advertisement) of a smokeless tobacco product.

(*c*) EFFECT ON LIABILITY LAW. — Nothing in this Act shall relieve any person from liability at common law or under State statutory law to any other person."

Under Sec. 8 (Reports), the Secretary of Health and Human Services is to transmit a report to the Congress not later than 11 January 1987, and biannually thereafter, containing (1) a description of the effects of health education efforts on the use of smokeless tobacco products; (2) a description of the use by the public of smokeless tobacco products; (3) an evaluation of the health effects of smokeless tobacco products and the identification of areas appropriate for further research; and (4) such recommendations for legislation and administrative action as the Secretary considers appropriate. The FTC is to similarly transmit reports containing (1) a description of the current sales, advertising, and marketing practices associated with smokeless tobacco products, and (2) such recommendations for legislation and administrative action as it deems appropriate. The terms defined in Sec. 9 (Definitions) include "smokeless tobacco" ("any finely cut, ground, powdered, or leaf tobacco that is intended to be placed in the oral cavity"), "package", and "sale or distribution" ("includes sampling or any other distribution not for sale").[a]

UNITED STATES OF AMERICA. Regulations under the Comprehensive Smokeless Tobacco Health Education Act of 1986. Part 307 of Title 16 (Commercial Practices) of the United States Code of Federal

---

[a] Regulations for the implementation of this Act were issued by the FTC in November 1986 (*Federal Register*, Vol. 51, No. 213, 4 November 1986, pp. 40005-40023).

Regulations. Dated 3 November 1986. (*Federal Register*, Vol. 51, No. 213, 4 November 1986, pp. 40005-40023) **USA 87.47**

The summary of this text reads substantially as follows:

"On February 27, 1986, the President signed into law the Comprehensive Smokeless Tobacco Health Education Act of 1986 (Smokeless Tobacco Act) [see *IDHL*, 1987, **38**, 67, **USA 87.1**]. The Smokeless Tobacco Act requires, among other things, that manufacturers, packagers, and importers of smokeless tobacco display health warnings on their packaging and in most of their advertising and submit plans to the [Federal Trade] Commission specifying the method used to rotate, display, and distribute the required health warnings.... This notice contains the statement of basis and purpose for the regulations implementing the Smokeless Tobacco Act and the text of the final regulations."

UNITED STATES OF AMERICA. Smoking regulations. Part 101-20 (Management of Buildings and Grounds) of Title 41 (Public Contracts and Property Management) of the United States Code of Federal Regulations. Dated 4 December 1986. (*Federal Register*, Vol. 51, No. 235, 8 December 1986, pp. 44258-44259) **USA 87.52**

The summary of this text reads as follows:

"This regulation provides for revised smoking regulations in buildings controlled by GSA [the General Services Administration].

Numerous studies have concluded that smoking adversely affects the health of those persons 'passively' exposed to tobacco smoke. In view of these findings and in the interest of protecting Federal employee health and well being, GSA proposed regulations to protect the non-smoking worker's and public building visitor's right not to be exposed involuntarily to secondhand tobacco smoke at the Federal work site. The proposed regulations also recognized the needs of those who smoke and permitted the designation of smoking areas. These areas were proposed to allow those who smoke to continue to do so conveniently and without affecting productivity. Hence, the policy attempted to recognize the rights, needs, and concerns of all employees.

The proposed regulations where designated to improve the overall quality of GSA-controlled space and to assure the health and safety of Federal employees and the visiting public. The General Services Administration received numerous comments on the proposed regulations. The comments were from the general public as well as from special interest groups, Government employees, unions, and Government agencies. All comments were considered.

General Services Administration believes the final regulations are responsive to the concerns raised by employee representatives, agencies, and the public."

UNITED STATES OF AMERICA. An Act (Public Law 100-202) making further continuing appropriations for the fiscal year 1988, and for other purposes. Dated 22 December 1987. (The Department of Transportation and Related Agencies Appropriations Act 1988). **USA 88.42**

Sec. 404 of the Federal Aviation Act of 1958 is amended by the insertion of a new subsection entitled "Prohibition against smoking on scheduled flights and tampering with smoke alarm devices". It is henceforth prescribed that, on and after the date of expiration of the four-month period following the date of enactment of this subsection, it is to be unlawful to smoke in the passenger cabin or lavatory on any scheduled airline flight in intrastate, interstate, or overseas air transportation, if such flight is scheduled for two hours or less in duration. The Secretary of Transportation is to issue such regulations as may be necessary to carry out the provisions of this subsection. The above provisions are to be repealed "effective on the expiration of the 28-month period following the date of enactment of this subsection".

UNITED STATES OF AMERICA. Smoking aboard aircraft. Parts 121 and 135 of Title 14 (Aeronautics and Space) of the United States Code of Federal Regulations. Dated 11 April 1988. (*Federal Register*, Vol. 53, No. 71, 13 April 1988, pp. 12357-12362) **USA 89.14**

The first two sentences of the summary of this text read as follows:

"This rule requires the no smoking sign to be turned on at all times on scheduled airline flights, except for flights between the United States and other countries, which are scheduled to be 2 hours or less in duration. This rule carries out a ban on smoking on such flights mandated by Pub. L. 100-202 [see *IDHL*, 1988, **39**, 865, **USA 88.42**]."

UNITED STATES OF AMERICA. An Act (Public Law 101-164) making appropriations for the Department of Transportation and related agencies for the fiscal year ending September 30, 1990, and for other purposes. Dated 21 November 1989. **USA 90.31**

Sec. 404(*d*)(1)(A) of the Federal Aviation Act of 1958, as amended by one of the provisions of the present Act, now reads as follows:

"... it shall be unlawful to smoke in the passenger cabin or lavatory on any scheduled airline flight segment in air transportation or intrastate air transportation, which is—

(i) between any two points within Puerto Rico, the United States, Virgin Islands, the District of Columbia, or any State of the United States (other than Alaska and Hawaii), or between any point in any one of aforesaid jurisdictions (other than Alaska and Hawaii) and any point in any other of such jurisdictions;

(ii) within the State of Alaska or within the State of Hawaii;

or

(iii) scheduled for 6 hours or less in duration, and between any point described in clause (i) and any point in Alaska or Hawaii, or between any point in Alaska and any point in Hawaii."[a]

---

[a] Regulations for the implementation of these provisions were issued by the Department of Transportation on 7 February 1990 (*Federal Register*, 13 February 1990, Vol. 55, No. 30, pp. 4991-4993). — ED.

UNITED STATES OF AMERICA. Prohibition against smoking; final rule. Parts 121, 129, and 135 of Title 14 (Aeronautics and Space) of the United States Code of Federal Regulations. Dated 28 February 1990. (*Federal Register*, Vol. 55, No. 45, 7 March 1990, pp. 8364-8368)
USA 90.37

The first paragraph of the summary of this text reads as follows:

"This rule implements the prohibition against smoking contained in Public Law 101-164 enacted on November 21, 1989 [see *supra*]. This legislation makes it unlawful for any person to smoke in the passenger cabin or lavatory of an airplane during most scheduled flight segments in the United States. The statutory prohibition applies to U.S. and foreign air carriers."

UNITED STATES OF AMERICA (CALIFORNIA). An Act (Chapter 193 of the Laws of 1980) to amend Sections 1235, 1290, and 25942 of, and to add Sections 1234 and 1286 to, the Health and Safety Code, relating to smoking. Approved 17 June 1980. (4 pp.) **USA (CA) 81.2**

Sec. 1 of this Act states that the Legislature "finds and declares that smoke is detrimental to nonsmokers' health, welfare, and comfort, especially to those who have allergies or who have cardiovascular or respiratory disease; that smoke may cause discomfort and physical irritation; and that regulation of smoking in health facilities and clinics is, therefore, necessary". Sec. 1234 imposes restrictions on smoking in "patient areas of a clinic", while Sec. 1286 imposes corresponding restrictions in "patient care areas, waiting rooms, and visiting rooms of a health facility". Neither Section is applicable to skilled nursing facilities, intermediate care facilities, and intermediate care facilities for the developmentally disabled. Various penalties for violations of the above-mentioned restrictions are likewise introduced.

UNITED STATES OF AMERICA (NEW YORK). An Act to amend the public health law, in relation to smoking restrictions and to repeal article 13-E of such law relating thereto. Approved by the Governor: 5 July 1989. **USA (NY) 90.1**

The following is an extract from a summary of the provisions of this Act (contained in a Memorandum on the Bill made available to WHO):

"Existing Public Health Law Article 13-E is repealed and a new Article 13-E is added to restrict smoking in public indoor areas and in the workplace. This bill would continue to prohibit smoking in public places such as libraries, museums, theaters and public means of mass transportation as provided by current Article 13-E, and would add provisions barring smoking in taxicabs, limousines, schools, hospitals, residential health care facilities licensed by the State, arenas, auditoriums, clubhouses, courthouses, elevators, restrooms, waiting rooms, waiting areas, ticketing areas, enclosed areas containing a swimming pool, food markets, stores, banks and commercial establishments. In some instances, the person controlling each such place would be permitted to designate a smoking area. Smoking would not be prohibited in conventions of private groups, private homes, residences and automobiles, private social functions, hotel and motel rooms rented to guests, limousines under private hire, private boxes in indoor arenas, tobacco businesses, and bars.

Trade shows could permit smoking if notice were given to the public that smoking would not be restricted. Smoking would be prohibited in the bowler settee area of bowling establishments and in at least 25% of the concourse area of such establishments. Bingo sponsors are required to provide a contiguous nonsmoking area sufficient to meet customer demand. Food service establishments are required to provide a contiguous nonsmoking area sufficient to meet customer demand. Demand will be deemed met if at least 70% of the food establishment's seating capacity is reserved for non-smokers.

In the workplace, employers must put into effect written smoking policies. Such policies, at a minimum, must provide nonsmokers with a smoke-free work area. Smoking must also be prohibited in auditoriums, gymnasiums, classrooms, conference rooms, meeting rooms, elevators, hallways, restrooms, employee medical facilities, and rooms or areas containing photocopying or other equipment used in common. Contiguous nonsmoking areas are required in cafeterias and lounges sufficient to meet employee demand. If at least 70% of the seating capacity in such area is set aside as smoke-free, demand will be deemed met. The article also applies to the legislative, judicial and administrative branches of state and local government."

URUGUAY

URUGUAY. Law No. 15361 of 24 December 1982 adopting provisions on the advertising and marketing of cigarettes, cigars, and tobacco products. (*Diario Oficial*, 14 January 1983, p. 51-A) **Ur. 83.3**

Sec. 1 of this Law prescribes that written advertisements for cigarettes, cigars, tobacco, and similar products must contain the following warning in clear, legible characters: "Warning: smoking is harmful to health. M.S.P.[a]". Oral advertising must include the same warning at the rate of one for every five advertising references to cigars, cigarettes, and tobacco, on an alternating basis. Television advertising must include the warning in clearly legible characters, and the advertising must appear for a sufficient period of time to enable it to be easily read.

Sec. 2 prescribes that, within 180 days following the promulgation of this Law, cigarette packets, packs of tobacco, and, in general, all types of containers of cigarettes, cigars, tobacco, and similar products supplied in Uruguay must display the same warning in conspicuous characters.

Sec. 3 requires manufacturers and importers of cigarettes marketed in Uruguay to publish in the major advertising media, once every three months, the maximum nicotine and tar levels per cigarette in the case of the brands which they offer for sale. Sec. 4 prescribes that the Ministry of Public Health is to verify the accuracy of the levels stated.

Sec. 5 prohibits the sale of cigarettes, cigars, tobacco, and similar products to persons under 18 years of age, while Sec. 6 prohibits the sale of loose cigarettes. Penal provisions are laid down in Secs. 7 and 8.

URUGUAY. Law No. 15656 of 10 October 1984 extending the interval for publishing the maximum contents of nicotine and tar by cigarette manufacturers and importers. (*Diario Oficial de la República Oriental del Uruguay*, 9 November 1984, No. 21848, p. 115-A) **Ur. 88.6**

The effect of Sec. 1 of this Law is to amend Sec. 3 of Law No. 15361 of 24 December 1982 by prescribing that the above-mentioned figures are to be published once annually. However, Sec. 2 empowers the Ministry of Public Health to publish them twice annually, taking into account new analyses.

VENEZUELA

VENEZUELA. Decree No. 849 of 21 November 1980 prohibiting, with effect from 1 January 1981, the transmission by television stations of any commercial advertising which directly or indirectly encourages the consumption of cigarettes and other products derived from tobacco manufacture. (*Gaceta Oficial de la República de Venezuela*, 21 November 1980, No. 32116, p. 242447) **Ven. 82.12**

VENEZUELA. Decree No. 996 of 19 March 1981 prohibiting, with effect from 1 April 1981, the transmission by radio stations of any commercial advertising which directly or indirectly encourages the consumption of cigarettes and other products derived from tobacco. (*Gaceta Oficial de la República de Venezuela*, 20 March 1981, No. 32192, p. 243092) **Ven. 82.14**

VENEZUELA. Resolution of 23 October 1984 establishing a Standing Honorary National Council attached to the Division of Chronic Diseases of the Ministry [of Health and Social Welfare] for studying health problems associated with smoking and with a view to formulating policies for the prevention of smoking and the organic diseases resulting therefrom. (*Gaceta Oficial de la República de Venezuela*, 6 November 1984, No. 33098, p. 250793) **Ven. 86.1**

Sec. 2 of this Resolution indicates the multidisciplinary nature of the abovementioned Council. In addition to representatives of specialized bodies (the Institute of Social Security, the National Academy of Medicine, the Cancer Society, etc.), the Council includes representatives of the following ministries: the Ministry of Health and Social Welfare; the Ministry of Agriculture and Livestock Breeding; the Ministry of Labour; the Ministry of Transport and Communications; the Ministry of Justice; the Ministry of the Environment and Renewable Natural Resources; the Ministry of Information and Tourism; and the Ministry of Youth Affairs.

Under Sec. 3, the Council is to be assisted by an Executive Committee, whose task is to evaluate the harmful effects of smoking on health. Details are given of the composition of the Committee. Sec. 4 provides for the establishment of a Technical Support and Coordination Unit, responsible for developing anti-smoking measures. The Unit is to be of a multidisciplinary nature and is to include medical professionals (epidemiologists), statisticians, sociologists, teachers, and experts in public relations and social communications.

COUNCIL OF EUROPE

CONSULTATIVE ASSEMBLY OF THE COUNCIL OF EUROPE. Twenty-fifth Ordinary Session. Recommendation 716 (1973)[1] on the control of tobacco and alcohol advertising and on measures to curb consumption of these products.

The Assembly,

1. Observing that the consumption of alcohol and tobacco is increasing constantly, and that these products can have serious effects on health;
2. Considering that the public is encouraged to consume such products by advertising which frequently connects tobacco and alcohol with success in life, unspoilt nature and a world of well-being;
3. Considering that such advertising exerts a considerable influence, particularly on young people who very often are misled into believing that it is essential to smoke and drink in order to belong to the adult world;
4. Considering that tax revenue derived from the sale of alcohol and tobacco is very substantial, and that member governments spend little in order to combat the dangers of excessive consumption whose financial consequences are to a large extent borne by the public authorities and often exceed the tax revenue itself;
5. Considering that many road accidents are caused by drivers who are under the influence of alcohol;
6. Considering that any government policy to improve the health of the population should include measures to reduce the dangers of the use and misuse of alcohol and tobacco, and in particular a determined information campaign;
7. Observing that, subject to legal restrictions, existing or projected, the fundamental responsibility for the use of tobacco and alcohol rests with the individual,
8. Recommends that the Committee of Ministers invite member governments:
   (*a*) to study the social and psychological causes of excessive drinking and smoking, in order to improve prevention and facilitate early detection of disease;
   (*b*) to provide a greater range of socio-medical services for the treatment of smokers and alcoholics who wish to put an end to their addiction, and to subsidise organisations active in the field;

[1]*Assembly debate* on 26 and 27 September 1973 (10th, 11th and 13th Sittings) (see Doc. 3323, report of the Committee on Social and Health Questions).
Text adopted by the Assembly on 27 September 1973 (13th Sitting).

(*c*) to subsidise organisations combating the abuse of alcohol and tobacco;

(*d*) to regulate strictly or forbid advertising of tobacco and alcohol on television and radio, and to limit advertising of these products in general, particularly in the press, theatres, streets, public places and sport stadiums, taking as a model Resolution AP (69) 3 of the Committee of Ministers of the Council of Europe entitled "Regulations governing the advertising of medicines to the public";

(*e*) to undertake, in view of the large tax revenue derived from these products, a determined information campaign on the risks involved in their consumption;

(*f*) to emphasise in this information campaign the extent to which children's behaviour is conditioned by that of their parents;

(*g*) to include in the school curriculum, throughout its duration, objective information on the dangers of tobacco and alcohol;

(*h*) to encourage teachers to attend regular information courses on drinking and smoking, and on psychological ways of reducing the consumption of tobacco and alcohol by young people, and to inform their pupils on the risks of alcohol and tobacco consumption;

(*i*) to forbid the use of tobacco on all forms of public transport and in waitingrooms of government services, unless a special non-smokers' compartment or room is provided;

(*j*) to promote research into ways of manufacturing less harmful cigarettes;

(*k*) to increase duties on particularly harmful products containing tobacco and alcohol;

(*l*) to make it obligatory that cigarette packets carry a health warning and information on tar and nicotine content;

(*m*) to apply fully the recommendations made in Resolution (73) 7 on "punishment of road traffic offences committed whilst driving a vehicle under the influence of alcohol", adopted by the Committee of Ministers on 22 March 1973, in particular its paragraph I, sub-paragraphs 1 and 2, recommending that the alcohol level in the blood at which any person driving a vehicle is liable to punishment should be fixed at a maximum of 80 mg/100 ml, and to take steps to reduce this limit to a level of 50 mg/100 ml;

(*n*) to prohibit the manufacture and sale of cigarettes containing more than 1 mg of nicotine or 15 mg of tar, and to encourage manufacturers to eliminate tar completely;

(*o*) to publish regularly a list of the various brands of cigarettes on sale in individual countries with an analysis of their harmful factors.

PARLIAMENTARY ASSEMBLY OF THE COUNCIL OF EUROPE. Fortieth Ordinary Session. Recommendation 1101 (1989)[1] on the protection of non-smokers.

The Assembly,

1. Recalling its Recommendation 716 (1973) on the control of tobacco and alcohol advertising and on measures to curb the consumption of these products;
2. Noting that cigarette smoking continues to be the largest single avoidable cause of premature mortality in Europe, where it is responsible for more than half a million deaths each year;
3. Considering that many studies have demonstrated that environmental tobacco smoke is not merely a nuisance to non-smokers, but may also be a serious health hazard to them;
4. Concerned about the damage done to the foetus and about the general complications caused by smoking and environmental tobacco smoke to women during pregnancy, as well as about its particularly harmful effects on children;
5. Concerned at the levels of smoking among young people;
6. Concerned that, whereas cigarette smoking is decreasing among men and no longer increasing among women in developed countries, it is dramatically increasing in Third World countries;
7. Concerned about the promotion of smokeless tobacco, which the World Health Organization (WHO) has found to constitute no safe alternative to cigarette smoking;
8. Considering that the benefits of taxation and employment in the tobacco industry are offset by medical costs on tobacco-related diseases and lost production;
9. Considering that government action is indispensable in order to encourage people to stop smoking, to urge young people to refrain from starting to smoke and to guarantee the right of non-smokers to be free from environmental tobacco smoke;
10. Noting and considering that the time when smoking had a symbolic function – from peace pipe to emancipatory manifestation – lies behind us;
11. Supporting Resolution EUR/RC37/R9 of the Regional Committee for Europe of WHO, unanimously adopted in September 1987, which encouraged member states to promote measures to protect non-smokers, in view of WHO's goal of "Health for All" by the year 2000;
12. Welcoming the decision by the European Parliament to ban smoking in all its meeting rooms as from 1 September 1988;
13. Desirous that its own committees should follow the example of the European Parliament by agreeing to refrain from smoking during their meetings,

14. Recommends that the Committee of Ministers:

A. urge member states:

i. to implement comprehensive multisectoral policies on tobacco, in co-operation with intergovernmental and non-governmental organisations;

ii. to promote education on the risks of smoking and on respect for the rights of non-smokers;

iii. to establish regulations to prohibit smoking in enclosed public places, public transport, airliners, health-care premises, education establishments, premises where food is handled, covered premises devoted to sports and entertainment, places of work (except in separate rooms meant for smokers) and in all other places where non-smokers need to be protected from environmental tobacco smoke;

B. initiate the preparation of a European charter on tobacco, as a binding legal instrument, as advocated by the Regional Office for Europe of the World Health Organisation;

C. guarantee the protection of non-smokers in meeting rooms and shared offices in Council of Europe buildings, as the European Parliament has done.

[1]*Assembly debate* on 3 February 1989 (25th Sitting) (see Doc. 5984, report of the Social, Health and Family Affairs Committee, Rapporteur: Mr de Puig).
Text adopted by the Assembly on 3 February 1989 (25th Sitting).

EUROPEAN COMMUNITIES

EUROPEAN COMMUNITIES. RESOLUTION OF THE COUNCIL AND THE MINISTERS FOR HEALTH OF THE MEMBER STATES, MEETING WITHIN THE COUNCIL of 18 July 1989 on banning smoking in places open to the public (89/C 189/01)

THE COUNCIL OF THE EUROPEAN COMMUNITIES AND THE MINISTERS FOR HEALTH OF THE MEMBER STATES, MEETING WITHIN THE COUNCIL,

Having regard to the Treaty establishing the European Economic Community,

Having regard to the draft recommendation from the Commission,

Having regard to the opinion of the Economic and Social Committee[1],

Whereas the European Council held in Milan on 28 and 29 June 1985 stressed the importance of launching a European action programme against cancer;

Whereas the Council and the Representatives of the Governments of the Member States, meeting within the Council, in their resolution of 7 July 1986 on a programme of action of the European Communities against cancer, set the objective of contributing to an improvement in the health and quality of life of citizens within the Community by reducing the number of cases of cancer and under this heading gave priority to measures against smoking;

Whereas, in addition to the potential encouragement to smoke and the unpleasant physical effects and the nuisance which smoke causes for non-smokers, there is an increased risk of respiratory illnesses for non-smokers involuntarily exposed to the smoke of tobacco products; whereas consequently, it is appropriate to protect the right to health of non-smokers against involuntary smoking;

Whereas, to ensure respect for the right to health of non-smokers, it is essential to ban smoking in public places in certain establishments and in forms of transport;

Whereas, however, in view of the extent of tobacco addiction affecting part of the population, it is appropriate to make provision to permit smoking in part of these establishments and forms of transport;

Whereas it is necessary to extend to the citizens of all Member States the protection they are afforded in some Member States against the damage caused by involuntary smoking;

Whereas, finally, the initiative set out in this resolution will have an even more beneficial effect on public health, particularly for the workers directly concerned, when coupled with health education programmes during the years of compulsory education and with information and public awareness campaigns,

INVITES THE MEMBER STATES:

to take the following measures by introducing legislation or by other methods in accordance with national practices and conditions:

1. Ban smoking in enclosed premises open to the public which form part of the public or private establishments listed in the Annex. Member States may add to the said list;
2. Extend the ban on smoking to all forms of public transport;
3. Provide, where necessary, for clearly defined areas to be reserved for smokers in the above establishments and, if possible, in public transport, particularly for long journeys;
4. Ensure that in the event of a conflict, in areas other than those reserved for smokers, the right to health of non-smokers prevails over the right of smokers to smoke;

to inform the Commission every two years of action taken in response to this resolution.

Public and private establishments referred to in point 1 of the resolution
(non-exhaustive list)

1. Establishments where services are provided to the public, whether for a charge or free, including the sale of goods;
2. Hospitals, establishments where health care is given and all other medical establishments;
3. Establishments where elderly persons are received;
4. Schools and other premises where children or young people are received or housed;
5. Establishments where higher education and vocational training are given;
6. Enclosed establishments used for entertainment (cinemas, theatres, etc.); radio and television studios open to the public;
7. Enclosed establishments where exhibitions are held;
8. Establishments and enclosed places where sports are practised;
9. Enclosed premises of underground and railway stations, ports and airports.

[1] Opinion delivered on 26 April 1989

EUROPEAN COMMUNITIES. Council Directive 89/622/EEC of 13 November 1989 on the approximation of the laws, regulations and administrative provisions of the Member States concerning the labelling of tobacco products. (*Official Journal of the European Communities*, No. L 359, 8 December 1989, pp. 1-4) **EEC 90.21**

Articles 1-9 of this Directive read substantially as follows:

"*Article 1*

The objective of this Directive is the harmonization of the laws, regulations and administrative provisions of the Member States concerning the warnings regarding health to appear on the unit packet of tobacco products and the indication of the tar and nicotine yield to appear on cigarette packets, taking as a base a high level of health protection by reducing the harm done to health by tobacco addiction.

Article 2

For the purposes of this Directive:

(1) 'tobacco products' means products for the purpose of smoking, sniffing, sucking or chewing, inasmuch as they are, even partly, made of tobacco;

(2) 'tar' means the raw anhydrous nicotine-free condensate of smoke;

(3) 'nicotine' means nicotinic alkaloids.

Article 3

1. The tar and nicotine yields that must be indicated on cigarette packets shall be measured on the basis of the ISO 4387 and ISO 3400 methods.

2. The accuracy of the indications on packets shall be verified in accordance with ISO standard 8243.

3. The indications concerned shall be printed on the side of cigarette packets, in the official language or languages of the country of final marketing in clearly legible print on a contrasting background so that at least 4% of the corresponding surface is covered. This percentage shall be raised to 6% for countries with two official languages and to 8% for countries with three official languages.

4. In January each year the Member States shall forward to the Commission lists of the tar and nicotine contents of the cigarettes sold on their markets. The Commission shall publish this information in the *Official Journal of the European Communities*.

Article 4

1. All unit packets of tobacco products shall carry, on the most visible surface, the following general warning in the official language or languages of the country of final marketing: 'Tobacco seriously damages health'.

2. With regard to cigarette packets, the other large surface of the packet shall carry, in the official language or languages of the country of final marketing, specific warnings alternating in accordance with the following rule:

— each Member State shall draw up a list of warnings taken exclusively from those listed in the Annex,

— the specific warnings selected shall be printed on the unit packets so as to guarantee the appearance of each warning on an equal quantity of unit packets, with a tolerance of around 5%.

3. Member States may stipulate that the warnings referred to in paragraphs 1 and 2 be combined with the indication of the authority that is their author.

4. On cigarette packets the warnings provided for in paragraphs 1 and 2 shall cover at least 4% of each large surface of the unit packet, excluding the indication of the authority provided for in paragraph 3. This percentage shall be increased to 6% for countries with two official languages and to 8% for countries with three official languages.

The required warnings on the two largest surfaces of each cigarette packet:

(*a*) shall be clear and legible;

(*b*) shall be printed in bold letters;

(*c*) shall be printed on a contrasting background;

(*d*) shall not be printed in a place where they may be damaged when the package is opened;

(*e*) shall not be printed on the transparent wrapper or any other external wrapping.

5. In the case of tobacco products other than cigarettes, the general warning laid down in paragraph 1 shall be printed in, or irremoveably affixed to, a conspicuous place on a contrasting background and in such a way as to be easily visible, clearly legible and indelible. It shall not in any way be hidden, obscured or interrupted by other written or pictorial matter.

Articles 5-7

[*Modalities for the adaptation of the provisions of this Directive to technical progress*]

Article 8

1. Member States may not, for reasons of labelling, prohibit or restrict the sale of products which comply with this Directive.

2. The provisions of this Directive do not affect the right of the Member States to lay down, in compliance with the Treaty, requirements concerning the import, sale and consumption of tobacco products which they deem necessary in order to protect public health, provided such requirements do not imply any changes to labelling as laid down in this Directive.

Article 9

1. Member States shall adopt the laws, regulations and administrative provisions necessary to comply with this Directive before 1 July 1990.

They shall forthwith inform the Commission thereof and communicate to it the provisions of national law which they adopt in the field governed by this Directive.

The Commission shall publish in the *Official Journal of the European Communities* the national warning lists drawn up in accordance with the first indent of Article 4 (2).

2. Member States shall bring into force the above laws, regulations and administrative provisions before 31 December 1991.

However,

— until 31 December 1992 cigarettes, and

— until 31 December 1993 other tobacco products

existing on 31 December 1991 which do not comply with this Directive may still be put on sale.

3. Member States which, after 31 December 1991, amend their warning lists drawn up in accordance with the first indent of Article 4 (2) shall notify the Commission of that amendment eighteen months before its application. The Commission shall publish it in the *Official Journal of the European Communities.*"

The following Annex (List of health warnings referred to in the first indent of Article 4 (2)) is appended:

"A. *Warnings which must be included on the national lists*

1. Smoking causes cancer.
2. Smoking causes heart disease.

B. *Warnings from amongst which Member States may choose*

1. Smoking causes fatal diseases.
2. Smoking kills.
3. Smoking can kill.
4. Smoking when pregnant harms your baby.
5. Protect children: don't make them breathe your smoke.
6. Smoking damages the health of those around you.
7. Stopping smoking reduces the risk of serious disease.
8. Smoking causes cancer, chronic bronchitis and other chest diseases.

EUROPEAN COMMUNITIES. Council Directive 90/239/EEC of 17 May 1990 on the approximation of the laws, regulations and administrative provisions of the Member States concerning the maximum tar yield of cigarettes. (*Official Journal of the European Communities*, No. L 137, 30 May 1990, pp. 36-37) **EEC 90.42**

Articles 1-4 of this Directive read as follows:

"*Article 1*

The objective of this Directive is the harmonization of the laws, regulations and administrative provisions of the Member States concerning the maximum tar yield of cigarettes, taking as a basis a high level of public health protection by the reduction of the health damage caused by tar.

Article 2

1. For the purposes of this Directive, 'tar' means the raw anhydrous nicotine-free condensate of smoke.

2. The tar yield of cigarettes marketed in the Member States shall not be greater than:

— 15 mg per cigarette as from 31 December 1992, and

— 12 mg per cigarette as from 31 December 1997.

3. For the Hellenic Republic, as a temporary derogation, the limit values and dates of implementation shall be as follows:

— 20 mg until 31 December 1992,
— 18 mg until 31 December 1998,
— 15 mg until 31 December 2000,
— 12 mg until 31 December 2006.

However, this derogation may not be used to justify controls at the Community's internal frontiers.

Article 3

The tar yield of cigarettes shall be measured according to ISO standards 4387 and 3400. Verification must be carried out according to ISO standard 8243.

Article 4

Adaptation of this Directive to technical progress shall be limited to the method of measuring tar yields and the method of verification referred to in Article 3."

Article 5 lays down that the Commission is to be assisted, in regard to the adaptation process mentioned in Article 4, by a committee of an advisory nature, composed of representatives of the Member States and chaired by the Commission representative. The working procedures of the Committee are indicated in Article 6. Articles 7-8 read as follows:

"*Article 7*

1. The Member States may not, for considerations of limitation of the tar yield of cigarettes, prohibit or restrict the sale of products which comply with this Directive.

2. This Directive shall not otherwise affect the right of the Member States to adopt, in accordance with the Treaty, rules concerning the import, sale and consumption of tobacco products which they deem necessary in order to protect public health, provided such rules do not imply any changes to limits on the tar yield of cigarettes as laid down in this Directive.

Article 8

1. Member States shall bring into force the laws, regulations and administrative provisions necessary to comply with this Directive within 18 months of its notification (1). They shall forthwith inform the Commission thereof.

2. Products existing at the dates referred to in Article 2 (2) which do not comply with this Directive may continue to be marketed for two years thereafter.

3. Member States shall communicate to the Commission provisions of national law which they adopt in the field governed by this Directive."

Other related titles

WHO, *Legislative Responses to AIDS*, Martinus Nijhoff Publishers (ISBN 0-7923-0128-5)